THE WESSEX ASTRUM

Sacred Geometry
In A Mystical Landscape

Peter Knight and Toni Perrott

Best wishes,

Peter Knight

Published in the UK by
Stone Seeker Publishing,
Dorset, England
website: www.stoneseeker.net
email: stoneseeker@waitrose.com

ISBN: 978-0-9560342-0-5

Cover design and photography © Peter Knight & Toni Perrott
Illustrations © Peter Knight and Toni Perrott, unless otherwise stated.

Also by Peter Knight

Ancient Stones of Dorset (1996)
Sacred Dorset - On the Path of the Dragon (1998)
Dorset Pilgrimages - A Millennium Handbook (with Mike Power - 2000)
Earth Mysteries - An Illustrated Encyclopaedia of Britain - CD-ROM (2004)
Thirteen Moons – Conversations with the Goddess (2007)

Visit his website for more details: www.stoneseeker.net

Also by Toni Perrott

London Dragon Paths – A Sacred and Mystical Landscape Revealed (in preparation)

Go to her website for further details: www.dragonseeker.co.uk

Cover images:
Front cover - left: St George at Iwerne Minster; bottom right: Stonehenge at
midwinter sunset; centre right: Glastonbury Tor; centre: detail of window at
Kingswood. **Back cover** – St Michael in a window at Iwerne Minster.

Printed in Wales by Cambrian Printers. www.cambrian-printers.co.uk

Dedication

We would like to dedicate this book,
with love and thanks, to our parents…

… and to Planet Earth, who is ultimately the Mother of all.

Acknowledgements

We would like to thank all those people, known and unknown to us, who have assisted our Quest. In particular, we thank Nicholas R Mann, for providing the Foreword, as well as for his inspirational books of wisdom over many years. He also gave permission to use his map of Sedona; we thank Tony Peart for granting permission to use his Temple Rockley map; we also thank Karen and Steve Alexander, for their kind permission to use their image of the *Silbury Fractal*.
Finally, we would like to say a special, heartfelt thank you to our dear friend Gary Biltcliffe, who initially pointed us in the direction of Robert Coon's work, which led to the discovery of the Wessex Astrum. His depth of knowledge, his wisdom, and his constant encouragement, has been so important to us.

Abbreviations

OS – Ordnance Survey; C – Century; ft – feet; m – metres; BC – before the time of Christ (i.e. prehistoric); AD – the Christian/historical period.

Contents

Foreword

by Nicholas R Mann

Humanity is currently at an extraordinary juncture where it is being asked to rethink and renew its relationship to the indwelling qualities of landscape and of place. Overlaid by harmful patterns of industrial culture that refer only to human economics, the vibrant inner landscape, the *anima mundi*, the 'soul of the world,' is nonetheless reasserting itself. This may be hard to accept. How can the land, the rivers, the woodland, the oceans, the Earth itself, be anything but passive in this secular age, where the forces once perceived to dwell within nature have been banished, and those who revere them regarded as upholders of irrational superstition? Today, however, the Earth Spirit is increasingly reasserting itself in the face of the human urge to exploit and control. Excessive demands made upon the world are now being met by forces far beyond human management ability. Definitions of the relationship between humanity and the living Earth are changing as events occur that show exactly who holds the upper hand in this relationship. Toni Perrott and Peter Knight are part of this change as they present a remarkable revelation from the Earth that belongs to an order far outside the current orthodoxy.

The revelation of the 'Wessex Astrum' will challenge many preconceptions as it asks humanity to realign itself not to human goals but to those of the Earth Spirit, the soul of life on Earth. Like the crop circles and other landscape temples emerging or re-emerging at this time, the Wessex Astrum demands humanity go beyond such issues as origin, ownership, authorship, economic value and re-enter dimensions that resonate with the harmonious patterns and structures of life on Earth itself. The gigantic Wessex Astrum is there in the landscape to imagine, investigate and co-operate with. Like all charged and sacred landscapes, it can enable those upon it to move to a level transfigured beyond reason; where the spirits of place, the *genii loci* so familiar to our distant ancestors, dance in the matrices of time and space that underpin creation.

Let Toni and Peter show you something 'outside the box.' As they say, these two motivated individuals are not asking you to believe in anything: just join the dots and ponder on this star for yourself. Let its historical and mythic contexts unfold; let its geometry work its magic; and remember what it is like to walk through a landscape with the beauty and power of its spiritual potentials restored.

Nicholas R Mann,
Glastonbury, August 2008.

5

Chapter 1
Ancient Wisdom Awakens

"The real magic lies not in seeking new landscapes,
but in seeing with new eyes" Marcel Proust

Wessex was one of the Anglo-Saxon kingdoms that preceded the formation of the Kingdom of England. Named after the West Saxons, it was situated in the South and Southwest, existing from the 6th C until the emergence of the English state in the 9th C. "Wessex" has not officially existed since those times, but has been a familiar term since Thomas Hardy revived it for his West Country novels and poetry. Today, it is generally regarded as encompassing the counties of Devon, Dorset, Hampshire, Wiltshire and Somerset, plus, many would contest, parts of Oxfordshire, Berkshire and Gloucestershire.

Wessex is an area exceptionally rich in prehistoric sites, and contains large tracts of beautiful countryside, including Salisbury Plain, the Mendips, Dartmoor, Cranborne Chase, the New Forest, the Purbeck Hills and much of the Cotswolds. It is home to the major spiritual centres of Glastonbury, Stonehenge and Avebury, and annually hosts the greatest concentration of crop formations in the world.

Yet for hundreds of years this ancient landscape, already regarded by many as the mythical land of Arthur, the Grail and Avalon, held another secret. A forgotten and vast geomantic phenomenon had, in fact, underpinned countless sacred sites, churches, villages, manor houses and moats. It had influenced the lives of people over many centuries, laid out on the land, unseen and unsuspected for many generations, awaiting recognition once more. The time, it seems, has arrived.

Many landscape enigmas have been proposed over the years, most of which have been rejected by a generally cynical academia. The St Michael Line, the Glastonbury Zodiac, the Belinus Line and various "Earth Stars" are pre-eminent in this heresy. Huge landscape vesicas have been advocated, defined by the precise positioning of churches and ancient features. Ley lines (alignments of sacred sites and natural features on the land) have been plotted across the whole of Britain and beyond, not to mention triangles and other geometrical forms defined by ancient and natural features, whose lines may march for hundreds of miles around the globe. Others advocate that stellar systems are mirrored in the layout of ancient sites, and it is also suggested that cities such as London and Washington DC were laid out to sacred geometrical principles. Around Rennes-le-Château, in France, it seems that an entire landscape has been utilised precisely according to ancient measure.

We waded through this vast volume of work, over many years, and visited many of the places involved, dowsing and walking the land to draw our own conclusions firsthand. Some of these leys and geometrical figures were compelling and convincing. Others were less so; there are a few, alas, that we feel have been carried along on a proverbial whim and a prayer. We do acknowledge, however, that it is a constant battle to ascertain what are relics of ancient wisdom and what are products of modern imagination.

We should, in fact, all be wary not to project our modern belief systems onto sacred sites and not to assume that we know the philosophy of our ancient ancestors. We are all becoming aware, however, that for decades we have underestimated the capabilities of our distant forebears. Thankfully, we are now re-assessing the abilities and belief systems of our prehistoric ancestors, and finding more and more evidence that they were accomplished astronomers, geomancers and mathematicians. We have no doubt that people *had the ability* to lay out a hexagram on the Wessex landscape *sometime in prehistory*, although we are not necessarily proposing such a sweeping theory. However, the Knights Templar and the Master Freemasons may have initiated the building of sites that would enhance or complete a hexagram. They may have laid these out based on existing sacred sites and natural hills that presented themselves as part of such a design. It is clear to us that at some time in the past it was *perceived* that certain hills and sacred sites formed alignments, and people may have sought to complete something they regarded as having already been initiated by Nature (perhaps in the form of an energetic imprint), or by the Earth Goddess, or perhaps, much later, by "God" as defined by Christianity.

Perhaps the one saving grace of even the less convincing proposals for landscape geometry is that they nevertheless encourage people to get out onto the landscape, to visit sacred sites, to reach out into the realms of myth and legend, to see our world with new eyes. This can only be positive, and perhaps it is the object of the whole exercise – to get us to deeply connect with the land again, in ways our ancestors once did. We are compelled to venture out into a land of magic, to bond with the Spirit of Nature. More than this, such pursuits encourage us to question what we had been told was historical fact, to unravel and pluck from obscurity concepts and experiences that some in authority wished to remain hidden, and still do.

It was a spirit of adventure and exploration, coupled with a healthy open-mindedness, which led us to the Wessex Astrum. Indeed, it was as if the Astrum had found us, inviting us to follow its Mystery. Neither of us had been involved in landscape geometry previously, other than in an incidental way. We had both acknowledged that many ancient and historic sites had been laid out with an intimate relationship to both the topography, and to other sites in the neighbouring landscape. We had also realised that geometry is present in all of Nature, and that certain natural principles, such as the Golden Section and the Fibonacci Sequence, had been mimicked by humankind when they envisioned sacred sites. But that was the extent of it, and we had no particular calling to delve into the complex, and often mathematical, minefields (or mindfields!) of sacred geometrical theorem. In fact, it was this left-brained, analytical emphasis of sacred geometry that had previously deflected us from deeper study.

However, all this was to change, through a series of *seemingly* unrelated events. Toni attended a sacred geometry workshop, and another about connecting with Elementals and symbols in the consciousness of the landscape, returning home enthused each time. At around the same time Peter was finishing off his novel, *Thirteen Moons – Conversations with the Goddess*, and he had incorporated a chapter about Sacred Geometry, which invited him to question all aspects of how Man related to Nature, and how geometrical principles had been, and still could be, applied to both sacred sites and personal enlightenment.

Around this time we also moved from Sturminster Newton, Dorset, to a farm on a hilltop above Stourpaine, a few miles away. Previously, we could only just see Hambledon Hill from our old house. But when we moved to the new home, on the other side of the hill, we were delighted that we were much closer, and the hill now loomed large and magnificent to the northwest. We had changed our view of the hill, from one side to another, but not just geographically, but also in terms of its added layers of significance; for little did we know then that this hill was to play such an important part in our lives; it is one of the six points of the Wessex Astrum.

Before we moved, we did a walk to the summit of Melbury Beacon, near Shaftesbury, noting an alignment of the hill with a church in the town, and a distant hill on the skyline further north. We discussed our interest in Shaftesbury with a close friend of ours, researcher and author Gary Biltcliffe. Gary mentioned the book, *Spheres of Destiny: The Shaftesbury Prophecy*, in which visionary Robert Coon proposed an ancient spiritual connection between Shaftesbury and Glastonbury. (The two sites are now regarded as the Heart Chakra of the planetary Rainbow Serpent.) Toni pursued this, and duly ploughed through its pages. Coon suggested the existence of certain landscape features, such as two eagles and a giant hexagram, the latter of which he called the *Wessex Star*. Toni checked these features on OS maps, but was

The moment we photographed the alignment of Melbury Beacon, a Shaftesbury church and a distant hill, which heralded the discovery of the Wessex Astrum. The arrow marks the alignment.

not convinced, and neither was Peter. The proposed hexagram is very misshapen (see image on page 23), despite being depicted in the book and on certain websites as symmetrical. But a spark had been ignited within us, and with it an excitement, a feeling that we were being led to something more tangible, a form that would satisfy our self-regulated levels of truth. Even at this stage we had no idea that we were being led to something monumentally magical. Melbury Beacon, by the way, is on one of the Astrum lines!

We were aware of the well-known Glastonbury to Stonehenge alignment, as well as the famous St Michael Line, which crosses England from Cornwall to East Anglia.

Writers before us had also commented on the alignment of sacred sites and hills connecting Stonehenge and Avebury. We felt drawn to plot these three lines on an OS map. We found that we had a virtually perfect right-angled triangle and that the longest side of the triangle was in fact the famous St Michael Line! But Coon's hexagram still lurked in the back of our minds. We wondered if the Glastonbury-Stonehenge alignment might be the baseline of an equilateral triangle. We plotted that the apex of such a hexagram lay in the Wotton-under-Edge/Holywell area of Gloucestershire. Tracing a line on the map westwards from Avebury at the same angle and distance as the Glastonbury to Stonehenge line, we came west to Brockley, which formed the top line of another, this time inverted, equilateral triangle, defined by an apex at Hambledon Hill! We stood back in wonder at what was before us.

It seemed that before our eyes had manifested an amazing figure, which represented the balance of Nature and the Universe - the polarities of female and male, yin and yang - laid out on the landscape. Traditionally and esoterically, interlocking triangles are regarded as the Blade (the male principle of the upright triangle) and the Chalice (the inverted triangle); the Blade is the point of the phallus, with the Chalice resembling the female pubic mound and a receptacle.

Neither of us was prepared, however, to be convinced. We were ever mindful that such "manifestations" could possibly be coincidental. We played Devil's Advocate on numerous occasions, for it is all too easy to see what one wishes to see. But even during our preliminary studies we found many more sacred sites located on, or very close to, the six hexagram lines, as well as still more along the six lines of the resultant hexagon. The twelve lines of the hexagram and hexagon passed through sacred site after sacred site, through Knights Templar localities, abbeys, long barrows, ancient moats, lonely chapels, prominent hill summits and places which we felt had significant names. For a couple of heady days we reeled with excitement as we fine-tuned the alignments, surmising over how wide the lines should be and exactly where they should terminate.

But one thing did concern us, however; although the hexagram was composed of two triangles of almost equal size, they were slightly too close together, and did not form a symmetrical hexagram. But we were soon to discover that not all sacred hexagrams are symmetrical, and that many featured in ancient sacred texts are also "elongated" or "compressed". We clearly had to delve further into the history and symbolism of this sacred icon that we call the hexagram.

Chapter 2
The Sacred Hexagram

T he six-pointed figure that we call the hexagram has had a long association with humankind, stemming from observations in prehistory that Nature is an expression of mathematics and sacred geometry. Our distant ancestors understood that much could be learnt from observing natural processes and that this could lead them to a closer contact with the Divine. For thousands of years, people have striven to incorporate sacred geometry, including the Fibonacci Sequence, the Golden Section and other Nature-based principles into their sacred sites. Pre-eminent amongst these sacred figures has been the hexagram.

The Hexagram in Nature
The hexagram can be experienced directly by anyone who stands outside during snowfall. Although snowflakes exhibit a variety of beautiful designs, the basic template is always six-pointed, a phenomenon recorded as early as 135 BC by the Chinese philosopher Han Yang. The hexagonal nature of snowflakes seems to have first been noted in the west by Englishman Thomas Hariot in 1591, and the astronomer Johannes Kepler in fact wrote a treatise in 1611 entitled, *De Niva Sexangular (On the Six-cornered Snowflake)*. We don't get much snow nowadays where we live in Dorset, but one night in April 2008 we had a fall. Next morning was bright and still and we went out for a walk in the fresh snow, which crunched underfoot. We marvelled at the snow as it clung to leaves and tree trunks, knowing that every one of the billions of snowflakes that had created this magical scene was a

The daffodil and the lily demonstrate six-pointed symmetry.

hexagram. Snowflakes are, of course, frozen water droplets, and anyone who looks at multiple soap bubbles gathered on the surface of water will see that they generally adopt a hexagonal pattern.

Many flowers show the hexagram, such as the daffodil and varieties of the lily family. There is even a lily named Solomon's Seal (*Polygonatum multiflorum*), after the six-pointed symbol of the Biblical king. The hexagram can be seen in the construction of bee's honeycomb, comprising hexagonal forms. The Greeks suspected that the bees possessed, *"... a certain geometrical forethought"*, as one philosopher put it. Charles Darwin declared that the honeybee dwellings were, *"...absolutely perfect in economising labour and wax"*, marvelling at the bees' instinct for such engineering.

On a more cosmic scale, the orbits of some of the planets, such as Mercury,

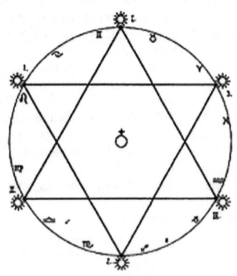

The orbit of Mercury traces a hexagram.

inscribe a hexagram against the stellar background. Mercury has a shorter orbit than Earth and completes three orbits in just less than fifty weeks, so that each year there are six solar conjunctions. If all six are marked on a circle then the result is a hexagram (shown here).

By an inexplicable coincidence, there are the same number of hexagrams on the Chinese I-Ching as there are loops on a strand of DNA. Perhaps these symbols describe something about universal reality. This seems to go right down to microscopic levels too; research by Eshel Benn-Jacob of Tel Aviv University has recently shown how several strains of bacteria grow in the form of a six-pointed star, and a Uranium atom also displays a hexagonal formation. Certain species of radiolaria, microscopic marine organisms, also grow in spheres that are made up of hexagons, one of which bears the name *Aulonia hexagona*.

The Hexagram in Prehistory

Six-pointed stars have been found on Dacian artefacts from Romania dating from c.6000 BC. One of the most stunning and profound images of the Egyptian Mystery School is the so-called *Flower of Life*, found carved on the wall of the Egyptian Temple of Osiris, at Abydos (left). The

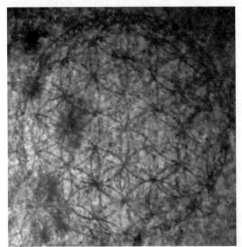

The Flower of Life, carved on the wall of the Egyptian Temple of Osiris, at Abydos.

Flower of Life is a series of interlocking hexagrams enclosed by circles, an ancient symbol of profound importance throughout history. It is also known as *The Genesis Pattern,* apparently demonstrating how life began. The Flower of Life can be found in temples, art and manuscripts all over the world. Although prehistoric images of the Flower of Life are rare, they occur in greater numbers in historical times, scattered across the globe, including such places as Masada in Israel, Mount Sinai in Egypt, the Forbidden City in China, in India at Harimandir, Hampi and Ajanta, at Roman sites in Turkey, various Japanese temples, as well as in Peru, Mexico and elsewhere. Furthermore, rock carvings of hexagrams enclosed by circles have been found at Uxmal, Central America, dating back to 1000 BC. In Pythagorean Theorum, the Greeks regarded the six-pointed star as representing justice. It was later drawn by Leonardo Da Vinci (see page 17), and in *The Ancient Secret of the Flower of Life (Vol. 2),* modern mystic Drunvalo Melchizedek places a hexagram over Da Vinci's iconic *Vitruvian Man.*

In India, hexagrams adorn temples dating from the Vedic Age, 1,500-500 BC, where the two triangles are said to be, "...locked in a harmonious embrace". The two components are called *'Om'* and *'Hrim'* in Sanskrit, symbolizing Man's position between earth and sky. Multiple interlocking hexagrams form the Sri Yantra, or *Yantra of Creation,* a geometrical diagram representing the universe, used in Hindu worship and meditation, especially in Tantrism. It is made of nine intersecting isosceles triangles of different sizes: five "female" triangles pointing downwards to symbolize the deity Shakti, and four "male" triangles pointing upwards represent Shiva. Since Vedic times the Sri Yantra has been the most powerful and mystically beautiful of all yantras. A yantra is similar to a mandala, but as well as a two-dimensional diagram, it can be a three-dimensional object of worship, imbued with the power of deity, used for procuring visions of the unseen. From these early Vedic uses, the hexagram was later to become a sacred symbol of Hinduism and Jainism. As well as temples, households in India today have a six-pointed star at their door, known as the *Star of Lakshmi,* after the Goddess of abundance and prosperity. The hexagram has also been called the *Drum of Shiva.*

In Buddhism, some versions of the *Bardo Thodol*, also known as The *Tibetan Book of the Dead*, contain hexagrams with a swastika inside. In Tibet the hexagram is called the *'origin of phenomenon'* (chos-kyi 'byung-gnas). It is especially connected with the Goddess Vajrayogini, and forms the centre part of her mandala.

Multiple interlocking hexagrams form the Sri Yantra, or *Yantra of Creation,* representing universal harmony in Hindu worship and meditation.

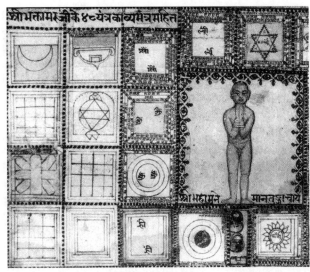

18th C ink drawing from Rajasthan. Note the two hexagrams; one is regular, the other compressed – like the Wessex Astrum!

Professor Gershom Sholem theorizes that the "Star of David" originated in the writings of the Greek mathematicians, and that the Greek philosopher Aristotle used triangles in different positions to indicate the basic elements. The superimposed triangles thus represented combinations of those elements. From Aristotle's writings, these symbols may have made their way into early, pre-Islamic Arab literature. A carving of a six-petalled flower was found at Beth-El, near Ramallah (Palestine), and was dated about 300 BC. Another was found on a Hebrew seal or signet, discovered in Sidon, later to become a Knights Templar port, dating from the 7th C BC. This consisted of a ring with a seal in the shape of a six-pointed star. Hexagrams, officially designated as examples of *The Star of David,* were found engraved on jar handles at Gibeon, Israel, and were dated as late First Temple Kingdom (c.1006-586 BC). They are regarded as copies of Greek emblems from Thasos and Carthage, used for marking wine vessels.

The Sacred Hexagram in Historical Times
On a visit to the British Museum in February 2008, we were delighted to find an

The Leningrad Codex, dated 1008AD.

exhibit featuring a Roman tombstone, dated c.60 AD, commemorating the death of a legionnaire from Macedonia. Near the top are three six-petalled flower decorations. In historical times, however, the most widespread association of the six-pointed star has been with Judaism.

It is not officially known, surprisingly, when the Shield of David first became the acknowledged symbol of Judaism. The first mention of the star in Biblical literature is in Amos 5:26, regarding the trek from Egypt to Canaan, when Yaweh angrily tells his people:

"I hate and despise your feast days…. You shall take up Siccuth, your king and Chiun, your images, the star of your God…."

So few ancient synagogues have survived from this period that it is impossible to draw conclusions regarding the *absence* of the hexagram in the archaeology. It begins to appear frequently on synagogues from the 16th C onwards, when the Kabbalistic influence of Isaac Luria was spreading. It appears side by side with the Menorah, the sacred candelabra, which until then had been regarded as the "Shield of David," and which it gradually displaced in synagogues and on religious objects. A Hebrew manuscript of 1564, the Hamburg *Stadtbibliothek*, shows the symbol accompanied by the words, *magen david;* it is further met with as a Zionist emblem, and as the symbol of the Red Magen David Society (the equivalent of the Red Cross).

Hexagrams in a beautiful window in a synagogue in Istanbul.

The Leningrad Codex, dated 1008 AD, is one of the earliest manuscripts of the complete Hebrew sacred scriptures. The Aleppo Codex, against which the Leningrad Codex was corrected, was the first such manuscript and is several decades older, but parts of it have been missing since 1947, making the Leningrad Codex the oldest complete version. The hexagram is illustrated in both manuscripts and shows that the Star of David, or the Seal of Solomon, was very much associated with Hebrew culture by that time, and this would eventually lead to it being adopted on the Israeli flag.

A particularly beautiful example of Jewish architecture is to be found in a synagogue in Istanbul (above). Within the hexagram there is another six-pointed star, which is actually formed by the intersection of curved lines of a six-petalled flower. It demonstrates how straight-lined geometry can contain curved lines, circles and vesicas.

The six-cornered *Star of Israel* shares its roots with Islamic tradition and in the Middle East we also find plenty of evidence that Muslims embraced the sacred hexagram. The hexagram crops up regularly in Islamic architecture, such as at the

Left: Christian Chi Rho. Centre: hexagonal plan at Ani. Right: Alet Cathedral, near Rennes-le-Château.

14

Dome of the Chain, dating from the 7th C, situated next to the Dome of the Rock on the Temple Mount in Jerusalem. It was built around the same time as its famous neighbour. The temple's small dome is supported by 17 internal columns, all of which can be seen from any one point. A prominent feature of the mosque is the magnificent tiled floor that has two interlocking hexagrams, enclosing two hexagons. Elsewhere, stone windows with hexagram frames survive at the Palace at Khirbet El-Mafjar, 3 km north of Jericho, and date from the 8th C AD.

Three concentric hexagrams at St Mary Redcliffe, Bristol.

The Christian Hexagram

The association between Christianity and hexagrams goes back to the very roots of the religion. In Genesis 1:1, God is said to dwell in the void; but how did God, the conscious intelligence, move out of the void into matter? Incredibly, the oldest Bibles contain the missing first sentence: 'In the beginning there were six'; some texts speak of the hexagram as the *Creator's Star*. The Bible makes no direct mention of a *Star of David*, although the *shield* or protection of both David and Abraham does appear (Genesis 15:1 and Psalms 18:36). Not until 528 AD does the Catholic Church refer to the star that led the Magi to Christ as the "Star of David". The "Shield of David" also denoted the seven days of the week, with the planets as their overlords. The hexagon in the centre, the most complete figure, was the Sabbath, the six outer triangles being the weekdays. It was divided into four rhomboids, corresponding to the four cardinal directions: north, south, east and west. As a Messianic symbol, the hexagram represents the zodiacal sign of Pisces (Feb 21 to Mar 20), the time of the year the Messiah is supposed to appear.

One of the earliest symbols associated with Christianity is the six-pointed Chi Rho cross, found at many Roman sites and seen in churches today (image above). In Armenia, the ancient city of Ani was known as the *City of a Thousand Churches,* and the church in the Citadel, which dates from the 10-11th C (see image above) reveals a hexagonal plan. Even the famous labyrinth in Chartres Cathedral even has a six-petalled flower design in its centre. On our travels around the Astrum, the hexagram was to be a recurring image, arising more often, we would suggest, than coincidence

15

would dictate. We found them on pulpits and miserichords, in stained glass windows, and carved into stone. One of the finest can be seen at St Mary's Redcliffe, in Bristol, where there are three interlocking hexagrams inlaid into the floor (see image above) and an old hexagonal-shaped porch. Surely some deeper, more esoteric, meaning is implied here; these are not just bibical symbols used merely as decoration.

Esoteric Meanings of the Hexagram

The frontispiece to Heinrich Madathanus' *"Aureum Seculum Redivivum"*, published in 1625.

There is substantial evidence that the hexagram has ancient occult and esoteric origins. From 800 to 600 BC, the hexagram was a general symbol representing the *'art of alchemy'*. Researchers have found the symbol in magical texts from the Byzantine Era, in medieval books of the occult, on Knights Templar relics, and in Freemasonry.

The two opposing overlaid triangles are the archetypal representation of the 'sacred union' of male and female principles, yin and yang, the 'hieros gamos', the chalice and the blade, the fire and water of alchemists. The spinning double tetrahedron has been seen as the symbol of the Creator. The hexagram is a potent symbol of the relationship between the macrocosm and the microcosm, between Heaven and Earth, and it has strong links to the Kabbalah and the Tree of Life. The star tetrahedron equates with the Star of David, the Philosopher's Diamond, the *Merkaba*, the two triangles representing heaven and earth, spirit and matter, 'as above so below'.

The hexagram is formed by uniting the Gestaltian Water Triangle with the Fire Triangle; the combination formed the symbol for *firewater*, the *essence* or *spiritus* of wine: *alcohol*. It was also the sign for *quintessence*, the *fifth element*, making it among the most important motifs from the world of alchemy, alongside gold, sulphur, mercury and the pentacle.

18th C Irish Masonic symbolism, with a serpent, vesica and hexagram.

The hexagram was used for protection in Babylonia around 2000 BC and early Babylonians divided the annual Solar cycle into six celestial animals. This is not an isolated example of the Sun's association with the number six, for other cultures around the world have described the Sun as being six-natured. In Zoroastrian astrology, the hexagram is known as the 'King's Star'. Some researchers have theorized that this hexagram represents the astrological chart at the time of King David's birth, or his anointment as king.

A hexagram ritual is part of Enochian ceremony, used during the consecration of temples, and occultist Alistair Crowley in fact called the symbol the *"holy hexagram"*. Some Orthodox Jewish groups go so far as to reject the use of the *Star of David,* because of its association with magic and the occult, and do not recognize it as a Jewish symbol.

The Rosicrucians use the hexagram, which, according to their teachings, was known to the ancient Egyptians, Hindus, Chinese and Peruvians. The illustration above is the frontispiece to Heinrich Madathanus' *"Aureum Seculum Redivivum",* or *"The Golden Age Revived",* first published in 1625. Madathanus was the pseudonym of Adrian von Mynsicht (1603-1638), an alchemist and Rosicrucian.

In alchemical tradition, the six-pointed star is called the Talisman of Saturn, as well as the "Stone of the Wise", which is often associated with the five-pointed star, the pentagram. Modern occultists regard the hexagram as a symbol of Thoth, the Atlantean, whose wisdom is told in the Emerald Tablets of Thoth. In Ritual Magic, the hexagram is called the Seal of Solomon, and represents Divine Union, comprising a female, watery triangle, and a male, fiery triangle. The traditional elemental triangles of earth, air, water, and fire are derived from the seal.

In Jewish, Islamic and Christian medieval legends, the Seal of Solomon was a magical signet ring said to have belonged to King Solomon (*Sulaman* in Islamic texts), which variously gave him the power to command demons (the Jinni) or to speak with animals. Today it is a common symbol in Islamic Middle East and North Africa, where it is thought to bring good luck.

Hidden symbolism is encoded in the Great Seal of the United States, which incorporates 13 small stars in a hexagram pattern, symbolizing the thirteen original colonies, above an eagle's head. Some claim that this appears in gratitude for the financial contributions of Haym Solomon to the American Revolution and American War of Independence of 1776, and some maintain that Solomon designed the great seal himself. Joseph Campbell writes; *"In the Great Seal of the U.S. there are two interlocking triangles. We have thirteen points, for our original thirteen states, and six apexes: one above, one below, and four to the four quarters. The sense of this might be that of above or below... the creative word may be heard, which is the great*

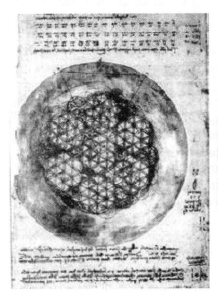

Left: the Flower of Life, as sketched by Leonardo Da Vinci. Above: the Flower of Life at the Golden Temple, Amistar, India.

thesis of democracy." (The Power of Myth, p.27). Hexagrams crop up in many modern U.S. state buildings, such as the one embedded in the ceiling of the Washington National Cathedral, and are encoded into street plans (see Chapter 3).

The hexagram in the seal of the USA. (c/o GreatSeal.com)

The Kabbalah is the Jewish magical tradition, dating back to at least the 6th C AD. Kabbalistically, the hexagram is the Sefirah Tifaret - meaning *"perfection".* It symbolizes the six directions of space plus the centre, under the influence of the description of space found in the Sefer Yetsira. Congruently, under the influence of the Zohar, it represents the Sixth Sefirot of the Male, united with the Seventh Sefirot of the Female. In the Kabbalistic Tree of Life there is often a hexagram placed at the top, with the yin and yang triangles either side of it, containing male and female faces respectively.

The modern cult of Raelism uses a hexagram, chosen by movement founder Claude Vorilhon, which has been the source of considerable controversy, as it resembles a Star of David, but with a swastika at its centre. According to official Raelian dogma, the swastika, *'represents infinity of time, and traces its origins to Sanskrit and Buddhist symbols, to the Chinese character for temple, and to ancient catacombs, mosques, and synagogues.'* In 1991, the symbol was changed to remove the swastika to deflect public criticism, as well as to gain acceptance for the building of a Raelian 'embassy' in Israel, built for the anticipated arrival of Elohim space vessels!

The Star of David is also used, less prominently, by The Church of Jesus Christ of Latter-Day Saints, the Mormons, chiefly in their architecture. To them, it symbolizes the Tribes of Israel and the Mormons' claimed affinity towards the Jewish people. The hexagram is also used in the seal and the emblem of the Theosophical Society, founded in 1875, and it was also adopted by Rudolf Steiner for his *anthroposophy*.

In the rites of Freemasonry the hexagram turns up frequently in the jewel that accompanies each degree, and as the highest degrees are reached, a mystical geometry lecture is given on its meaning. The lecture describes the hexagram as the "Seal of Solomon" and by combining it with the value of the triple Tau, in a difficult-to-follow numbers game, one connects it to all the Platonic solids. Perhaps the coded message here is that the "Seal of Solomon" itself represents a three-dimensional object, namely the star tetrahedron. The hexagram in the jewel is, after all, circumscribed by a circle. The carpets of the Freemasons Lodge in Bristol are covered in hexagrams (see pages 203-4) and they are often found as stonemasons' signs, and in the various coats of arms of Freemasonry.

Extending from the hexagram is of course the hexagon, which is created connecting the six points of a hexagram, making a total of twelve lines. Twelve is a magical number on so many esoteric, religious and mythic levels; the twelve apostles, the number of months in a year, the twelve tribes of Israel, Odin's twelve sons, the Etruscans' twelve cities, King Arthur's twelve great victories against the Saxons, the number of signs in the zodiac, and so forth. This is one reason why we paid great credence to the six hexagon lines of the Astrum. Indeed, we were to find many wondrous sacred sites on these lines, justifying our decision.

Sacred Geometry and the Hexagram

The usual explanation for the use of the hexagram by the Church is that it is out of reverence for King Solomon, and his attributes of great wisdom. But we often found the symbol out of context, in windows and on carvings that appeared to have nothing to do with the Old Testament figure. To us, some deeper meaning is implied. The Knights Templar, the Masons and the Freemasons have, over many centuries, ensured churches, cathedrals and secular buildings were built to the correct proportions and contained images to reflect sacred geometry. For instance, a hexagram and a sword are carved on a stone at Kirkwall Cathedral, which is accredited to the Knights Templar (see image page 20). In her new book, *The Spiritual Purpose to Rosslyn: Key to a Hidden Matrix,* Jackie Queally has laid out a hexagram around the altar at Rosslyn Chapel, associating it with one of several initiatory stages. She sees this *Star of David* as, *"... a two-way flow between matter and spirit... vertically there is a central Matter-Spirit pole above the chapel here, but in the vaults below there is the complementary Spirit-Matter pole."*

Pioneering researchers such as John Michell and Nigel Pennick have found 'sacred number' and geometry in buildings of various dates throughout history, some of which go back to 4,000 years ago, such as at Stonehenge. It was Inigo Jones who first overlaid a hexagram on to Stonehenge in 1655, and William Stukeley did likewise in 1723. We found an elongated hexagram within Stonehenge, one of which is shown here alongside one by John Michell, the other on page 56.

More recently, we have found similar geometry in our research, such as at Temple Church in London. This was the headquarters of the Knights Templar in Britain, and was so important that it was opened in 1185 by no lesser person than Heraclius, the Patriarch of Jerusalem. The Round, at the west end of the church, houses stone

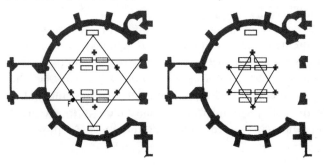

Plan of the Round in Temple Church, London, showing an elongated hexagram (left) and a regular hexagram (right), both plotted by Peter Knight. (From *London Dragon Paths* by Toni Perrott).

Hexagram and sword carved by the Knights Templar at Kirkwall Cathedral.

effigies of benefactors, clad in armour, famously featured in *The Da Vinci Code*. As at Stonehenge, Peter found evidence of both elongated and regular hexagrams, where the lines pass through the effigies and stone columns. Adrian Gilbert had previously suggested a hexagram here, but in his diagrams some of the columns are in slightly the wrong place. Bligh Bond overlaid a hexagram, with its integral vesica piscis, circle and square, over the plan of the Lady Chapel within Glastonbury Abbey. Nigel Pennick has overlaid two hexagrams on the plan of the Abbey, one of which has its centre under the Omphalos, the crossing of the building (see Chapter 9).

In his book *The Sacred Art of Geometry,* Pennick gives several more examples of hexagonal geometry in church design. He actually describes the number six as, *"... the perfect number..."*. Pennick laid two hexagrams over the ground plan of St George's in Bloomsbury, London, one of which is set 45° to the other. He also illustrates multiple hexagrams laid into the floor of San Giovanni Laterano, in Rome, again showing many set at an angle of 45° to the other. We found an identical interaction between hexagrams in the windows of Fonthill Gifford church, on one of the Chalice lines (see Chapter 13). Pennick also shows a 15th C illustration showing two triangles, one inside the other, which are very unequal in size. Again, we found this in another window in the same church at Fonthill Gifford. Pennick has also convincingly overlaid a hexagram onto King's College Chapel, Cambridge.

In Juan Garcia Atienza's excellent work on the Knights Templar, *The Knights*

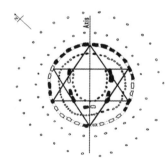

Stonehenge. Left: compressed hexagram involving the sarsen circle (Peter Knight). Right: regular hexagram (after John Michell). Compare with another Stonehenge hexagram on page 56.

Templar in the Golden Age of Spain, he notes that the walls and vaulted ceiling arches of the rotunda area of the Temple in Paris, prior to its destruction, prescribed a hexagram (an old map is reproduced below). He sees the temple as key-shaped, the round being the handle, the nave as the key, and the Lady Chapel at the side of the nave as the teeth, "… that opens the lock". On our visits to Astrum churches we often found that the Lady Chapel felt the most sacred and was the focus of powerful energies. Sometimes we found these chapels protruding out from the nave, as at Wotton-under-Edge.

In our fieldwork on the Astrum we were to encounter many examples of hexagram symbolism in churches. But now we need to digress briefly. Before we ventured out onto the Wessex landscape, we researched to see if there were any precedents for landscape hexagrams. We were not to be disappointed.

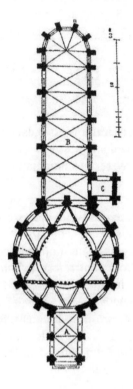

The Knights Templar encoded a hexagram into their Temple at Paris.

Chapter 3
Hexagrams on the Landscape

S uspecting that a hexagram laid out on the Wessex landscape had revealed itself to us, we naturally looked for precedents. As well as manmade phenomena, we were also drawn to look into the mysterious enigma of crop circles.

Crop Formations

In recent years some notable formations have revealed very complex sacred geometry involving both hexagrams and hexagons. The famous *"Stonehenge Snowflake"* appeared in June 1997, and displayed a classic six-pointed geometry. In August 1997 a formation appeared at Milk Hill in Wiltshire (close to one of our Astrum lines), where a huge hexagram was inscribed in the field, with smaller hexagrams at each of the points. That same summer, the *"Fractal Star of David"* appeared at the foot of Silbury Hill, just yards from another Astrum line. It consisted of a hexagram with a circle at each point, as well as a large circle in the middle of the formation. This was complemented by a six-pointed formation, known as the *"Silbury Flower"*, which manifested close to the Neolithic mound in June 1996.

In June 1997, yet another formation appeared close to Silbury, called the *"Silbury Fractal"*, once again comprising a hexagram with smaller hexagrams at each point. Not far away the *"West Overton Kasket"* appeared on 24th June 1999, in which there were ten hexagrams connected by triangles, and on 24th July 2005 another hexagonal crop formation formed in a field next to Avebury henge.

In 2007, two crop formations appeared directly on Wessex Astrum lines and we wondered if these were in response to our studies. Hexagram formations have often manifested on flows of earth energies, a notable example being the *Mayan Glyph,* which materialized on the Elen current of the Belinus Line in 2005, close to Wayland's Smithy (information c/o Gary Biltcliffe).

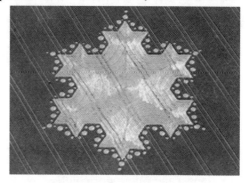

The *Silbury Fractal* formation of 1997.
© Steve and Karen Alexander:
www.temporarytemples.co.uk

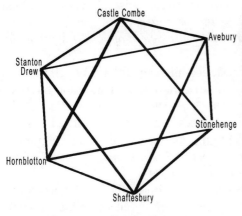

"Star of Peace" (after Robert Coon).

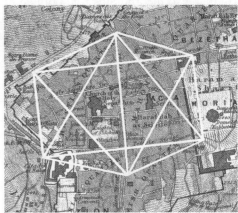

"Elongated" hexagram overlaid on Jerusalem.
(After John Michell.)

Landscape Hexagrams

We have already mentioned how Robert Coon had advocated a landscape hexagram, his six-sided *"Star of Peace"*, which involves Avebury and Stonehenge, two defining Astrum localities. Coon's focus and preoccupation had been on Shaftesbury, concerning "Byzant rituals" involving the hilltop town and Glastonbury. When we plotted the hexagram we found that it was clearly skewed, and that his main line from Stonehenge did not go to Glastonbury, but rather the church of the Somerset village of Hornblotton. His parallel line from Avebury terminates at Stanton Drew, indeed a major stone circle complex, but we noted the discrepancy between the distances of the two parallel lines from the apex points of the hexagram. Clearly, Shaftesbury is several miles more to the south of the Hornblotton-Stonehenge line than Castle Combe is north of the Stanton Drew-Avebury line. Whilst we do not fully embrace Coon's hexagram, we acknowledge his vision and his work as being one of the catalysts for the revelation of the Wessex Astrum.

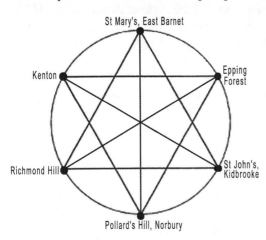

Hexagram on the landscape of London. (After Christopher Street; our version of the *Hexagonal Star* in Street's book *Earthstars*.)

Christopher Street has published a comprehensive work on the sacred geometry of London in his seminal book, *Earthstars – The Visionary Landscape.* His work seems to confirm William Blake's vision of London as the *New Jerusalem.* Street has painstakingly and accurately mapped out numerous geometrical shapes on the landscape, defined chiefly by the siting of churches. Amongst these are hexagrams, notably the one involving Richmond Hill (our version of his Figure 95 being shown here). The hexagram results from the axial lines of a 30-point star, a form that also incorporates five-pointed pentagrams. Street incisingly comments that, *"In sacred geometry, successfully combining the pentagram and the hexagram is regarded as something of an alchemical act and a marriage of opposites symbolising the union of forces that create life."*

In his book, *City of Revelation,* earth mysteries pioneer John Michell maps a hexagram in Jerusalem, based upon the location of certain sacred sites and the street plan. What is significant is that his hexagram is *"squashed or elongated"*; just like the Wessex Astrum, it is not symmetrical. He does not comment further on this, raising no objections to the fact that the hexagram is asymmetrical. The hexagrams of Coon and Michell suggest the existence of at least two *non-symmetrical* hexagrams that, should they be authentic, appear to be of some antiquity.

Henry Lincoln is well-known for his controversial work on the landscape around the village of Rennes-le-Château, in the foothills of the French Pyrénées. In his book, *The Holy Place,* he describes his discovery of, *"... an immense geometrical temple, stretching for miles across the landscape, a constellation of pentacles, circles and hexagons: a Holy place of enormous size and significance"*. One of his hexagrams is centred on Esperaza (illustrated below) whilst another has its centre at La Valdieu, the *"Valley of God"*. He also found several hexagrams and hexagons in the architecture of churches in the area, notably the *"Seal of Solomon"* in the window of the church at Alet (shown on page 14).

Nicholas R Mann has produced a scholarly work, *The Sacred Geometry of Washington DC,* in which he puts forward convincing arguments that the US capital was deliberately laid out to geometrical principles incorporating precise measure and proportion; hexagrams and pentagrams are defined by the orientation of streets and the positioning of prominent state buildings and monuments. Mann has also produced a guide to the sacred sites and the sacred geometry of the Sedona district of the USA, entitled *Sedona: Sacred Earth* (1989). There he found more landscape hexagrams, along with pentagrams, laid out in a sacred landscape, and one of his maps is shown below (page 26).

Henry Lincoln's "Seal of Solomon".
(After Lincoln.)

In his thought-provoking book *Pi in the Sky,* published in 1992, Michael Poynder advocated several hexagrams, so-called *Earth Stars,* on the landscape of Ireland and Brittany. In this lavishly illustrated work, he makes some convincing arguments that our prehistoric ancestors must have processed, *"... a wealth of ancient knowledge of astonishing sophistication"*. In the Boyne Valley, he maps out two encircled *"energy stars"*, hexagrams involving the great Neolithic complexes of Newgrange and Knowth. At Carrowkeel, in County Sligo, he proposes a hexagram involving a variety of sacred sites, including cairns, standing stones and ponds, which he sees as mapping out the

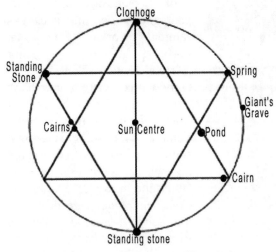

Michael Poynder's *Carrowkeel Star*. (After Poynder; our simplified version of his original.)

positions of the planets of the Solar System. He extends this out into the larger landscape, seeing the *Carrowkeel Star* as an element of a much larger hexagram, the *"Lough Arrow 8.3 mile Star"*, that involves further standing stones and a dolmen. Poynder has also mapped another hexagram around Carnac, in Brittany, an area strewn with huge megaliths and chambered tombs; as in Ireland, he again proposes planetary associations with several sites, and argues that the Neolithic builders must have had a deep knowledge of mathematics, including the concept of Pi.

Inspired by Henry Lincoln, Dorset researcher Jonathan Harwood has carried out a detailed study of the Dorset landscape over many years, and in 2000 self-published a summary of this work in his booklet, *Sacred Geometry in the Dorset Landscape*. He proposes that, *"... churches and certain older sacred sites have been deliberately placed at measured distances from each other... in order to create patterns and relationships that are meaningful."* Harwood suggests the existence of several pentagrams and hexagrams, which share a common unit of measurement. One of the most convincing is his *Up Cerne Hexagram,* which is centred on the village of Up Cerne, not far from the famous Cerne Giant. It consists of two hexagrams, surrounded by a slightly irregular hexagon, the latter of which is defined by six churches (see illustration below). Like Poynder, Harwood came to the conclusion that the geometry he found, *"... relates, at least in part, to the movements of the Sun and Venus and has to do with ideas and rituals associated with death, re-birth and fertility."*

Dorset researcher Gary Biltcliffe has recently published the seminal work about the Isle of Portland in Dorset. In *Secrets of the Masonic Isle – Uncovering the Magic and Mystery of Ancient Portland,* he outlines evidence that several Portland churches are positioned so as to

The Up Cerne Hexagram, proposed by Jonathan Harwood in self-published paper, 2000. (From J Harwood, simplified for clarity, due to scale)

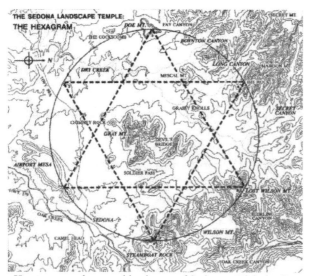

Hexagram on the sacred landscape of Sedona – Nicholas R Mann. © (From *Sedona – Sacred Earth*. With permission.)

define hexagrams and pentagrams on the Isle. His seminal work shows that Portland was once a major spiritual centre.

Only whilst writing this book did we come across the work of Tony Peart. His website, Templar Mechanics, is a great source of maps of sacred geometrical figures on the landscape in the UK and on the Continent. One page describes the area around Temple Rockley, just east of Avebury. The continuance of the St Michael/Beltaine Line beyond our terminal point at Avebury goes straight through the area, which was a major Knights Templar preceptory (see image next page). Tony has plotted a six-petalled *Flower of Life* created by six overlapping circles (vesicas) all 5.15 miles in diameter incorporating hexagrams. He also plotted a hexagram defined by Windmill Hill, Woodhill ancient settlement, the White Horse, Milk Hill, Martinsell hillfort and Chiseldon church. He demonstrates other hexagrams around the Lincolnshire village of Templar Bruer, on the Isle of Wight, and yet another on Malta; all of these were Knights Templar centres.

Tony's work confirmed three things for us. Firstly, we had proof that the Knights Templar had employed sacred geometry on the landscape. This gave more credence that the original designers of the Astrum *may* have been the Knights Templar. We were to encounter more major Templar sites along Astrum lines, notably at Bristol and Templecombe. And secondly, and of great relevance, was that the Temple Rockley geometry actually adjoins our Wessex Astrum; his sacred geometry incorporates Wessex Astrum sites, such as Avebury, Silbury Hill, Windmill Hill, Milk Hill and Oliver's Castle.

Landscape Serpents

It is interesting that Hamish Miller and Paul Broadhurst found energy 'signatures' at node points along the St Michael line, which manifested as three concentric twelve-pointed stars, each one being two hexagrams! (See *The Sun and the Serpent,* page 207.) Later work by Miller and other dowsers on energy nodes and these energy signatures has revealed that these patterns can change form, apparently by human interaction through healing at sites. Miller and Broadhurst visited the labyrinth of Chartres Cathedral and described it, in the *Dance of the Dragon,* as being, *"a nexus of earth energies"*. At its heart is the six-petalled flower! In the same book, diagrams show the two currents of the trans-European Apollo-St Michael Axis as being composed of six flows of current – the sacred six once again.

26

Ley Lines and Landscape Hexagrams

Having explored some landscape hexagrams, it might be worth pausing briefly to look at such figures with regards to ley lines. These controversial alignments of sacred sites and natural features were first advocated by Alfred Watkins in the 1920's.

Since then many authors, notably John Michell and Paul Devereux, have studied in fine detail the whole concept of landscape alignments. In fact a whole sub-culture has since arisen, birthing groups and societies that roam the world searching for these enigmatic lines. We would like to make the clear distinction here between ley lines (alignments) and the *energy leys* (flows of earth energies) of dowsers. The two may

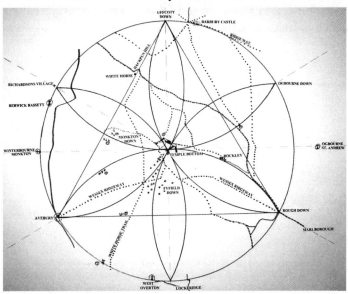

The six-petalled star and triangle on the landscape around Avebury and Temple Rockley. © Tony Peart, from his website: www.templarmechanics.com.

coexist, such as with the St Michael Line as we shall see later, but they are different beasts. Leys are manmade, if Divinely inspired, whereas currents of earth energies are natural, if spiritual, elements of a living landscape.

So we must ask the question as to whether a landscape hexagram is in fact a set of conjoined ley lines. Clearly, some could be classed as such; aligned sites are often found in between the terminal points of many landscape hexagrams. Others cannot be so classified, as there may be no other sites at all between the apexes. With regards to the Astrum, we would have to regard each of the fifteen lines described in this book as ley lines, for each one has at least a dozen aligned sacred sites. Researchers and critics in the past have argued regarding how wide a ley line should be, and how long, and the minimum numbers of sites it should have, and so forth. We deal with this further in Chapter 5, when we define the Wessex Astrum. But for now we are satisfied that Alfred Watkins would be happy with our lines, and we pay homage to his pioneering work, acknowledging the savage academic backlash he endured.

Around many ley lines, such as the Belinus Line and the St Michael Line, there are accompanying flows of earth energy. Although we dowsed powerful energy flows and vortices at many of the sites on the Astrum line, we do not advocate for one instance that there are flows of energy accompanying each line across the landscape. Quite the contrary; the Astrum is essentially a man-made construct, although we acknowledge that its designers would surely have been influenced by what they experienced at localities. The St Michael Line (see Chapter 22) is one of the components of the Astrum, and it does indeed have the well-documented Mary and Michael flows dancing around its axis. We leave others that follow us to draw their own conclusions on the other possible Astrum configurations, and connections with earth energies. We do suggest, however, that such studies are undertaken with an open mind, and that care should be taken not project onto the Wessex Astrum that which individuals expect to find.

Chapter 4
Our Quest Begins

"You need to be the change you wish to see in the world."
Mahatma Gandhi

With an adventurous spirit we set off in the footsteps of Miller, Broadhurst and Watkins, and all the other seekers of Truth who had ventured out before us into the magical landscape of Wessex. Indeed, the Land and its sacred sites were beckoning us – and we eagerly obliged. From the outset, we were determined to keep an open mind, not to manifest "confirmations", through wrongful interpretation of imagined "discoveries", that the Wessex Astrum might be for real.

The Astrum comprises the six lines of the hexagram, six of the hexagon, the Beltaine Line, the Samhain Line, and the Central Axis, and we were determined to travel up and down each of these fifteen alignments. This was a daunting task, with some 514 miles to investigate and visit; this is longer, in fact, than the axis of the St Michael Line that crosses Southern England! This statistic took us by surprise somewhat as we never imagined the unravelled Astrum lines would be so long. We clearly had to go about our study systematically, taking one section at a time and travelling as best we could along as many miles as was possible, bearing in mind that many places were out of bounds to us, such as private land, inaccessible terrain and MOD ranges. But we were not deterred and, looking back now, we have a sense of pride that we largely succeeded in our Quest.

Although we knew that the ultimate Truth lay out there on the landscape itself, we nevertheless did extensive research beforehand, using Google, local libraries and our own library of books to good effect. The magic thus began even before we stepped out onto the landscape. For instance, we found records of hexagonal and hexagram-shaped crop circles that had manifested on or very near our proposed lines. We found precedents for irregular hexagrams, such as the layout for Jerusalem proposed by John Michell, as already mentioned. We located several places on our lines that were associated with the Knights Templar, which we thought relevant, knowing how sacred geometry, and the hexagram in particular, was incorporated into their symbolism and architecture. We found that some of the megaliths Peter had uncovered previously now stood on the proposed lines. We also perused local village and town websites, which revealed sacred wells, lost sacred sites and other significant records not shown on modern maps. We also used to great effect the 19th C OS maps, many of which are now online, which show former churches and stones, long since gone. We soaked it all up like sponges, champing at the bit to venture out into the sacred Wessex landscape, in search of the Wessex Astrum.

In true *Sun and the Serpent* style, we decided to keep chronological records of our excursions, to tell of our exploits and site visits in the order they happened, hopefully getting across some of the sense of wonder and discovery, a journal of our thoughts and conversations on site, with wonderful examples of synchronicity and "chance" meetings, as well as our subsequent reflections on returning home. This is the form in which we have chosen to tell our story.

We hope this format will encourage a similar sense of adventure, to inspire the reader to venture out into landscapes, familiar and alien, with the view of connecting with the Land in a spiritual way. We have come to realise that this may have been the point of the whole journey for us. We were enticed out into ancient landscapes, to hidden corners of rural England, and went willingly and open-eyed. What we found was far in excess of our original expectations. We found the Planetary Spirit, no less, reflected in and underpinning everything we encountered, from holy chapel to sacred well, from hallowed hill to humble wayside cross, from ancient folklore, to our own experiences.

We set out to find the Wessex Astrum, but in the end we realised that *it* had been showing *us* the way. And more than that, we truly found ourselves again. Our experiences on our Journey reinforced the realisation that we and the Land really are one - we are umbilically connected no less. Time and time again we found evidence that our ancestors must have had this realisation too, confirmed by the way so many sites had been deliberately, and so exquisitely, positioned on the landscape. Our ancestors had also been as one with the Land, and we feel we have also forged a closer link with them; this has made our forebears into real people, whose footsteps we were following; we were to build a very personal relationship with them.

Ultimately, perhaps the point of the exercise is not so much whether the Astrum is of ancient origin or not, nor if the lines are intentional or coincidental, but rather what has been re-discovered and experienced during our site visits and research. Unrecorded megaliths were made known to us; we offered local people new interpretations of their churches, showing them relics they had not been aware of; we were drawn to lonely hills and stood on deserted summits we may never have frequented; we were blessed with exploring out-of-the-way villages and deserted mounds, hidden corners of England, which would never have been our quarry but for this project; we found more evidence that the Knights Templar had left signs of their wisdom; and we frequented overgrown wells and springs, and equally forgotten caves; megaliths were revealed in churchyards and lonely crossroads; we found several instances of former churches that were located on or near Astrum lines, which had since been either demolished or turned into non-religious buildings. All this, and more, was revealed to us.

If our work leads to more people treading the landscape, visiting forgotten ancient places and looking with new eyes at the world around them and, in the process, treating the Earth with more respect, then it will all have been worthwhile. To us personally, it already has been worthwhile; we walked in the footsteps of ancestors who had 'long since fallen on sleep', yet so often felt their presence amongst us.

For Toni it was also something of a personal pilgrimage to her ancestral places. It seems likely that a certain *William De Perrott,* from Castel Perrott in Brittany, came to England in 957 AD and obtained land in Wessex. Later, Seigneur de Perrott, from Brittany, furnished William the Conqueror with a quota of ships and men for the Conquest. From this we have the naming of North and South Perrott and the River Parret in Somerset. In the Domesday Book we have records of Perrotts (and its many variant forms, such as Perrot, Parrot, Perritt, Perrett and so on), scattered all over Wessex and beyond. It turned out that the Astrum lines went through several places where the ancient Perrotts resided, a big concentration being in Wiltshire, around Rowde and Seend.

Peter also felt connected with some other Astrum places, such as West Kennet Long Barrow, inside which he had recently scattered the ashes of his departed father. Because of this, he could really appreciate how ancient peoples must have felt when they left their own relatives in these sacred chambers. And the more he looked back at his life, the more it seemed that he had been prepared for this work. He had only come down to Wessex looking for work 20 years before, due to redundancy in his native Birmingham. Looking back now, it is clear to see how the Universe was, even way back then, conspiring to steer him to that day, standing alongside Toni on top of Melbury Beacon, when the Wessex Astrum began to reveal itself.

Chapter 5
The Wessex Astrum Defined

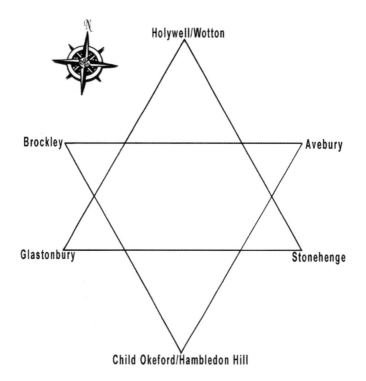

S o we had stumbled upon, or indeed were guided to, a giant hexagram straddling the counties of Gloucestershire, Dorset, Wiltshire and Somerset, embodying ancient Wessex. As there was no historical name for the figure, we had to choose one, which we feel mighty privileged to have been chosen to do so.

A Star is Born

Although they were our initial preferences, *Star of Wessex* and *Wessex Star* would have caused confusion with that described previously by Robert Coon. We also considered *The Wessex Magen*, from the Hebrew term for the Seal or Shield of

Solomon, but felt that this would also inadvertently link it with Jewish and Hebrew symbolism. *Shactona* is the Hindu word for a six-pointed star, but this term did not seem suitable for a hexagram laid out across the South of England! Closer to home, the Welsh word for star is *seren*, whilst the Gaelic is either *reannag* or *reul*. None of these appealed. The Greek for star is *astron*, from which we get *astronomy*. For this reason we rejected it, as it would have perhaps implied that we were advocating some sort of *stellar map* laid out on the landscape.

The Latin for star can be *stella, sidus* or *astrum*. The term *Wessex Astrum* was eventually chosen above other contenders. Although Latin is very much associated nowadays with Roman Catholicism, and has been so for centuries, we must remember that it was spoken centuries before the birth of Christianity, and has been the *lingua franca,* or universal language, of educated people around the world.

A Tale of Two Triangles

The Astrum is composed of two interlocking equilateral triangles. The E-W lines of these triangles are around 3-3.5° off east-west. The north-south axis of the Astrum is approximately 5.5° off N-S regarding the OS grid. The dimensions and lines of the hexagram, hexagon and the central axis, are defined by a number of critical factors.

The hexagram clearly takes account of:

1) **The course and length of the Glastonbury to Stonehenge alignment;**
2) **The course and length of the Stonehenge to Avebury alignment;**
3) **The section of the St Michael Line between Glastonbury and Avebury;**
4) **The location of several prominent and sacred hills (see map below), such as Glastonbury Tor, Beacon Batch, Hambledon Hill, Melbury Hill, Tan Hill, Win Green, Gare Hill, Eaker Hill, and the Neolithic monument of Silbury Hill;**
5) **The passage of one of the hexagon lines through Templecombe, the Knights Templar preceptory in Somerset;**
6) **The passage of one of the hexagon lines through Bristol, which has Knights Templar associations;**
7) **The location of certain abbeys and priories, such as Lacock, Keynsham, Glastonbury, Longleat, Kingswood, Maiden Bradley and Fonthill.**

The following discoveries also help convince us that the Astrum is authentic:

1) **The Samhain Axis (which includes Stonehenge) extends to Winchester in one direction, and the Preseli Mountains, in Wales, in the other;**
2) **The continuation of the eastern Chalice line projects to Milton Abbas Abbey, in Dorset;**
3) **An extension of the top, E-W Chalice line goes into the heart of London;**
4) **The continuance of the eastern line of the Blade goes to the centre of the Isle of White (around Godshill);**

5) A continuance of the Beltaine alignment from Avebury goes along the ancient ridgeway track to the site of the Knights Templar preceptory at Temple Rockley.

All these factors combined would determine that the Astrum could not be symmetrical – in other words, the inverted triangle would have had to be 4-5 miles further north to make it a perfectly symmetrical hexagram. As already mentioned, although Stonehenge, Avebury and Glastonbury are key elements of the Astrum's shape, it is dozens of *NATURAL* prominent and/or sacred hills that really defines the directions of the lines to the remaining three apexes.

The Hills of the Wessex Astrum
Some sixty significant hills help define the Wessex Astrum, and the main ones are shown below. They include Glastonbury Tor, Beacon Batch, Hambledon Hill, Melbury Hill, Tan Hill, Win Green, Gare Hill, Little Solsbury Hill, Cow Down, Maesbury Castle, as well as the Neolithic monument of Silbury Hill; in addition to

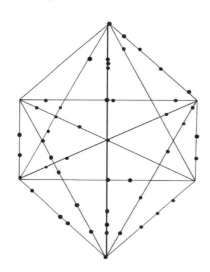

The defining hills of the Wessex Astrum. (Some others were omitted due to scale.)

these, the Beltaine alignment passes through Oliver's Castle, and hexagon lines go through Windmill Hill and Milk Hill. By *significant hills* we do not necessary mean those that are particularly high above sea level (although many are) – it's all relative. For instance, on the Somerset Levels, Windmill Hill stands prominent when viewed from the north, although it only rises to 58m above sea level. So too at Hartgrove (in Dorset) where a 118m ridge is a prominent feature, as it rises out of the low meadows of the Blackmore Vale. Sometimes it is a prominent *spur* of a hill that is the feature of note, such as those at Wotton-under-Edge, Vincent's Rock (Bristol) and the one east of Mere. At Wotton-under-Edge, the hillside spur protrudes into the surrounding lowlands like a huge landscape phallus, and the Central Axis is aligned to it.

The Chalice and the Blade
We have called the upright △ triangle the *Blade*, in line with convention as a figure symbolising the sword, fire and the male/yang principle. We have termed the inverted ▽ triangle the *Chalice*, as it is by tradition an archetypal image of the Divine feminine/yin principle, in line also with esoteric symbolism. As outlined in Chapter 2, these two symbols, either separate or interlocking, have an ancient, almost universal history. It will also be observed that the interaction of the Chalice and Blade triangles also defines another three smaller upright △ triangles and three smaller inverted ▽ triangles. These four triangles are equilaterals, with dimensions of around 10 miles on

each side; the small differences in their dimensions due to the unsymmetrical nature of the Astrum.

Naming the Astrum Lines

It seemed appropriate to name the six Astrum lines, if only to help us make a more profound, personal connection with them, energetically and in our hearts. We make no assumptions that these are the original names; but perhaps these are what they are meant to be called at this time. We took the naming of the lines seriously, realising that they would be used by people who would come after us. We hope that those who follow in our footsteps will appreciate our reasoning.

The Blade

Beginning with the Blade, we have called the Glastonbury to Stonehenge alignment the **Dod Line.** This seemed suitable for two reasons. Firstly, the alignment goes along Dod Lane, which famously runs east from Glastonbury Abbey. Secondly, the name *Dod Men* was suggested by Alfred Watkins, in his book *The Old Straight Track,* for the surveyors of the ley line system. In a way, we feel we are honouring Watkins, as well as John Michell, who saw the relevance of Dod Lane and uncovered much about the alignment when little was known.

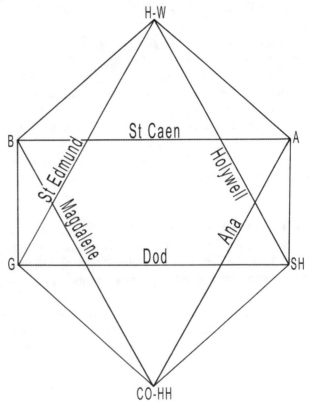

The names given to the lines of the Wessex Astrum.

We have named the Glastonbury to Wotton Blade alignment the **St Edmund Line**. This is due to the fact that the line passes right through Edmund's Mound at Glastonbury, only recently discovered by Nicholas R Mann and Philippa Glasson to have been an astronomical observatory, as outlined in their excellent book, *The Star Temple of Avalon.*

We have called the Wotton-under-Edge to Stonehenge alignment the **Holywell Line**. It passes through, or close by, seven sacred wells and springs, as well as a moat (all significant water features), as well as through the Holywell area of Wotton.

The three Blade lines, then, are associated with two male characters plus a holy well.

35

The Chalice

As for the Chalice, we have named the Brockley to Avebury configuration the **St Cain Line**, after St. Cain (later St Keyne), the 5th C saint who gave her name to Keynsham, through which this line passes. She was a learned young woman who wished to remain a virgin, crossing from her native Wales to settle in a solitary wooded abode where Keynsham now stands, where she was said to have changed an infestation of serpents into the fossils now known as ammonites. We wonder if these *serpents* really represent the Old Ways, pagan beliefs surviving in the area driven out by Cain. Her nephew was St Cadoc, who later persuaded her to return to Wales, where she lived, *"... in a hillock at the roots of a great mountain,"* where a healing well sprang up.

We have called the Brockley to Hambledon Hill alignment the **Magdalene Line.** This is not only out of reverence for the biblical and archetypal lady, held in such high esteem as the bride of Jesus by the Templars and other heretical groups, but also after the village of Fifehead Magdalen, which stands on the alignment. We name this line in honour of this much maligned and misunderstood wise woman.

We have termed the Hambledon Hill to Avebury line **Ana**, after the primeval British Mother Goddess; her sacred hill, Tan Hill, stands directly on this line. This was formerly St Anne's hill, a corruption of Ana or Anu.

To sum up, we have named all three Chalice lines after three legendary women or deities.

How Long is a Piece of String?

We were astonished to find that the sum of the alignments was over 500 miles, considerably longer even than the famous St Michael Line. But we were undaunted, for we knew we had been given a unique opportunity to reveal this sacred figure, dedicating ourselves to doing the best we could. We knew we would be guided to where we were meant to be, meet people who would help us, see whatever was to be revealed to us. From our very first field trip this turned out to be the case. We would have several "chance" meetings with people who, although total strangers to us, imparted just the information we needed.

Dimensions of the Wessex Astrum

The Blade has three sides of 40 miles = 120 miles
The Chalice has three sides of 39.5 miles = 118.5 miles
The six sides of the Hexagon = 138 miles
Central Axis from Holywell to Hambledon Hill = 52 miles
St Michael Line from Glastonbury to Avebury = 43 miles
Samhain Line from Brockley to Hambledon Hill = 43 miles

Total of 514.5 miles

But How Wide is a Piece of String?

Well, we knew how long our pieces of string were, but how wide were they? In his book, *Twelve Tribe Nations,* John Michell speaks of certain alignments as, *"Axes of Vision... corridors of visionary places,"* which could be over a mile wide. But it was Hamish Miller and Paul Broadhurst, in *The Sun and the Serpent*, who were to champion the concept, confirmed by dowsing, that ley lines should be regarded as corridors, rather than narrow sight lines. A good analogy of this is how a river might forge a wide river valley, with its meanderings and all the other related features that lie just *beyond* the present flow of water, yet which are intricately bound to its history. We concluded, therefore, that rather than regarding the alignments as thin sharp lines, we would consider them more as corridors, each around ⅓ of a mile (approx. 1km) in width, within which we would scrutinize anything we thought relevant.

This gave us a leeway of 500m either side of each axis. It turns out that statistician Robert Forrest had noted a similar width corridor all along the St Michael Line, within which 63 churches were located. Considering we were following lines up to 52 miles in length, we would propose that this "margin of leeway" is acceptable, especially as the lines pass through hills, springheads and other natural features that were preordained, and could not be moved; they had to be *worked with*. More than this, those who had either designed, or at least recognised, the Wessex Astrum would have perhaps seen these defining features as being Divinely positioned, by forces greater than Mankind. Man was merely enhancing *predestined holy lines*.

At times we looked outside this "corridor" parameter, such as when lines passed through the edges of certain towns; centres of habitation often move over the centuries and many churches can also be relocated. On several occasions it was not the modern centre that was relevant, but rather the *former* centre of habitation, or perhaps a lonely chapel, the site of a former abbey, or a forgotten ancient well, cross or megalith. Sometimes a line would only skirt a town, but its local history would nevertheless betray relevant folklore or archaeology.

Looking For a Direction

Robert Forrest also concluded that the curvature of the Earth over the entire length of the St Michael Line would only deviate its course by a matter of several yards, so this effect would certainly be negligible for the Wessex Astrum, which only followed the St Michael Line for 43 miles. This angle is around 62-63° off true north, and 65-66° off our Glastonbury-Brockley line. This Beltaine line also forms one side of a triangle, defined by Glastonbury, Stonehenge and Avebury, one angle of which is almost exactly 90°

Near the end of his seminal book, *The Keys to the Temple,* David Furlong casts a critical eye over the accuracy of the St Michael alignment using computer analyses. He found that although Burrowbridge Mump, Glastonbury Tor, Avebury and Ogbourne St George line up to within metres, other sites do not; St Michael's Mount, The Hurlers and Bury St Edmunds are out of alignment by between 700 and 2700 metres. Apart from the section mentioned, he concluded that *"...the rest of the St Michael Line is merely wishful thinking."* We find it compelling that the only truly straight section of the St Michael Line is that which falls within the Wessex Astrum!

This warrants the question as to which came first – the St Michael Line or the Wessex Astrum. It's "chicken or the egg" time again - food for thought, folks!

But Where Does it End?

And what of the terminal points of each alignment? We were struck by how the lines of the Astrum took in most of the major sites as they approach the apexes. For instance, the five lines converging on Glastonbury between them pass either through the Tor, the Chalice Well, the Abbey, St John's Church, St Benedict's Church or Edmund Hill Mound; some lines pass through more than one of these sacred sites. To answer any possible detractors, it is in fact possible to bring five random lines into Glastonbury *without* passing through *any* of these sites!

The same happens at Avebury, where the five convergent lines between them variously pass through Avebury Henge, Silbury Hill, Avebury Church, West Kennet Long Barrow, Waden Hill, Tan Hill, Milk Hill or Windmill Hill (see the map on page 130). Again, sometimes lines go through more than one of these sites.

On Hambledon Hill, in Dorset, all five lines terminate in the hillfort within the space of half a mile, an incredible fact considering the lengths of the lines and that they start their journeys from radically different directions (see map on page 117).

Although Stonehenge is a very tight focus for all the lines that converge on it (see map on page 184), it is apparent to us that the remainder of the Wessex Astrum apex points are not well-defined tight geographical localities, but rather extended areas. In

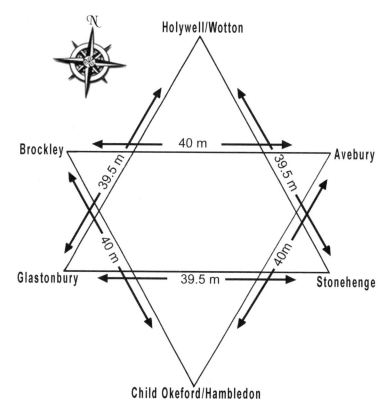

fact, we were at times concerned as to whether we were taking our lines out across the landscape from the correct spot. Take Glastonbury, for instance, from which five of the Astrum lines diverge; the Abbey, St Benedict's, the Tor, the Chalice Well and St John's church all variously act as terminal points. So too at the southern point of the Chalice, where lines converge on various points on Hambledon Hill. Avebury is similar, its sacred landscape extending over several square miles. Five of the six terminal points had to be taken, therefore, as extended areas, rather than precise foci. We have no problem with this, for the world has many precedents of sacred landscapes covering several square miles. The Giza Plateau, the Carnac area of Brittany, and the Boyne Valley in Ireland are just three of countless examples. Some scholars, and alternative researchers, may be unhappy with this *lack of precision,* but it sits well with our concept that sacred sites are not isolated and insular on the landscape, but rather are facets of something holistic; everything is connected.

As mentioned previously, the perceivers of the Astrum were restricted by the position on the landscape of various sacred hills and major prehistoric sites, which ultimately determined the alignments. We actually feel it incredible that two 40-mile alignments converging on Hambledon Hill hillfort, from Avebury and Brockley respectively, should converge with three others, from Stonehenge, Glastonbury and Wotton-under-Edge, in an area less than ½ mile across. Likewise, at Stonehenge five lines converge on an area less than ¼ mile across. This was surely beyond the realms of coincidence.

Further Conclusions and Statistics

It is only too easy to make statistics fit what one wishes to find. We found statistical analysis to be fraught with problems, however, due to rededications of churches, lost churches with no record of dedication, and other factors. The results below do not prove or disprove the Wessex Astrum, but make interesting reading all the same.

> The 15 Astrum lines pass through over 60 hill summits, triangulation points or other prominent topographical features, which is more, we feel, than coincidence would dictate.
>
> Silbury Hill stands on one of the Chalice lines, which fits perfectly with the fact that it is generally regarded as symbolic of the Divine Feminine.
>
> Likewise, Tan Hill (sacred hill of the Goddess Ana or Anu) stands on a Chalice line.
>
> Stonehenge is one of the apexes of the male Blade triangle. We have long felt this to be more of a solar temple – male symbolism again.
>
> Avebury stands at one point of the female Chalice triangle. We have for some time believed this to be predominantly a Goddess temple.
>
> To complement this, the prominent spur of Coombe Hill at the northern apex of the Blade, above Wotton-under-Edge, projects out of the Cotswold Edge like a huge phallus.
>
> We came across several churches along Astrum lines that are dedicated to John the Baptist and Mary Magdalene, two misunderstood characters highly venerated by the Knights Templar.

Other Templar localities, such as Bristol, Templecombe and Temple Rockley, are on or close to Astrum lines. We tentatively suggest that this *may* indicate the period when the Astrum was conceived, or at least recognised.

On the three lines that comprise the Blade, we found a strong bias towards male saints, with 17 churches dedicated to men, 8 to women and 4 to both. Two of the female dedications were to St Margaret, the dragon slayer. On the three lines of the Chalice, we found 19 male dedications, 6 female, and 3 to both; the percentages are similar to the Blade lines, with a bias towards male saints. These figures match the averages found in other areas of England, where there is usually an inclination towards male dedication.

We did notice, however, a marked bias towards churches dedicated to St Mary and other female saints near rivers or holy springs/wells, suggesting that they replaced ancient pagan sites associated with female deities, i.e. site evolution.

Along the St Michael Line axis we visited nine parish churches, seven of which were dedicated to male saints, with only one to a female; one other was dedicated to the Holy Cross. This is a greater bias towards the masculine than along other Astrum lines.

There were more moated sites on Chalice lines than on the Blade lines, suggesting a bias; water sites are generally regarded as places of the Divine Feminine.

Our rediscovery or confirmation of some twenty stones on Astrum lines, either surviving or else recorded but now lost, suggests that these were taken into account regards the hexagram, or else marked old tracks.

The discovery of megaliths in churchyards, and sometimes even within the fabric of churches, suggests that such sites were sacred prior to the arrival of the Church – they were ancient holy places.

On Ley Lines and Energy Leys

It needs to be stated from the outset that we do not regard the lines of the Astrum as *Energy Leys* (a term we personally dislike anyway, because of the confusion it causes) but rather they are *Ley Lines* or alignments, drawing a distinct difference between the two phenomena. It could be said that the Astrum is a series of fifteen conjoined *ley lines*. Although we felt and dowsed powerful earth energies at many sites, we would like to state here and now that…

… we are not advocating at this moment in time that earth energies are in any way, shape or form flowing down the AXIS of each alignment. (It may later be discovered that energies do so; that remains to be seen.)

With the St Michael Line, the Mary and Michael energy flows were found accompanying the axis, but this alignment is, above all, a manmade construct, even if it does follow a *natural* phenomenon, defined by the direction of the rising sun at Beltaine. Dowsers advocate that this is also part of an energy matrix that goes around the entire planet. We do not see the Wessex Astrum as part of this phenomenon directly, although the St Michael Line influenced the designers of the Astrum, to a certain extent, and they may well have been aware of the Planetary energy flows. Ultimately, everything is connected, and our ancestors did regard themselves as part of a living landscape and of a conscious Universe, where everything is one. So in that sense, the Wessex Astrum *is* part of the planetary matrix. Perhaps the form of the hexagram resulted from an energetic imprint, which influenced both Man and nature. Our distinction is this: although influenced by the location of hills, and sacred power sites such as Glastonbury, Avebury and Stonehenge …

> *… the Wessex Astrum is a man-made construct, a human conception.*

The hexagram was, we acknowledge, envisaged by people who had a close link to the Land, its energies, its Spirit and to the ethereal forces of the Earth. But, at the end of the day, although inspired by Nature, and influenced by certain natural sites *and* involving sacred geometry, it is manmade.

We hope that these two clear statements, expressed in bold italics, will be appreciated by those who come after us, and that they will stop in its tracks any misinterpretation of our findings and concepts. We welcome, of course, further work by those who may wish to follow in our footsteps, to study aspects of the Wessex Astrum further, and we shall be making web pages available for such a forum. We do not imagine for one second that we have uncovered everything that there is to be found. We believe that more magic still awaits discovery on the ancient and sacred landscape of Wessex.

Chapter 6
The Blade Defined

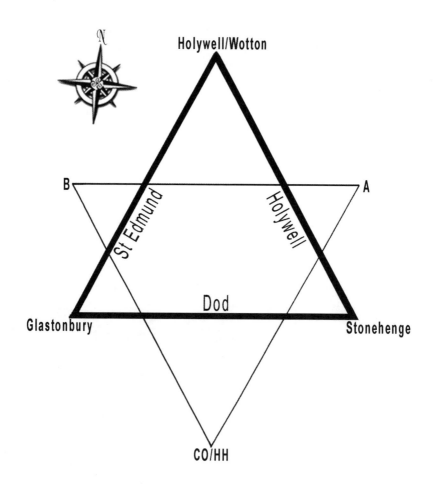

The Blade of the Wessex Astrum is an almost exact equilateral, upward-pointing triangle with sides of around 39.5 miles. The apex points are at Glastonbury, Stonehenge and Wotton-under-Edge. In esoteric traditions the upright, pyramid-like triangle is symbolic of the male, yang principle, and it seems fitting that the three apexes hold facets of this; Stonehenge is the world-famous and unique *Temple of the Sun,* famously aligned to the midsummer sunrise. We have long felt that Stonehenge is more solar and masculine, as opposed to Avebury, which feels to us like the place of the Goddess; Glastonbury is dominated by the Tor, crowned by a chapel dedicated to the solar archetype St Michael, as well as the town's Arthurian folklore; and lastly Wotton-under-Edge, overshadowed by a spur which juts out into the plain below like a giant phallus.

The sacred "blade" triangle is expressed in pyramids across the planet, such as here at Giza in Egypt.

It is impossible to create a closed shape with only two lines, making the triangle the most basic enclosed shape after the circle. Triangles are present in sacred geometry on many levels, from the Platonic Solids, to the ratios of the King's Chamber of the Great Pyramid. A hexagon can be divided into six equilateral triangles, and the Pythagoreans were particularly interested in polygons because each triangular number forms an equilateral triangle.

The upright triangle has been symbolic of the solar logos for thousands of years. The great pyramids of the Americas, Bosnia and Egypt had their focus on the sun, the male ruler of the heavens and the Earth. In alchemy, the upright triangle represents fire, complementing the feminine 'water' properties of the inverted triangle. As already examined in Chapter 2, this triangle variously symbolises male deities, such as Shiva, and the Zeir Anpin of the Kabbalah. The Dogons of Mali have long regarded it as representing the male principle. The Greek letter Delta is a triangle, representing wholeness and completion. The Hittites regarded this upward pointing triangle as the symbol of a king, and of health. It is the alchemical symbol of fire, the point being the tip of upward-reaching flames. In both Hinduism and Buddhism, the upward-pointing triangle represents the lingum, or phallus. Freemasonry has a triangle enclosing an eye, symbolising divine knowledge, most famously seen on the US dollar bill. In Christian symbolism, the upward-pointing triangle represents the three aspects of the Holy Trinity.

The pyramid on the US dollar bill.

It seems fitting to us to have named two of the

lines after male characters, the other being Holywell, due to the location from which it starts and the number of holy wells and springs along its course.

As we have already discussed, we have called the Glastonbury to Stonehenge alignment the **Dod Line,** the Glastonbury to Wotton Blade alignment the **St Edmund Line**, and the Wotton to Stonehenge alignment the **Holywell Line**. The three Blade lines are thus associated, at least in terms of symbolism, with two male characters plus a holy well.

We will now begin our description of our pilgrimages and discoveries along the fifteen alignments of the Wessex Astrum. We hope you will enjoy the journey!

(Note: As a reference aid, the places shown on the location diagrams at the beginning of each chapter are later given in **bold type** in the text, as and when the main section describing them is encountered.)

Chapter 7
The Blade – The Holywell Line:
Holywell/Wotton to Stonehenge

x Holywell/Wotton
x Synwell
x Tor Hill

x Hammouth Hill
x Tumulus
x Chilbury Hill

x Luckington
x Alderton
x Grittleton

x Allington
x Chippenham
x Moat

x Hillfort

x Chittoe
x Bromham
x Rowde

x Pottern Field (summit)
X Eastcott

x Summer Down (tumuli)
x Tumuli

x Tumuli
X Stonehenge

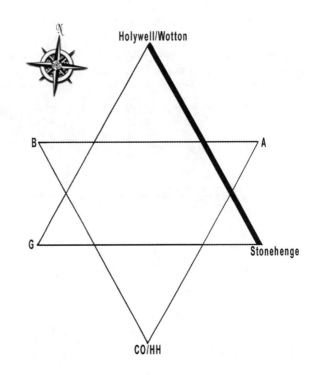

Five Astrum alignments diverge from the **Wotton-under-Edge** area, so here may be an appropriate juncture to look into the town's history.

The 'Edge' element is the steep scarp of hard, Jurassic, Inferior Oolite limestone. The views from Wotton Hill or Coombe Hill are superb; one can see both the suspension bridges of the Severn Estuary, the Black Mountains of Wales, the Mendip Hills south of Bristol, or one's eye can follow the southern line of the Edge as it runs east towards Bath. Much of the area is designated as an Area of Outstanding Natural Beauty.

There are three prehistoric barrows in the parish: a long barrow and a tumulus near Symonds Hall Farm (NE of the town), and a long barrow on Blackquarries Hill, the latter of which is on one of the Astrum hexagon lines (see page 187). A few finds of worked flints and arrowheads have been made locally, and there is evidence of human activity in the Roman period, proven from finds at Tyley bottom, near Symonds Hall, and at the Roman Villa at Wortley.

Wotton is traditionally associated with the wool trade, and it is a common misconception that the name derives from "Wool Town". In fact the first record of the town is in a Saxon Charter of King Edmund of Wessex, who in 940 AD leased land in 'Wudeton' to the Theign Edrick. "Wudetun" means the enclosure, homestead or village (tun) in or near the wood (wude). The hill above the town was the site of one of early-warning beacons used during the approach of the Spanish Armada in 1588.

The Church of St Mary's is a Mercian church, established around 940 AD as a Saxon place of worship. The Domesday Book of 1086 describes Wotton under the name of Vutune, a royal manor ruled by the Lords of Berkeley. During the reign of King John,

The Ram Inn, Wotton, is said to be haunted and to stand on an ancient site on a ley line.

and possibly as a result of Thomas de Berkeley's part in the barons' revolt, Wotton's Old Town (still so called) was burnt to the ground. However, by 1243 Thomas had built a manor house near the church and in 1252 his widow, Jone de Somery, established an annual fair and a weekly market. The town supported almshouses and a house of friars (one of nine in Gloucestershire), but never held a monastery or nunnery.

It was a prosperous community in the middle ages, thriving on the wool trade, and receiving municipal privileges from Henry III. Weaving and cloth-making was the main occupation of the inhabitants of Wotton from the 13th C onwards. The Industrial Revolution brought to an end many cottage industries, as several mills sprang up along the Little Avon. The cloth industry persisted through the 19th C, even after the disastrous slumps of the 1830's and 1840's; over a long history it has brought considerable prosperity to Wotton.

The Ram Inn is said to be haunted and has been the subject of research by dowsers and ghost hunters. Folklore says two people were murdered on the premises. The Inn is thought to have been built around 1145, and sits in a dip on Potters Pond, now one of the side streets running down from Church Street and the High Street. It is a substantial building, with two stories of Cotswold stone and a timber framed *Weavers' Attic* above. The Inn stands on a ley line running between Ley Farm and Hetty Peglar's Tump, a late Stone Age burial mound; the alignment is said to run directly through the *Witch's Room* of the Inn, then on through the Church, eventually reaching Stonehenge. Dowsers have found that the Ram stands on top of a pagan burial ground, as well as a henge.

We shall return to Wotton later, when we track the other Astrum lines that diverge from the area.

Looking from the top of Coombe Hill, along the Holywell Line to Tor Hill. The Holywell spring nestles in the valley below.

The Holywell Line begins high on **Coombe Hill**, just south of the Old London Road. Old antiquarians spoke of, *"a triple earthwork called the Ring of Bells,"* on top of Coombe Hill, although the exact location is uncertain. Near the spot, we found an elongated mound, described on page 213, which marks the Central Axis. The line plunges down steep slopes into Holywell. When we originally plotted the Astrum we were fascinated that this place name should be near the northern apex of the hexagram, and wondered whether or not a well survived. Whilst we were up on Coombe Hill we were approached by a man named Paul, who had just moved to the area, who then gave us the location of the spring. This was just one of many "chance" meetings with people unbeknownst to us who pointed us in the right direction.

We first approached **Holywell** from the church of St Mary's, which we shall return to on page 215, via a back street known as Valley Road, along which the Cotswold Way runs. Two footbridges cross streams before Holy Well Lane is reached. We turned left and very soon saw the depression that marks the ancient well to our right, immediately in front of allotments. Four overgrown stone steps lead down to the waters, which still flow beneath overhanging foliage. We could hear a trickle below and wanted to partake of the waters, as we had done at many other sacred wells and springs, but a sign warned us not to drink. Despite the abandonment of this sacred place, it still felt holy and we wondered what events had transpired here over thousands of years; a Roman coin dated 259-68 AD was found in a garden near the well. Toni dowsed a strong energy current, which led her to the cottages and allotments behind the well; it seemed to carry on up the steep hill beyond.

We then followed winding lanes up to **Synwell**, the next destination on the Holywell Line. This is now a modern estate, and the line crosses the recreation ground before passing through Warren House, to the southeast. From this open park we could see Coombe Hill towering above us to the NW. Nothing now remains of Syn Well, but old records speak of it as being, *"...east of the stream, beyond the church,"* and that it was renowned for the quality of its waters. We did, however, see water gushing beneath a drain grill next to a post box, just outside the Full Moon Pub, and wondered if this flowed from the source. The former importance of this area is confirmed by the fact that most of Wotton-under-Edge was once known as Synwell.

The line then goes across both **Tor Hill** and **Hammouth Hill**. Just south of the line is *Knight's Grove*, an ancient wood listed in English Nature's *Ancient Woodland Inventory (June 1994 Amendment)*. The next stop is a Bronze Age tumulus (grid ref: 807877) NNW of Worcester Lodge. The line proceeds through the grounds of the latter before crossing Chilbury Hill, and then through three farms before going through the very centre of **Luckington**. The 17th C antiquarian John Aubrey recorded of Luckington, *"... In this village is a fine spring Hancock's-well, which is mentioned by Dr. Chilrey... it cures the Itch and Scabbe; it hath done much good to the eies"*. It is situated at the NE end of the village (grid ref: 841847).

Luckington parish church, east of the village centre, is dedicated to St Mary and St Ethelbert. It was used for the marriage scene in a BBC TV dramatisation of Jane Austen's *Pride and Predjudice*. The church is usually locked but we found the graveyard to be atmospheric, particularly under the branches of a huge yew south of the tower, where we stood in semi-darkness, midst forgotten tombstones. Just to the

Serpent and broken hexagram at Alderton.

east of the tree, next to the farm, is a low mound, which we thought might possibly be ancient, which dowsing confirmed. Back at the car park, we looked south and could see the spire of Alderton church on the skyline, our next destination. Luckington once had three churches; the Providence Chapel survives in the centre of the village and is dated 1866 on the front.

Alderton is described in the Domesday Book as *Aldrintone*. Aubrey describes a destroyed manor house, north of the church near the fishponds. Sir Charles Hedges of Alderton was Queen Anne's secretary and he had the same crest and arms as the City of London. Manor Farm is on the line and is a beautiful 17th C building. The church and the village pond, 300yds SW, seem to define the edges of the line. The church is dedicated to St Giles and was rebuilt in 1844 by Joseph Neeld of Grittleton House (see below), who was at one time MP for Chippenham. It is only open on Sundays from April to October, between 10.00am-4.00pm.

But there is much to see around the outside of St Giles'; there are several interesting roof decorations in stone, such as a Templar cross, a triangle and, of relevance, a hexagram on the south side (with the top point broken off). There are also weird grotesques and an unusual curvi-triangular window, with four vesicas within. Other small windows at the west end show a single serpent entwined around a staff as well as a chalice with a dagger emerging from it. On the south side, a small window shows another hexagram, and also of interest is a dragon in foliage at the west end. At the SE corner of the churchyard stands a large redwood and Toni dowsed a strong energy flow going from the tree to the church, entering through the wall below two great grotesque carvings. At the west end of the churchyard a sunken path can be seen going south, which continues in the field beyond.

The Holywell Line then crosses the Fosse Way at Dunley Wood, and passes the 402ft spot height on the road going north from Grittleton. The line then strikes through the village of **Grittleton** itself, the parish church of which marks the axis.

Grittleton has two churches and a large manorial estate. The grand buildings of the private school (formerly Luckington House) are seen from the churchyard of St Mary and St Ethelbert. The oldest surviving stonework of the church is 12th C, although there was an earlier church. Up the 14th C tower we could see fine winged gargoyles and inside there are some interesting stained glass windows. One shows St John holding a chalice out of which is emerging a winged dragon, and a crucifixion window shows Jesus enclosed within a beautiful blue vesica piscis, an ancient symbol of the Divine Feminine. But the most unusual window is one near the font showing St Luke, who is holding a caduceus, a staff around which are entwined two serpents. We had never before seen any Biblical characters associated with the caduceus. Usually it is being wielded by either Mercury or Hermes; we had encountered Hermes at Iwerne Minster. Miller and Broadhurst found this symbol to represent the yin and yang energy currents that entwine the St Michael Line.

St Luke holding a caduceus at Grittleton.   Dragon emerging from a chalice at Grittleton.

The next village on the line is **Sevington,** a small hamlet which held more unexpected treasures. Just east of the centre of the line is the beautiful Victorian School, built by Joseph Neeld in 1849. It is very elaborate, with fine embellishments that we did not expect to find in such a small village. Its porch and tower give the impression of a chapel rather than a school. Next to the school Toni was drawn to a small mound, created around the stump of a large felled tree, and she dowsed an energy flow going from the mound to the school.

We then passed through a nearby gate which gave access to two lakes to the north, used for fishing. Tall trees formed an avenue down to the lakes, and on 19th C OS maps this avenue extends for nearly a mile to Grittleton House. The beauty of the lakes is spoilt somewhat today by the traffic of the M4, which thunders by to the north. Further on, the line passes east of the ancient moat at Fowleswick. The property was described by antiquarian John Aubrey in the 17th C as:

The Victorian School at Sevington.

" ...an ancient howse with a faire mote about..". He queried whether the property had once belonged to Wallingford Abbey.

The line then passes through **Allington,** which has a church and the fine Bulidge House. Allington was given by King Stephen to the nuns of Martigny in the Valais, and through them later transferred to Monkton Farley Priory.

The line then passes into the **Chippenham** area, which formerly stood wthin the huge woodland known as Pewsham Forest. The Holywell Line crosses Frogwell, a lane going west out of Chippenham. It gets its name from the well/spring of that name, which is shown on old maps at grid ref: 903734, on the north side of the road. This may be the spring that antiquarian John Aubrey spoke of: *"... a spring called Holy-well. Medicinal waters were taken anciently... dedicated to some Deity or saint to whom they imputed virtue...".* To the west of this is the parish church of St Peter's, opened in 1967 by the Bishop of Bristol. We stood opposite the church in awe as we realised that the church was hexagonal! We felt it incredible that a church built in the 1960's, just yards from the centre of the line, should have a six-sided symmetry. Just next to the church, the road divided at a spot

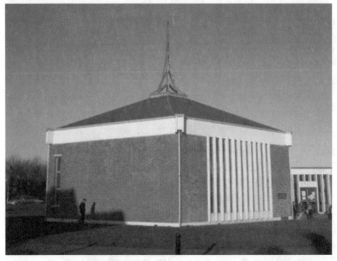

St Peter's church at Frogwell, Chippenham, was built in 1967 to a hexagonal design, and stands just yards from the axis!

51

called Lord's Mead.

At the end of Rowden Lane is **Rowden**, a charming collection of well-kept cottages around a small green. Rowden Manor is the site of the original Rowden House, described by Aubrey as, *"..a large, well built Gothique house...about the house is a mote... and a fair hall, very well furnished with armour,"* A seige took place here during the Civil War. The site was originally enclosed by a moat and vestiges of this can still be seen, particularly of the north side behind The Manor, where water flows along the moat from a nearby spring. This was to be just the first of several moated sites we were to visit on Astrum lines. On the large lawn of the property (visible from a footpath around the south side, or through the wrought-iron gates) stands the sculpture of a stag.

Dragons and a griffin adorn the west gatehouse at Spy House

From Rowden the line then crosses the winding River Avon three times, before going straight through the hillfort at Naish Hill (grid ref: 936694). A visit to the site revealed a flat field with no visible surviving banks. The line then passes through Bowden Park Farm, a fine old building with slit windows. The Holywell Line then skirts east of Bowden Church, which is dedicated to St Anne and is worth a visit if only for the fine views to the south.

The line then goes through the huge estate of Spy Park, whose grand west gatehouse is finely decorated with a large griffin and several small dragons (at grid ref:

Inside the lavish interior of Bromham Church.

942679). At the north gate is White Lodge, perhaps a memory of a holy site in the vicinity. The route of a Roman road runs east-west through the estate, passing within yards of the house. The line continues through the estate to **Chittoe**, passing west of the old village church. This is now a private dwelling, *The Old Church*, but it can be viewed from the road, from where can be seen a fine stone building with an external bellcote. The line crosses the lane to the west, at the southern entrance to Spy Park House, an area of pleasant woodland and public bridlepaths.

The corridor of the line takes in both churches at **Bromham**, which seem to define its boundary. The Domesday Book records an earlier wooden Saxon chapel here, and the present 12th C parish church of St Nicholas has the most wonderful collection of gargoyles. The spire of the tower is a well-known landmark and rises to 180ft. Inside the church, the peaceful Blessed Virgin Mary Chapel (also known as the Beauchamp Chapel) is on the north side. In the Chantry Chapel there are exceptional painted ceiling panels, with gold leaf tracery and a fine Alabaster effigy of Sir Thomas Tocates. Other grand monuments and high quality carvings confirm that local dynasties here had great wealth and influence; it was Sir William Beauchamp who built St George's Chapel at Windsor. The two chapels divide the church almost equally in two, so it is not clear which is the high altar, which is unusual. Peter dowsed a female energy current passing through the south chapel, whilst a male current ran into the north chapel.

Outside, hidden behind the church on the north side, is a tall Celtic-style cross, a memorial to the Irish poet Thomas Moore; it has Celtic knotwork that terminates with the heads of dragons. At the southeast corner of the church, Peter spotted a large reddish stone protruding from the base of the buttress – was this an ancient megalith? Next to the stone, the east end of the Chantry Chapel is richly decorated, including a stone dragon, be it with tiny wings!

There is also a Methodist Chapel close by, near the top of Church Hill, and there is

The church at Rowde, which is said to be haunted.

53

Stockwell, a tiny spring that flows beside the footpath known as Stoney Lane (formerly Stockwell Lane). The water from it was claimed to cure eye infections. Some older inhabitants can remember as children having their eyes bathed with the waters and in recent years people have again been visiting the well to obtain water to use as an eye lotion.

The next destination is **Rowde,** a compact yet ancient village, situated on the main Devizes to Chippenham road. An extensive Iron Age and Romano-British settlement stood northeast of village, close to Rowde Farm. The parish name means *a reedy-place,* presumably referring to a settlement near the Rowdeford stream. Rowde had a resident priest in the Domesday Book, and so presumably a church, although the present building, apart from the 15th C tower, is an 1831-3 rebuild. In 1548 it was documented that the *"Hospital of St John the Baptist in Devizes"* owned property in Rowde, and land was also held by Malmesbury Abbey. The turnpike (one of the earliest in Wiltshire) ran from Devizes, through the village, to Rowdeford (where the Beltaine Line crosses), where a small but elegant three-arched bridge (repaired and widened in 1815) marks the parish boundary. The village has a triangular green, forcing a swerve in the main road, with the stately perpendicular church tower perched above it. The church of St Matthew (formerly St Mary) is approached along a track next to the George and Dragon pub. It has a plain exterior, with few decorations, and we found it to be locked outside Sunday services, with no contact

The war memorial in Rowde churchyard, where some of Toni's distant ancestors are remembered.

numbers for keys. The church is said to be haunted by a tall lady, who sits in the pews praying before disappearing! Rowde is an ancestral place for Toni, as this area of Wiltshire was where some of her distant forebears lived. Parish records from the 16th C onwards show numerous examples of her lineage. For example, in Rowde between 1735 and 1869, there were 119 baptisms involving the name Perrott, Perrot, Perrat or Perrett, and 85 burials between 1759 and 1904. As one enters the churchyard the war memorial shows two Perretts who died in WWI (see image above), and gravestones also bear the Perrett name.

The Wesleyan Chapel is to the southeast, on the B3101, and is dated 1838 over the door. To the north of the village is the parkland of Rowdeford House, an 1812 mansion, through which the alignment passes. It is now a residential school for children with special needs. Close to the house, a headless ghost is said to haunt

54

Lock's Ford, and Rowde vicarage is also said to be haunted, this time by a spectral man, seen by the vicar and members of his family. Of interest is the fact that the Beltaine Line and the Holywell Line cross paths near Rowdeford House (grid ref: 976632) and this is precisely where Hamish Miller and Paul Broadhurst dowsed an energy node on the Michael flow, where it crosses the A342.

The alignment then ascends to the summit of **Pottern Field,** another area that was frequented by Toni's ancestors. A total of 79 baptisms involving her forebears took place in the parish of Potterne between 1725 and 1881. The line then passes through a collection of houses called **Eastcott**, before crossing the Wessex Ridgeway, through the northern end of a small wood which is shown on older maps. The line then crosses the Ana Chalice Line (the Hambledon to Avebury alignment).

For over three miles the Holywell Line then goes through MOD land, closed to the public. Study of the 1889 OS map, however, shows features that were present prior to the takeover by the military. The alignment goes just south of a stone marked on the old map (grid ref: 043539) and just north of some earthworks (grid ref: 058512) before passing right through a boundary stone (grid ref: 061509) and two tumuli. The line then goes through a milestone that stands on the old road across Salisbury Plain, now a public bridleway which, after miles of out-of-bounds land, at last allows access. The stone states, "Devizes 9, Salisbury 14". For the next mile the old road follows the Blade Line, passing through an important ancient crossroads, before reaching another milestone ("Devizes 10, Salisbury 13") and a boundary stone next to the track (grid ref: 083478), both shown on the 1889 map.

The line then passes just yards east of the cottages at **Bustard**, an ancient hamlet, which survives in the form of the Bustard Inn, Bustard Cottages, and a well. We can thoroughly recommend this pub for the charismatic, friendly Yorkshire landlord and the good food. A public track taken east from Bustard for a mile will take you to the Neolithic enclosure Robin Hood's Ball, as well as nearby long barrows and tumuli.

The line approaches the Stonehenge environs through MOD land between Larkhill and Rollestone army camps, passing by tumuli either side of the road linking the

The Cursus Group of round barrows, through which the Holywell Line passes.

camps (see map on page 184). These mounds can be seen to the north and south from the road. Passing east of Fargo Plantation, the line crosses the **Greater Stonehenge Cursus**, the Neolithic ceremonial way that lies to the north of Stonehenge. Terence Meaden has shown that all ten long barrows in the vicinity are within sight of the cursus, and that they align with either the western or eastern end of the monument, proving that these long barrows post-date the latter; it was the construction of the cursus that prompted the subsequent positioning of these long mounds. The cursus was built about 5,300 years ago and an explanation of it is given in Meaden's excellent book, *Stonehenge: The Secret of the Solstice*.

We sat in the middle of the cursus, where the Holywell Line crossed it, NW of the Cursus barrow group (see below) and tuned in. Toni got the image of a moonlit night, stirring memories of nocturnal rituals long ago. Peter got a strong image of a giant pulling a huge stone behind him. The stone was rough and craggy – he felt it was the Heelstone! This stone was one of the very first to have been erected at Stonehenge, long before the famous sarsen circle, and we thought that the vision meant that this stone was brought up the sacred cursus, perhaps as a ritual blessing before it was erected. This image was certainly unforeseen, and was not the result of any expectation; we do not know of any previous speculation that stones might have been transported down this ceremonial avenue.

The line then goes right through a prominent row of aligned round barrows, seen and accessed from the car park at Stonehenge (see photo above). These five Bronze Age mounds are known as the Cursus Group, and are aligned east-west. All the mounds contained cremations, as well as grave goods such as bone and amber beads, bronze knives and even gold. The axis of the line passes through the middle mound of the three that are fenced off together.

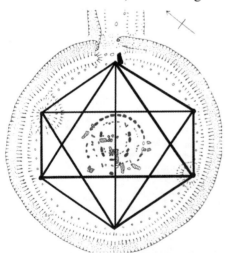

The compressed hexagram overlaid onto the plan of Stonehenge, defined by the four station stones (compare with page 20).

knives and even gold. The axis of the line passes through the middle mound of the three that are fenced off together.

We visited the mounds the day after the 2008 Summer Solstice, which was a beautiful sunny and blustery day. We scrambled onto all three mounds, but settled on the top of the centre one. We lay down and again tuned in. Toni got the image of two young boys peering over the top of the mound, looking to the east, where a fire glow illuminated the night sky, Perhaps they were witnessing ancient fires, lit to signal processions into Stonehenge, in the direction of the Avenue and the Old King Barrows.. We then stood up and sent out healing back down the Holywell Line to Wotton, and then down to the mighty monument of Stonehenge itself.

We both dowsed three spirals of energy at the middle of the mound, next to where we had been sitting. Dowsers over many years have found barrows to be sited on powerful energy nodes. (In the summer of 2008 we led a group from the Surrey Dowsers onto the mounds, and they confirmed the presence of powerful dowsable energies on the barrows, including spiralling nodes.) From this mound Stonehenge is almost lost behind the intrusive mess of the car park, and the woods behind. We marvelled at how the ancient stones, midst all this chaos and ugliness before us, even now retained some of their dignity. At one point, lying on our backs, Toni pointed out a cloud in the shape of the head of a huge, open-mouthed dragon. We felt our prayers had been appreciated!

The alignment goes right into the heart of the sarsen circle of **Stonehenge**, which really needs no introduction (see map on page 184). We have already described how hexagrams can be overlaid onto the plan of the monument, as shown in Chapter 2. We show another hexagram above, which we found hidden within the design of the monument. This time it involves the four station stones that stand outside the main sarsen circle. Of interest is the fact that it is a "compressed" hexagram, complementing the two regular hexagrams shown in Chapter 2. We are not aware that the four station stones have been linked with a hexagram before.

Every now and again we get invited to lead groups or tours into the heart of Stonehenge, for "Special Access" time. No matter how many times we walk amongst the mighty sarsen stones, we are filled with awe, and we ponder as to what rituals and spectacular ceremonies took place here long ago. Dowsers have proven that the monument sucks in energy like some kind of black hole, and the site is alive with the planetary life force. Toni dowsed and physically felt the strongest energy flowing between the central mica altar stone and the Heel Stone, then across road and along the Avenue. Ley lines also converge on Stonehenge like the spokes of a gigantic wheel. As we stand within the monument and look out across the landscape beyond, we now know that five more alignments also diverge from here – the lines of the Wessex Astrum.

Toni experiencing the energies between two of the Bluestones inside Stonehenge.

Chapter 8
The Blade
St Edmund Line:
Wotton to Glastonbury

x Wotton-under-Edge
x Kingswood

x Bury Hill

x Yate

x Rodford
x Roman road/Shortwood
x Warmley

x Moat
x Hanham Court
x Queen Charlton

x Publow
x Pensford
x Stanton Wick
x Stowey
x White Hill
x Coley

x Eaker Hill

x Tumuli and henge

x Haybridge
x Coxley

x Edmund Hill
x Glastonbury Abbey

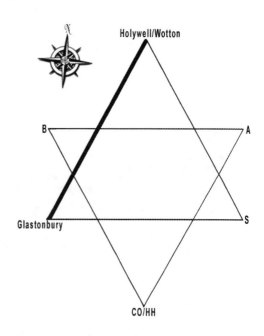

The St Edmund Line runs from the prominent hill above Wotton-under-Edge to Glastonbury Abbey, a distance of almost 40 miles. It is one side of the equilateral triangle that forms the "masculine" Blade of the Astrum. We visited sites along the line, starting at Wotton and working our way across Gloucester into Somerset, and we shall describe the alignment in this order. We named the line from the prehistoric astronomical observatory at Glastonbury. It was only *after* we had plotted this line that we found it went through the Edmund Hill Mound (detailed below), and that there was also an almost identical alignment on Palden Jenkins' map *The Ancient Landscape Around Glastonbury* (Gothic Image, 2005). His line starts at the Tor, whereas ours goes from the east end of the Abbey. Both alignments include Stowey, Eaker Hill and White Hill, and to us this independent corroboration only serves to confirm the authenticity of our alignment.

The terminal point of the line is the prominent spur overlooking **Wotton-under-Edge**, which is occupied by a group of pillow mounds, as well as two unmarked mounds (see page 213), which we had found to stand on the Central Axis. The St

Left: the hexagram in the window of the Independence Chapel, Wotton. Right: Toni dowsing at the war memorial cross. The site is a powerful omphalos of the town.

Edmund Line actually passes right through the westernmost pillow mound (grid ref. 760938). These mounds are thought by archaeologists to be medieval rabbit warrens, following the introduction of bunnies into Britain by the Normans. Others see a more duel purpose for these mounds, one perhaps being as observational platforms. Many are on the tops of hills, such as those at Old Sodbury to the south. The mound at Wotton is exactly aligned with the Astrum, just as two others on the same hill align with the Central Axis. All three show up excellently on Google Earth. Is it possible that the Normans took advantage of mounds that were already available, into which rabbits could burrow? The views from this point are breathtaking.

As the line of the Blade sweeps down the hill it passes between two churches, which seem to "channel" the line through the town. Both are on the road called Old Town, to the west of the War Memorial. We first visited the RC Church of the Holy Cross, a modern building with an almost N-S orientation – aligning itself with the St Edmund Line! A banner near the entrance describes it as "Salvatorian" and around its walls are displayed the Stations of the Cross. The other church is more interesting. Officially the chapel is called the Old Town Meeting House and stands over the road from the War Memorial, the modern Omphalos of the town where main roads meet. Although one stone is dated 1904, a notice board says its origins date back to 1701-3 and that it is an *Independent* church. We noted a hexagram in the west window (visible through an iron gate next to the bus shelter), suggesting to us that the builders of the church

may have been aware of the special locality. We also noted how the chapel, the War Memorial and the parish church of St Mary are in alignment; the tall golden tower and hexagonal clockface of the latter illuminated by the late afternoon sun. Toni picked up an energy current, flowing from the Old Town Meeting House, through the War Memorial, past the Surgery to St Mary's parish church. St Mary's and our dowsing of it is dealt with in Chapter 21, as it stands close to the Central Axis.

Also in the town, not far west of the line, is the Tabernacle, formerly a church but now an auction room. The church is visible from the spur above

Hexagrams at the entrance of The Tabernacle, Wotton.

and has a fine six-pointed window at the north end, through which the light illuminates beautifully rich colours. It was originally built as a Methodist Chapel in 1783 by Rowland Hill, but was rebuilt in the Gothic style in 1850. It is a "box chapel" and seated up to 800 people. What struck us were the dozens of hexagrams in the tiles at the entrance, reminding us of the whole magical journey we were on. In his book *The Sacred Art of Geometry,* Nigel Pennick illustrates multiple hexagrams laid into the floor of San Giovanni Laterano, in Rome. Inside the Tabernacle there are replicas of Roman tesselated pavements on the walls. The building is open on viewing and auction days, when admission is free; contact Wotton Auction Rooms Ltd (tel. 01453 844733).

Leaving Wotton, the St Edmund alignment passes through the school, and then skims the main buildings of both Hawpark Farm and Park Mill Farm. The line then skirts the village of **Kingswood**, located to the SW of Wotton. In reality, the line passes through an area historically prone to flooding, which forced the settlement further west. Kingswood Abbey was a Cistercian foundation, founded in the 12th C by William of Berkeley, in accordance with the wishes of his uncle Roger II of Berkeley; it was populated from the Cistercian foundation at Tintern. All that survives now is the 16th C gatehouse, which is in the care of English Heritage. Calcot Manor, to the north, was an annex of the abbey, used by the Monks during floods. The original 1300 datestone survives in the porch of the tithe barn.

The church at Kingswood is St Mary's, and stands close to the Abbey site, on the corner of the High St and Golden Lane, within sight of the Gatehouse. The church feels "large" inside, with a high roof and tall white-washed walls. For us, the chief feature of the church is the east windows. In each window are six flowers and other geometrical shapes, including

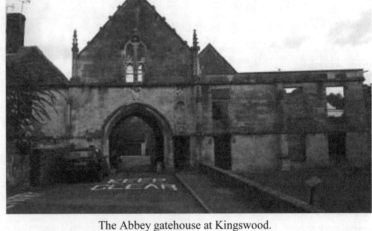

The Abbey gatehouse at Kingswood.

two hexagrams! The one on the left caught our attention (see image on the next page, and colour image on the cover), as it has the Blade coloured red, and the Chalice triangle in blue, the divine male and femainine colours matching their appropriate triangles! We stood there elated. We found another small hexagram in a window on the south side, and two dragons on a wall monument near the altar.

Out in the churchyard, we were immediately drawn to a small mound to the east of the church, on which two high-status graves stood. Toni dowsed a powerful energy current which ran from the mound, through the nearby yew and into the church, flowing directly under a window displaying one of the hexagrams!

The St Edmund Line then heads across gentle countryside for the next few miles, passing through Upper Barns Farm, Chaselane Farm and traversing Chase Hill, before crossing the Little Avon River, east of Wickwar.

The next rise is **Bury Hill**, north of the old quarries at Yate Rocks. The alignment then crosses the Wickwar to Hawkesbury road at Chaselane Farm, old roadside buildings supported by ancient wooden wall supports (grid ref: 737889).

The Hexagram and other geometrical symbols at Kingswood Church. The hexagram above has the red blade and the blue chalice! (See colour version on the book cover.)

The line then passes through **Yate**, now an overspill town for Bristol, which also marks the southern reaches of the Cotswolds. The first mention of Yate is as a religious house about AD 770 when land was given by Bishop Ecquine of Worcester, to a man called Eanulf, to found a monastery close to St. Mary's. The name is derived from the Saxon word *Giete* or *Gete* meaning "a gateway into a forest area". During the Saxon period and into medieval times most of this part of south Gloucestershire was covered with forest, which was later cleared for farming. Yate is recorded in the Domesday Book and in 1218 King Henry III granted permission for a market. In 1299 authorization was given for the manor to be surrounded by a moat and fortifying walls, with a gatehouse, drawbridge and portcullis. The castle remained in the Wyllington family until 1397, and with the end of the male line then passed through several families, becoming the Berkeley Estate. During the Civil War, some of Cromwell's troops, led by a young colonel called Edward Massey, camped at Yate Court, but on leaving they turned their cannons and razed it to the ground. Their destruction was so thorough that it was never rebuilt, though a farmhouse was built around the ruins and still remains. The manor house is represented today by Manor Farm, which stands on a large moated site east of the Bristol road. The surviving house is a large two-storied H-shaped building.

In Yate, the line passes the church at Goose Green (ref: 711834) and all three churches SW of St Mary's are near the line. On old maps, Goose Green Farm (grid ref: 714837) stands in isolation north of the village and marks where the alignment comes in from the north. There is a Templar Rd heading from the church and into the

Left: the stone next to St Mary's church, Yate.
Right: the alignment of Templar Rd with the parish church at Yate.

line, which crosses a stream. From here the alignment of the road to the church can be seen (see image above, right).

The town's parish church, St Mary's, dates back to Norman times, although a church at this site was recorded in 770 AD. Its tower forms a prominent landmark and the other walls are a mixture of stone, some an attractive red hue. On entering the churchyard one is struck by how crowded it is, with bushes and trees jostling for limited space. At the east end of the church we found a small stone, about two feet on each side, and wondered if it were a former megalith, or the vestiges of an ancient cross (site continuity again!). The church was largely rebuilt in the 14-15th C, though suffered, like many churches, at the hands of Cromwell's troops - the windows of the North Chapel are made up of smashed fragments of glass. Unfortunately the church is locked except for services, and we could find no contact details for key holders, but from the outside we could see stained glass windows, which may repay inspection.

St Mary's Primary School, situated outside the churchyard walls, was built on the site of a former poor house and next to the church is the Yate Heritage Centre. Locally, both Stanshawes Court and Kingsgate Park have been sites of paranormal activity, although in modern times Yate is more associated with J K Rowling, author of the Harry Potter books, who was born in the town.

The line then crosses the east edge of Westerleigh Common, before going through the tunnel that takes the road under the railway to **Rodford**. Just east of the tunnel formerly stood Rodfordhill Farm, which stood exactly on the centre of the line. Even today, Rodford is just a small cluster of homes, but at the southern end is the Independent Chapel, as marked on the 1889-1905 OS maps, surviving today as the Grace Evangelical Church Westerleigh (grid ref: 699804). The chapel is in stone rather than the more common brick construction for this type of chapel, and there is a small churchyard at the south end. Standing as it does, almost isolated in a rural setting, it is even more striking that the St Edmund Line goes precisely through the chapel!

The alignment then passes through the west edge of Westerleigh, 600m west of St James' Church. The church is usually locked, but does not have any notable stained glass windows, although fine gargoyles grace the tower. The road south from a 78m spot height follows the alignment for 500m, before it crosses the M4 and goes through Lydegreen Farm.

The course of the Roman road either side of **Shortwood** runs parallel and in places exactly matches the course of the alignment, which crosses the road east of the Methodist Chapel, a stone building dating from 1876. South of Shortwood the alignment follows the Roman road for over a mile, crossing the golf course, Siston Hill and then Siston Common, from where we could see the lengthening tentacles of Bristol's sprawl. The line then crosses through the main traffic island at Walmley, west of the Congregational Chapel in Chapel Lane.

The St Edmund Line then proceeds straight through **Barrs Court Moat,** a major site on this alignment. The two-acre site has been designated an ancient monument, 80% of which is surrounded by a well-preserved moat. The site once stood within Kingswood Chase, a royal hunting preserve and the successor to the much larger Forest of Kingswood, which was deforested in the 13th C. The moat is in fact the single most important medieval relic of the former Chase. Water-filled moats were a common settlement feature of wooded areas in medieval England and we have encountered them elsewhere on Astrum lines. We believe that some of them may have a more ancient origin.

The broad waters of the impressive Barrs Court Moat, all that remains now of a grand manor on the St Edmund Line.

Little is known of the early history of Barrs Court Moat, and the earliest documentation is that of 1340. One corner of the moat is now filled, and following the demolition of a mansion a farmhouse was developed from what were originally outbuildings. One of these buildings, a large cruciform barn, was converted into the public house in the 1980's. The four internal banks of the moat were constructed with a retaining wall, much of which remains, making it one of only two surviving walled moats in the UK. The original walls of the large 17th C farmhouse can be viewed along the western side. The best viewpoint is from the area of the small weir and plank bridge.

The name comes from Sir John and Lady Jane Barre who owned the land in the mid-15th C. In the 16th C, the Newton family enlarged Barrs Court and built a large mansion in the centre of the moat field, which stood there until around 1750. Barrs Court was an excellent example of a large middle-late medieval house, which would have consisted of a large house, with courtyards, stables, orchard and gardens, surrounded on four sides by the moat. Early manuscripts reveal a few brief details of a manor house enclosed within a high wall. There were niches all around the outside of the house, filled with colossal leaden statues, and a large and lofty entrance hall showing the Newton arms (a Moorish king on his knee, delivering up his sword). The Great Hall was richly carved and gilded, particularly the fireplace, the shelf of which was supported by two large figures in wood. The hall was paved with black and white marble squares, which is the characteristic flooring in Freemasonry, and there was also a chapel. Reference is also made of a drawbridge over the moat.

The moat can be viewed by parking at the Barrs Court Pub in Stevens Way. The old stone ruins next to it are the remains of the farmhouse and inside can be found a plaque displaying information and some drawings of different stages of the site's history. The moat surrounds the large open ground and can be seen particularly well behind the pub and the playground, and at the south end where footbridges cross. Weeping willows overhang the waters and ducks swim by at this very

This reproduction map of the old manor and moat at Barrs Court can be seen inside the front door of the Barrs Court pub.

pleasant recreational locality; the moat is wider than most we had encountered elsewhere. Inside the front door of the pub is a wall displaying a pictorial map of the old manor and the surrounding area. It clearly shows the manor house in the middle of what is now the open ground within the moat. This site is one of several moated sites on Astrum lines, but easily the most impressive. We ask the question again as to whether at least some of these had a more ancient origin.

The line crosses the Roman road and goes along the lower slopes of Stone Hill. Traces of a Roman station were found locally. Some coins from 240 AD and a monastic token of A.D. 400 were found at Hanham Abbots and in recent years a Roman well was also found nearby.

With pinpoint accuracy the alignment then goes through **Hanham Court,** which is mentioned in the Domesday Book. It is a former monastery site, one mile NNW of

Keynsham Abbey, which between 1330 and 1539 owned the original Hanham Court and much of the surrounding land. It was they who built the chapel of St George in 1350 to serve their needs, and that of local families. Folklore speaks of tunnels running from here, under the River Avon, to the Abbey. The present building is considered to be one of the finest mansions locally and dates from the 16th and 17th C. It was the seat of Sir Henry Creswicke, Sheriff of Bristol in 1643, who subsequently became Mayor. In 1660 Charles II created him a Knight for his services. The present owners are the Bannermans, garden designers by appointment to Prince Charles. The adjacent tithe barn dates back to the 15th C, when it would have been used by the monks of Keynsham Abbey to store the 'tithes' collected from the occupiers of the land.

We were really looking forward to visiting Hanham Court. After taking Down Court Road, we came to Court Farm, whose walls are buttressed. This property also stands on the alignment. Continuing along the road, we turned off at a sharp bend and continued south. There was a signed footpath that led to the house and church, which is locked except for services. The dedication is that of Christchurch and St George, the dragon slayer. Amazingly, the house is actually joined to the tower of the church, a most unusual affair, the tower having been converted to living rooms. An interesting sign on the wooden gate reads:

Hanham Court, which is adjoined to the tower of the church of St George. The alignment runs right through the property.

TAKE NOTICE THAT FROM TODAY'S DATE
POACHERS SHALL BE SHOT
ON FIRST SIGHT AND IF PRACTICABLE
QUESTIONED AFTERWARDS.
DUKE OF GUMBY 1868

The Duke of Gumby sounds like he was a really nice guy! Please note that Hanham Court itself is strictly out-of-bounds, so heed the warning!

The alignment then crosses the River Avon and goes up the slopes to Keynsham Cemetery, at **Stockwell**, passing right through the mortuary chapel. We rolled up here not really expecting to find much, as the cemetery was only founded in 1877, as an overflow for Keynsham. However, when we arrived on site we found a plinth next to the chapel which, to our delight, showed that when the cemetery was founded a major archaeological site was uncovered - the Durley Hill Romano-British Villa! It was partially excavated in 1922-24 and revealed a large site that was in use for about a century from around 1st C AD. The villa stood on a main artery linking Aqua Sulis (Bath) and Abona, at Sea Mills in Bristol (see page 200). The notable finds were mosaic floors linked by a flight of stone steps and a grandiose suite of bathhouses, suggesting a high status establishment. Water channels may mean that the villa had its

own spring on site. So this may have been a sacred ritual site prior to the building of the villa. Of interest to us was the fact that two of the rooms were hexagonal! These were said to have been inspired by the Imperial Palace on the Palatine in Rome. Finds from the site have been preserved in the museum at the Cadbury's Chocolate Factory nearby.

The line then cuts across the St Caen Chalice line, connecting Brockley and Avebury, before reaching **Queen Charlton** and its gem of a church, dedicated to St Margaret, the female dragon slayer. It dates from the late 12th C, with alterations in the 13th and 15th C. The church is usually

St Margaret with dragon, along with the sword of sovereignty and the Grail, all together in this window at Queen Charlton.

locked but keys can be obtained from either Penhill Cottage or No. 2 Orchard Cottages, both near the church. And it is certainly well worth obtaining said keys, as the interior of this church is a delight. The focal point is a window at the east end where there is a six-petalled design! Powerful energies were dowsed in front of the altar, and it is at this end that old arches survive, decorated with foliated heads and Otherworldly creatures. Behind the altar, St Margaret can be seen in the main window, slaying a green dragon, accompanied by St Dunstan of Glastonbury. The

Grail and the sword of sovereignty are being held by other figures. Above can be seen the six-pointed window, formed by three sets of smaller tripartite panes. There is a late-medieval cross on the village green nearby, shown on older OS maps, at the crossroads (grid ref: 632668), next to an oak tree. Peter dowsed several lines of energy coming into the cross, which seemed to be attracting energy as if it were a standing stone.

The alignment goes through both the church and the medieval bridge at Publow.

The line then goes on to cross Wansdyke, before scaling Publow Hill, passing right through the 382ft summit, before crossing Priest Down. The alignment then goes through both the bridge and the church at **Publow.** The Church of All Saints dates from the 14th C and has a 15th C tower with fine gargoyles. Repairs were carried out in 1860 and it has a notable Jacobean pulpit. Unfortunately, the church is usually locked.

The bridge over the River Chew (above) dates from the medieval period, restored in 1788 and 1810. It is home to two protected species, Daubenton's Bats, which roost in cavities under the bridge, and the White Clawed Crayfish.

Chew is believed to have originated in France, the *'ew'* element most likely derived from the French word *'eau'*, meaning water, and may have arrived with the Normans. The word *'Chewer'* has also been known to denote a *narrow passage*, whilst *'Chew'* can also mean *winding water*. Other possible explanations suggest it comes from the Old English word *cēo*, used in the transferred sense of a raven, in a similar way to Old Norse *gil*, or possibly a derogatory nickname from Middle English 'chowe' or 'chough', Old English *cēo*, a bird closely related to the crow and the jackdaw. Interestingly, some see it as being named after the Viking war god Tiw or Tyr, the son of the Norse God Odin. This gives us a connection with the crow and the jackdaw, in that Odin's familiar was a raven, another black bird.

The Wesleyans and Calvinists both had chapels at Publow, making a total of three places of worship in such a small hamlet. Toni noticed that a line from Publow church to the trig point at nearby Maes Knoll hillfort aligns with the summer solstice sunset.

The church of Thomas à Becket at Pensford, remarkably, stands on an island.

More than this, the section of Wansdyke that approaches the hillfort embankments is also aligned with this midsummer event.

The line continues to the nearby hamlet of **Pensford**, where St Edmund pops into the appropriately named George and Dragon Inn, which is exactly on the axis! We noted how a line joining the churches of Publow and Pensford is aligned to the winter solstice sunset and the midsummer sunrise.

The church of St Thomas a Becket Pensford, remarkably, stands on an island, one of only a handful to do so in England. The small churchyard is bounded on all sides by the waters of the River Chew, which flows swiftly by. The scene was idyllic as we entered the churchyard over a small bridge. Even the presence of the huge railway bridge behind the church could not distract from the fact we were standing on an ancient site. We were greeted immediately by a five-pointed star, the pentagram, in the upper part of the main east window, an ancient pre-Christian symbol. The church was being converted into a private residence and the new owner was on site when we visited and kindly granted us admission to inspect the interior. At the door a floor covered in tiles in the shape of hexagons greeted us! (see image on page 152). We wended our way through a maze of scaffolding to the east end, where a beautiful window shows Christ in Majesty, enclosed in a vesica piscis with vivid blue and purple clouds swirling around him. The central decoration in the stonework behind the altar is a golden hexagram!

The St Edmund Line then passes less than a mile east of Stanton Drew, a major prehistoric complex of stone circles, worth diverting to visit. The River Chew flows past these circles too and perhaps some of that ancient vitality is being transferred to both Publow and Pensford via its waters. Dowsers have for many years found how water can be a conduit for energies to travel across the landscape.

The line then follows the direct road to Stanton Wick, climbing up a steep gradient from Pensford. It then passes Broadoak Farm (shown on old maps), through Stanton Wick and up to the 480ft summit of Round Hill, through which the line passes. Next up is the church of St Nicholas and St Mary at **Stowey**. It dates back to the 13th C, although the present building is from 16-17th C. A small stream trickles by and the waters are collected in a large pond nearby. It is a pleasing stone building with some gargoyles up the tower, but, like so many in the Bristol area, is locked outside church services. Three large yews stand in the churchyard, offering shade and good energy. Next to the church, Stowey House retains some original 17th C features. Sutton Court, ½ mile west of the line, was built on the site of a 14th C castle, and retains 15th-16th C sections and has its own chapel. From the church at Stowey can be seen the tree-covered hill across which the St Edmund Line traverses, passing just east of the ancient *Castle Earthworks*.

The line then crosses **White Hill** (meaning *Holy Hill),* passing right through a famous local viewpoint, the Prospect Stile (grid ref: 587567). The panorama from here is truly stunning, from the west around to the north. Chew Valley Lake (the fifth largest artificial lake in the UK) is only a mile away, and Blagdon Lake can also be seen to the west. The church at nearby Hinton Blewett is dedicated to St Margaret, the dragon slayer.

From Prospect Stile, the line goes through the summit of Widcombe Hill, before descending to the small hamlet of **Coley**. Travellers descend to the village via a steep sunken road, an ancient route. From this road we can look back up to Widcombe Hill to the north.

This tumulus in the field, west of the Drove Cottage Henge site, marks the alignment.

Coley is a charming place, with an old stone bridge that crosses a bubbling, fast-flowing River Chew. The axis of the St Edmund Line goes straight through this ancient crossing.

Eaker Hill is one of the defining hills of the Wessex Astrum. Rising to over 290m (959ft), the centre of the line passes just yards west of the summit and the trig point. The pond west of the summit is shown on the 1891 OS map and may be very old. The Magdalene Line of the Chalice also crosses the hill, north of the summit, and the intersection is at a point marked on the 1891 OS map as *Soft Well*, just south of the road that passes through Bendall's Grove. We could not locate the water source on a site visit.

Beyond the summit of Eaker Hill, the line crosses the pleasantly wooded slopes of a coombe, before ascending again to the less severe contours of the Mendip Hills plateau. The line crosses Tower Hill, before passing through, with great precision, a group of three Bronze Age tumuli (grid ref: 555497), which themselves stand just west of the Drove Cottage Neolithic Henge, also known as the Hunters Lodge Inn Henge (grid ref: 558497). The mounds and the henge are part of the great ceremonial landscape that includes the famous Priddy Circles and Priddy Nine Barrows of North Hill, northwest of here. The henge and one of the barrows can be seen from Hillgrove Road, just to the north of them. The overall diameter of the henge is 54m comprising a circular bank 11.5m wide and 0.4m high, inside which is a ditch 6m wide and 0.3m deep. Both bank and ditch are broken by a single entrance on the NW side and enclose a circular central area 19m in diameter. Near to the entrance on this central area was a low oval mound. Today, only slight undulations can be seen in the field south of the road, just west of the entrance to Mountain Ash. Although only around 80 henges are known in Britain, they are considered to be of international importance. Google Earth clearly shows the henge, just SE of farm buildings. Two fields further west one can see the most prominent of the tumuli in a field boundary, the stone wall passing over the mound. This mound marks the St Edmund Line (see photo above).

Water gushing from underground at Holes Ash Spring, north of Wells, which once offered refreshment to pilgrims.

71

The line then descends from the Mendips down the steep coombe at **Rookham**, a charming wooded descent. Halfway down, as the slope lessens, a small parking area will be found on the right (west) side of the road. This is the access point for a small waterworks, accessed through a gate marked "151" (grid ref: 546482), near where a public footpath crosses the road. Through the gate a track can be followed into the woods and where it bends left, water will be seen gushing from the ground, channelled by a pipe (see image above). This is the site of **Holes Ash Spring**, which is named on old OS maps, and on the present 1: 25,000 scale. The water flows off the Mendips through a wood full of ferns and fallen moss-covered tree trunks. This road was formerly the main road north to Bristol and the spring must have been welcomed by people coming up the steep hill from Wells. It was very gratifying to find this major water source precisely on the St Edmund Line.

The line then descends from the Mendips, crossing the east end of Milton Hill, with its mysteriously named Arthur's Point. Nearby are Wookey Hole Caves, the hills around here being peppered with prehistoric cave sites. St Edmund then skirts the edge of Wells, the great cathedral city, passing by the two churches in the cemetery at **Haybridge**. The alignment then skirts Hay Hill, before passing through the west side of **Coxley**, known as Coxley Wick. The line crosses the A39 just west of Christ Church. The church is normally closed outside services, but from its churchyard the previous site, Hay Hill, can be seen rising to the north. Further north along the main road a spring can be found at the entrance to Littlewell Farm. The actual source of Little Well is in the field opposite, and the waters are now piped under the road. The waters are wonderfully refreshing and can be accessed through a wrought iron gate.

The alignment then goes straight through the mound on the top of **Edmund Hill** (grid ref: 506394), plus the chapel to the northeast of it. The hill is named after St Edmund of East Anglia, who was martyred in 869, and it is Avalon's only hill named after a saint. In the past it was called Windmill Hill, from a windmill that once stood on the mound (shown on a 17th C engraving). In their excellent book, *The Star Temple of Avalon,* Nicholas Mann and Philippa Glasson describe how the little-documented mound once played a key role in Glastonbury's ancient rituals and spirituality. Through

Glastonbury Tor rises into the skies, as seen from the ancient observatory that is the Edmund Hill Mound.

precise reckoning and diligent observation, they have proven how the mound astronomically aligns with the northern slopes of the Tor at midwinter. They have also plotted that, when observed from Wearyall Hill, the midsummer sun rose out of the Edmund Hill mound and, conversely, that the midwinter sunset is in alignment with Wearyall Hill when viewed from the mound. Other alignments occur, making this little known mound one of the most important local sites in prehistoric times, although the age of the mound has yet to be confirmed. The 1885 OS map also shows four stones in the vicinity of the mound.

Looking to the future, Mann and Glasson see it as significant that at the winter solstice of 2012 the galactic centre will rise over Glastonbury Tor. We are both humbled and gratified that this major site should be on our St Edmund alignment, which runs from Wotton-under-Edge to Glastonbury, and we duly named this alignment after the saint.

The terminal point of this alignment is in the grounds of Glastonbury Abbey, which it enters via the Abbey House gateway. This arched monument is decorated with a dragon and also stands on the Dod Line (see image page 77), and is dealt with in detail in Chapter 9.

Glastonbury – The Sacred Heart of Avalon

This is the first of five Astrum alignments that converge into, and diverge from, Glastonbury, and individual sites which are involved are detailed later. A brief introduction to the town, however, might be in order at this point.

Glastonbury is steeped in history, legend and spiritual heritage, so much so that it draws an unceasing variety of pilgrims. Christians, Druids, Pagans, Buddhists, and a whole clutch of weird and wonderful cults, all share Glastonbury, gathering on its hallowed soil to celebrate their faith and beliefs. The appeal of Glastonbury, like Jerusalem and Chartres, is a multi-religious phenomenon, possessing as it does the capacity to absorb and reflect various spiritualities, bestowing on all-comers their personal desires. There can be no denying that the landscape in and around the town has an aura that is both evocative and magical.

Referring to Glastonbury in his book *Avalonian Quest*, Geoffrey Ashe speaks of the *"...mighty pagan presence that underlies Christianity"*. Indeed, the seeds of Glastonbury's spiritual connection were sown long before the advent of the Church, when it was undoubtedly a major centre for worship of the Earth Mother/Goddess. The red-staining waters issuing from the foot of the Tor at Chalice Well are seen by many as Her life-sustaining blood. The Tor is said to be the home of Gwynn ap Nudd, King of the fairies and Lord of the Otherworld. The name Nudd has links with Nodens, an old British god who ruled over the nearby River Severn, and the Fairy King has similarities with King Arthur, who is said to wait inside the hollow hill.

Before the draining of the Somerset Levels, the Tor and its immediate hinterland was an island, the Isle of Avalon, also known as Ynis Witrin, or the Glass Isle. This gives it a tangible connection to the Glass Castle, which housed the Grail. This chalice has a symbolic link to Cerridwen, goddess of the Cauldron of Plenty. Arthurian myth speaks of the mortally wounded king being carried by boat to the Isle to be healed by the Priestesses of Avalon. The tales of the famous Lady of the Lake, who bestowed Excalibur to Arthur, may have originated from the fact that Glastonbury was once surrounded by water, and was also an ancient centre for Goddess worship; such places are frequently found in the vicinity of lakes, springs and rivers.

Glastonbury is thought to be the site of the first Christian chapel in Britain, a wattle structure still standing in the 7th C, which stood on the site of the Glastonbury Abbey. The Abbey became one of the richest and most powerful in the land, with pilgrims flocking from all over Europe to view the tomb of King Arthur. His body and that of Queen Guinevere were reputably found by the monks in 1191, although many scholars consider the "discovery" to have been a lucrative money-making ploy. The plan of the Abbey appears to be based on the geometry of the sacred vesica piscis symbol, consisting of two interlocking circles, incorporating hexagrams. The vulva or yoni-shaped area in the centre of the two circles corresponds to the position of the Lady Chapel, which contains a well in one corner, a place of great sanctity. Behind the Bishop's Kitchen, in the eastern corner of the Abbey grounds, sits a large stone with a hollowed out upper surface, found during excavations, and is regarded as an ancient omphalos or egg stone, similar to others found at sacred sites across the world (see page 83, in Chapter 9, for more details). The main Abbey itself is aligned with the Dod Line of the Blade, but three other alignments converge on the grounds.

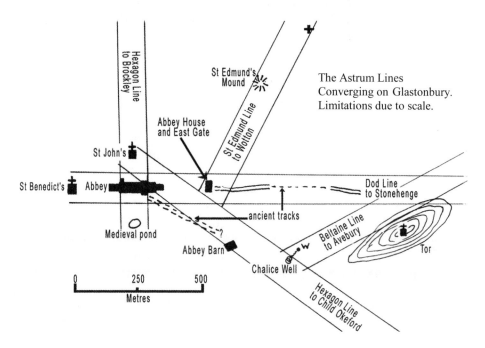

One of the most endearing and influential myths is that of Joseph of Arimathea. Legend tells of him bringing the boy Jesus to Glastonbury; Joseph later returned to England, bringing with him the Holy Grail, soon after placing Christ's body in the tomb. On Wearyall Hill Joseph thrust his staff into the ground and it took root and flourished, becoming known as the Holy Thorn. Although the original was cut down by Cromwell, who considered it an idolatrous symbol, cuttings were taken and various descendants can be seen on the hill, in the grounds of St John's Church, at the Chalice Well, and at the Abbey. The Arms of Joseph of Arimathea (a cross with two cruets) can be seen in St John's. Gracing the exterior of the church are winged dragon gargoyles, further symbols of pre-Christian beliefs. St John's stands on the Brockley to Glastonbury hexagon line (see Chapter 20).

One of the most sacred and peaceful localities around Glastonbury is the Chalice Well and its gardens. The waters rise from the earth at a steady rate of 25,000 gallons per day and have never been known to dry up, even in the severest drought. Wells and springs, particularly those near sacred sites or hills, were regarded as magical places of the Goddess. A priestess or anchoress would often have attended them and even lived on site, to be on hand to administer healing and divination. The water at the

Peter with other pilgrims standing around the ancient Omphalos of
Glastonbury, half-forgotten behind the Bishop's Kitchen, in the Abbey.

Chalice Well has a very high iron content, leaving a red deposit on rocks, viewed symbolically as either as the blood of the Goddess or that of Christ. Legend speaks of Joseph of Arimathea burying the Holy Grail beneath the Well, the chalice bestowing healing powers into the water. The Well is the start point of the Beltaine Alignment to Avebury (see Chapter 22) and is covered in more detail there.

Robert Coon saw Glastonbury as one of the Heart Chakra points of the Earth, on the flow of the global Rainbow Serpent. And it is well-known that Glastonbury Tor stands on the St Michael Line, one of the greatest and best documented of ley lines, which runs from Cornwall to East Anglia and aligns with the direction of the Beltaine sunrise. This alignment is followed in detail in Chapter 22. In *The Sun and the Serpent*, Hamish Miller and Paul Broadhurst describe how the currents of energy associated with the ley pass through Glastonbury. They show how the Mary (feminine) and Michael (masculine) currents, that weave around the axis of the line, flow around the Abbey. The Mary current sweeps down the axis of the Lady or St Mary Chapel, whereas the Michael cuts across the Abbey through the high altar. Fittingly, both the Michael and the Mary energies pass through the Chalice Well and its gardens, homing in on the lion's head, the waterfall and the vesica piscis symbolism of both the wellhead cover and the lower pool. Both flows then ascend the Tor, but they do not beat a direct path to the summit, rather they travel in serpentine paths, often following the processional ridges. Surprisingly, at the top the currents make a point of avoiding the tower, before descending the hill to resume their journey to Avebury and beyond. Miller and Broadhurst saw the pattern of the Mary currents as forming a Grail cup, into which the Michael energies flowed; this is a conjoining and a "harmonious marriage" on the sacred hill. This is graphically displayed on many stained glass windows showing John the Apostle; he is frequently depicted holding a chalice containing a dragon or serpent, echoing the very pattern found by Miller and Broadhurst on the Tor!

On the lower northern slopes of the Tor stand two old and gnarled oak trees, known as Gog and Magog, which are reached via a footpath from Wick Hollow. Their names derive from legends of two giants (although some tales speak of Gogmagog being a

The ruins of St Michael's at the summit of Glastonbury Tor, a place of great sanctity and powerful energies.

single entity) said to reside in Britain back in prehistory. Druids worshipped in oak groves rather than in temples and Glastonbury may have had its own Druidic grove. It is said that Gog and Magog are the last two oaks of an avenue marking a processional route up the Tor. The oaks stand together as symbols of a spirituality that revolved around nature and the turning year, witness to a belief system that saw trees as being alive with spirit.

Another enduring legend is that of the Avalonian John Goodchild (1851-1914). He brought a blue bowl back from Italy, which he buried under a thorn tree at Bride's Well, a lesser-known sacred corner of Glastonbury, in 1898. He had a vision that the chalice would be recovered by women, to help heal the world.

In the 1920's, Katherine Maltwood wrote her controversial book *A Guide to Glastonbury's Temple of the Stars*. From a study of Ordnance Survey maps, she advocated that the signs of an ancient earth zodiac were laid out in the topography of the Somerset landscape. Her circle of zodiacal effigies is 10 miles wide and includes Glastonbury, regarded by her as Aquarius. The zodiac figures are formed by the arrangement of hills, hedges, watercourses, dykes, woodland and other natural and man-made features. Place names and local legends also seem to tie in with her findings. However, its critics, including some earth mysteries writers, point out that many of Maltwood's zodiacal signs include transient features, such as rivers, streams and tracks, which were prone to gradual yet constant change over the centuries.

Glastonbury holds many more pleasures for the soul than have been covered here, and one is encouraged to obtain more detailed information on this magical place. Glastonbury does seem to be capable of potentially providing that which is sought, seeming to possess the capacity, and indeed the willingness, to give whatever is required of it. Despite the commercialism suffered in recent years, Glastonbury still retains that intangible "something", that air of mystery and legend that is the essence of sacred sites the world over.

The map above shows the five of the Astrum lines converging on, or diverging from, Glastonbury, which seem to take account of the significant archaeological and historical features around the area. It should be remembered that the width of our alignments is somewhat arbitrary, and the map is also limited by scale. We shall return to Glastonbury later, as we follow the other four alignments that diverge from the sacred heart of Avalon.

The Abbey House gate marks both the Dod Line and the St Edmund Line of the Astrum, and has a carved dragon (inset).

Chapter 9
The Blade
The Dod Line:
Glastonbury to Stonehenge

x St Benedict
x Glastonbury Abbey
x Glastonbury Tor

x Piltown
x Sticklinch

x Street-on-the-Foss

x Ford at Stoney Stratton

x Honeycliff

x Gare Hill
x Maiden Bradley Priory
x Round Hill
x Longbridge Deverill

x Whiten Hill
x Tytherington
x Corton/Upton Lovell

x The Coniger/tumuli

x Tumuli
x Stonehenge

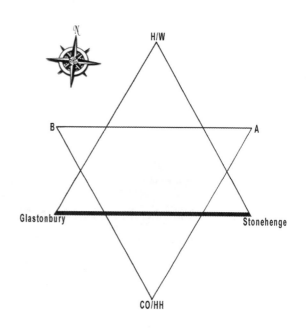

Serpents of the caduceus. in St Benedict's.

The Dod Line is the horizontal alignment of the Blade of the Wessex Astrum. This Glastonbury to Stonehenge alignment was described by John Michell in his seminal work, *The View Over Atlantis*. He noted that the axis of the Abbey is aligned to Stonehenge. He concluded, *"It can hardly be by chance that the sacred geography of Glastonbury was arranged to indicate Stonehenge with such precision... Glastonbury Abbey was conceived as the spiritual successor of Stonehenge"*. In *The Measure of Albion*, Michell calculates the length of the line from Stonehenge to the original church at the Abbey as 38.66 miles, whereas we have extended the alignment to 39.5 miles, to include St Benedict's. Palden Jenkins also includes the alignment on his popular and informative map, *The Ancient Landscape Around Glastonbury* (Gothic Image, 2005). We named this alignment for reasons already explained, but which are reiterated below.

Some authors have stated that the Glastonbury to Stonehenge line is exactly east-west, marking the equinox sunrises and sunsets. This is not strictly true, as Michell confirmed. The line is a few degrees north of due east, in line with the angle at which the Astrum is orientated! However, from many sites along the alignment the sun may indeed rise or set over the next site at the Equinoxes, due to the height of skylines. At the end of the day we are splitting hairs.

John Michell has also advocated that the alignment is one of the lines of the *Circle of the Perpetual Choirs,* an immense decagon whose points include (in clockwise order) Glastonbury, Llanwit Major, Carno, Llandovery, Ellesmere, Uttoxeter, Croft Hill, Stony Stratford, Goring and, finally, Stonehenge. The centre point is Whiteleafed Oak, where three counties meet. Perpetual choirs were an ancient tradition, used to

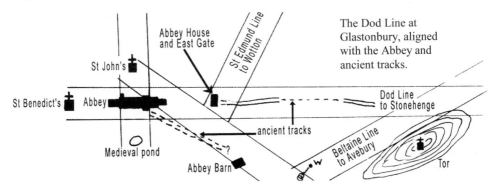

The Dod Line at Glastonbury, aligned with the Abbey and ancient tracks.

ensure that the magical enchantment of the land was maintained, through constant chanting.

The Dod Line starts at the church of **St Benedict**, in Benedict St (see map above). The present church dates from the 14th – 16th C, but it replaced a much earlier 11th C chapel, dedicated to St Beningus. Previous researchers have noted how the church and the Abbey are aligned almost east-west. It is this alignment that the Dod Line almost perfectly mirrors. We visited St Benedict's (having obtained keys from Millers, the nearby hardware shop) on a bright winter's day and inside we were greeted by sunlight streaming through beautifully decorated windows. The interior was light, airy and the energies felt good. We soon found much in the way of ancient symbolism. One window showed three women representing Faith, Hope and Charity, whom we recognised as the Christianisation of the ancient Triple Goddess. Two stone roof supports caught our eye. One showed an angel holding a shield, on which was carved a single serpent, whilst the other had a long-haired figure holding a shield displaying a caduceus (see image above). This symbol of two snakes entwined around

The Dod Line goes through Glastonbury Abbey, which is aligned with Stonehenge, and is a powerful and ancient sacred site.

a sword, staff or spear, is an ancient one, and one that many dowsers see as representing the yin and yang energies that flow in serpentine manner across the land. The quality and colours of the stained glass images is noteworthy, including the animal icons of the Apostles.

The alignment then enters **Glastonbury Abbey**, whose roots as a spiritual foundation go back to prehistory. The Abbey replaced earlier church buildings, which in turn almost certainly superseded a major pagan centre. Wandering around the massive walls and broken arches, the sheer size of the Abbey is realised, its length and height being truly immense. The doorway to the Lady Chapel is decorated with zodiacal and magical symbols, as one enters the sunken holiness of its interior.

The site is one of the most sacred sites in all Christendom, as it was here, c. 37-63 AD, that Joseph of Arimathea founded a wooden and wattle church, the *Vetusta Ecclesia*. Missionaries sent to Britain by the Pope built a stone church in AD 160, dedicated to Christ and St Peter, fragments of which were dug up in Bligh Bond's excavations in the early 20th C. Joseph of Arimathea's building had not in fact been replaced, but was restored. Around 540 AD St David founded another church on the same axis, quite possibly to commemorate the burial here of King Arthur. One tradition states that St Patrick, patron saint of Ireland, ended his days at Glastonbury Abbey, and that his bones were relics of great sanctity.

In 601 AD, the Isle of Avalon was a monastic

The Lady Chapel, through which the Mary current of the St Michael Line flows. The area around the altar and at the well is very powerful energetically.

island and by 633 AD the *Vetusta Ecclesia* had been walled up in order to preserve its sacred, but crumbling, stonework. In 704/8, the Saxon King, Ine of Wessex, founded a new church, demolishing some ruins, and erecting a totally new building dedicated to St Peter and St Paul. At this time the *Vetusta Ecclesia* was still standing, as it is recorded that King Ine signed a charter concerning it in 725. The monastery was ravaged by the Danes in 878 but the *Vetusta Ecclesia* was not burnt, possibly due to its sanctity.

In 943, St Dunstan placed the monastery under the Benedictines, linking all the old church buildings into a single larger construction. This Saxon church extended from what was then St Mary's Chapel (the *Vetusta Ecclesia*) to a point in line with the north porch of the later church. The axis was then changed to better align with Stonehenge. The orientation of the Abbey is about 3.5° north of east, whereas Stonehenge is 3° 38', which may have been the intended orientation of the geomancers, according to John Michell.

The new Abbey, built in 1082, was itself demolished in 1110 so that an even more magnificent edifice could be erected. In 1184 a major fire destroyed the *Vetusta Ecclesia* and the rest of the building, initiating a major rebuilding project. The internal geometry of the later buildings, however, still reflected the earlier structure. The final version of the Abbey survived and prospered until the Dissolution. One reason why the Abbey became so powerful and a centre for pilgrimage was the reputed discovery by monks of the bodies of King Arthur and his Queen, Guenivere. Once one of the richest in England, it was savagely attacked and sacked in 1539 and was almost totally demolished.

The Abbey is noteworthy in that the ground plan combines various systems of Masonic sacred geometry. John Michell did the early notable work on the sacred geometry, finding six-pointed stars and vesicas hidden within the ground plans. Of note is the sacred geometry of the Lady Chapel, which includes a hexagram, first noted by Bligh Bond. We refer the reader to the works by Michell and Nigel Pennick,

This doorway into the Lady Chapel is decorated with Biblical and alchemical symbolism.

who do more justice than we can to the complexities and beauty of the sacred geometry of the Abbey.

Miller and Broadhurst (in *The Sun and the Serpent),* and other dowsers, have plotted, over many years, the Michael and Mary flows of the St Michael Line through the Abbey. The male current cuts across the high altar, whilst the female flow runs the entire length of the axis of the Abbey, including the Lady Chapel. Going down into the lower levels of the Lady Chapel can often be a powerful experience, what with the flowing energies, and the atmospheric well in one corner adding to the mystery and sanctity. We dowsed the crossing of the Michael and Mary flows at the High Altar, from where the Michael flow headed towards a huge copper beech nearby. Toni dowsed that there was a surviving megalith below the High Altar, marking the place where the two energy flows cross.

Behind the Bishop's Kitchen is an ancient stone, which was possibly on site before any of the other visible stonework, and was discovered during the 1912 excavations by Bligh. Roughly egg-shaped, the boulder measures around 3ft x 2ft. The top surface bears a depression, possibly to take the menstrual blood of an oracle as she sat on its surface in pre-Christian times (see image page 75). We believe this to be the ancient heart or Omphalos of Glastonbury, possibly once marking the main crossing point of the Norman building, perhaps the spot revered as a powerful pagan centre.

As we stood within the main body of the Abbey and looked with wonder at the length of the building, we also reflected on the alignment, knowing that Stonehenge lay down the line, some 39 miles away. The Abbey is perhaps *the* classic example of how a sacred and powerfully energetic pagan site was Christianised, and yet still retains its sense of place and ancient sanctity. Perhaps the design of the Abbey even enhanced the locality, as the builders took into account, as they surely did, the energies that flow through this hallowed ground.

Many publications have been written about the history and energies of this major sacred site and some of these are listed in Further Reading. The Abbey has an admission charge, as well as a shop, a café (in season) and toilets. We shall return to the Abbey again in Chapter 15 and 20, as it also stands on two of the hexagon lines of the Astrum.

The Dod Line leaves the Abbey grounds via the Abbey House. Interestingly, just west of here is the Methodist church, whose main round window contains not one but eight hexagrams. The Dod Line heads out into the street via an arch, which is decorated with a dragon (see photo page 77), and heads off up Dod Lane opposite, which marks an ancient route. Alfred Watkins named the ancient ley line surveyors *Dod Men*.

Dod Lane turns into an ancient track that skirts the Tor, following the Dod Line that ultimately leads to Stonehenge.

Michell comments that Dod Lane is, *"...partly causewayed and was evidently part of a processional way to the Abbey... it was a spirit path"*. He finds it relevant that King Arthur was buried in the Abbey on the axis of this *death road*. We have named this alignment in honour of both Watkins and Michell.

Dod Lane turns into a track (see map) that goes over Chalice Hill. Ascending the track, we could see the ancient green way to the right, shaded now by trees. We pondered over the countless pilgrims who must have walked up and down this hallowed pilgrimage way. Further up the slope, we looked left across Bushey Combe to Edmund Hill (where the St Edmund Line comes into Glastonbury) and behind us down to St John's Church. Continuing eastwards, there are fine views of the Tor, and the track traverses the northern slopes of the hill, along Stone Down Lane. Paul Devereux and Laurence Main give a detailed map of this section on page 86 of their book, *The Old Straight Tracks of Wessex*. Bligh Bond wrote an imaginative account of Christian missionaries walking to Stonehenge along this ancient route, their goal being to convert the pagan priests there. He also expressed his belief that Glastonbury and Stonehenge were linked on esoteric levels.

The Dod Line then crosses the Somerset Levels, passing through **Piltown** (not to be confused with Pilton) and on to **Sticklinch**, where it runs parallel with, and just north of, the road through the village. It then goes through Street-on-the-Foss, crossing the Roman road, and then to the ford at Stoney Stratton. The line then crosses the prominent hill overlooking Batcombe before passing through another rise just south of Witham Friary. The Friary was founded in 1182 by Henry II and was one of only nine Carthusian Friaries in Britain, possibly the earliest. The order was founded by St Bruno and included both monks and nuns. St Mary's church once served the Friary,

St Michael's crowning the summit of Gare Hill, a key site on the
Glastonbury to Stonehenge alignment.

but the ruins of the other buildings were demolished in 1764.

The line then proceeds to **Gare Hill**, a crucially important locality on the Glastonbury-Stonehenge alignment, and one marking not only parish boundaries, but also the Somerset-Wiltshire border. The hilltop church of St Michael (now a private residence) replaced an earlier medieval chapel and stands just yards from the county line. A Roman road passes through the village crossroads, yards south of the church, continuing on its way east through the intriguingly named Penstone Wood. In Welsh, *Pen* variously means *head, chief, summit or capital.* So we may have a distant memory of an important stone in the vicinity.

St Michael and the dragon at Gare Hill.

Antiquarian Sir Richard Colt Hoare, in his mammoth *The Ancient History of Wiltshire,* describes the locality as *Gaer Hill.* He considered that, *"... the word Gaer is too well known, especially in Wales, as a Camp, &c. to require any comment".* In Welsh, the words Gaer and Caer both mean *fortification* or *citadel.* Alfred Watkins agreed, citing several examples, such as Y Caer, the Roman settlement at Brecon.

John Michell and others have found Gare Hill to be on several alignments and it is a fine example of the many hilltop chapels dedicated to the archangel that are located on ley lines. In his classic work, *The View Over Atlantis,* Michell regards Gare Hill as, *"... an important ley centre and still clearly recognisable as the sighted landmark for a number of ancient roads... a prominent centre for Roman roads and stretches of old track throughout the district".* As well as standing on the Glastonbury-Stonehenge line, Michell has the church standing on other alignments going to sites such as Wells Cathedral, the Roman Temple east of Maiden Bradley, the Stonehenge Cursus and Woodhenge (ibid, shown on two maps). In *The Measure of Albion,* he adds that, *"The prominence of Gare Hill in the ancient alignment system suggests that the original structure upon it was some kind of surveyor's mark."* The site *must* have been used long before the arrival of Christianity. Interestingly, another line goes through Gare Hill, Longleat House (see Chapter 21), and the church at Temple nearby - a perfect alignment.

When we viewed the area on Google Earth (which enabled us to do an accurate measurement) we discovered that the chapel is aligned to the summer solstice sunrise, which we have not found recorded elsewhere. It is a common misnomer that all churches are orientated east-west, a fact that does not stand up to close scrutiny in the field. We have found many churches aligned with the point of sunrise on ancient festival dates. One local tradition here, recorded in the 18th C, is that of the Beating the Bounds; all male residents walked the whole of the parish boundary of Maiden Bradley (which included Gare Hill church), for it was important that everyone knew where the boundaries were. Places bearing the name *Maiden* were often ancient gathering centres, such as at Maiden Castle in Dorset.

We first explored Gare Hill on a damp, overcast, atmospheric early spring day, arriving from the southwest along the road from Kilmington. This road goes through woodland for over two miles, hiding Gare Hill and giving no clues to the wonders to come. Suddenly, at the top, the chapel came into view, perched on a sharp, mound-like summit. We approached the chapel via a stile and the footpath that crosses the field from the north. An avenue of large oaks channelled a reed-covered sunken way, betraying springs bubbling from the earth. The chapel itself was resplendent on the hilltop, inviting us onward and upward. The chapel is now Churchfield House, and a sign near the entrance told us it ceased being a church in 1981. A public footpath enables access to the churchyard and the views from here were stunning, even under overcast skies. The land opens up to the northwest and the north, with the summit of Postlebury Wood on the skyline in the centre of the vista. We could now see how elevated we were, which we could not appreciate from the other side of the hill.

Six-fold symbolism in a window of the former church of St Michael's, Gare Hill.

By a wonderful stroke of synchronicity, the owners rolled up just as we arrived and they very kindly offered to show us around the inside of the chapel. The experience was incredible as we explored rooms that were energetically powerful and uplifting, with dowsable hotspots, such as at the east end, where the altar had once stood. Stunning high-quality windows depicted images such as Jesus in a vesica piscis, Mary Magdalene holding her jar, and, of course, St Michael holding his spear over a red dragon. In the main window we also found a small animal-like human head, with a serpent issuing from its mouth, as well as six yellow flowers bordering a vesica, each with six petals; they were hexagrams! We also noticed that Jesus' gaze was only directed toward one person – Mary Magdalene, reputedly his wife. She was returning his gaze with eyes full of love and devotion.

Back outside, we thought we would track the course of the Roman road as it approached Gare Hill from the SE. A footpath goes into the woods from the road junction and we could see the slight rise of the Roman road through the field east of it, which still shows faintly on Google Earth. The path enters woods and before long crosses a stream at a ford, just as it may have done in ancient times. The place was peaceful, the waters clear and cool. Back at the road, just next to the junction, a gate enables access into the field south of the chapel, and we could see a sunken way, overshadowed by a line of ancient oaks. This track had been the predecessor of the modern road, which now passes just west of it. The track led us back to the chapel, by which two trees intertwined their roots like embracing lovers.

Old OS maps show a Wesleyan Chapel NE of the church, which is strange when one considers the small size of the hamlet and its isolation. The whole impression we got from Gare Hill was that of a major ancient site at the crossing of ancient tracks and alignments, one of which we were following to the *Temple on the Plain.*

The Dod Line crosses into Wiltshire just yards east of the chapel and with great precision passes through the site of **Maiden Bradley Priory** (grid ref: 799403). Maiden Bradley was already a large manor prior to the Conquest, belonging to Tostig Godwinson, brother of King Harold. The Domesday survey assessed the manor at 4,000 acres and it was later home to the powerful Dukes of Somerset between the 12th and 17th C.

The parish takes its name from the leper hospital (or Lazar House) for maidens, founded on the site in 1152 by one of England's most powerful barons, Manser Bisset. King John granted the hospital an annual six-day fair, held in *Pley Street,* the track now going down to Priory Farm, on St Matthew's festival. This is on September 21st – Equinox! In 1189, the Bishop of Salisbury changed the hospital to an Augustinian Priory, dedicated to St. Mary and St. Lazarus, and which enjoyed royal protection. The Augustinians, or Black Canons, first came to England some forty years after the Norman Conquest. In its heyday, the Order had 217 houses across England, which were often on energetic sites, as with the Benedictines.

Maiden Bradley Priory was virtually self-supporting, with its own mill, corn barns, brewery, malt houses, a butchery, tannery and dyeing vats, which produced the saffron dye obtained from the crocus, cultivated in a 4-acre "saffron field".

Through the early part of the 13th C the Priory flourished, with local gentry vying with some of England's greatest nobles to bestow it gifts. Although a chapel had been built in 1179, it was decided that a grander church should be erected, which was completed by 1249. Oaks for the tower came from the Royal Forest of Gillingham, by special license. In 1376 a new Prior, Edward of Frome, set about rebuilding the Priory. Edward may not have lived to see his work completed, however, for it was not until 1390, a year after his death, that the Archbishop of Canterbury attended the formal blessing.

In 1535 a certain Richard Layton reported back to Thomas Cromwell, who had been appointed by Henry VIII to oversee the Dissolution of the Monasteries, about the relics he had found at Maiden Bradley Priory. Pronouncements by religious foundations that they possessed genuine relics were commonplace (producing income from pilgrims); Maiden Bradley seems to have been particularly well-endowed. Somewhat tongue-in-cheek, Layton wrote,

"I send you reliquaries… ye shall also receive a bag of relics, where in ye shall see strange things, as shall appear by the scripture: God's coat, Our Lady's smock, part

1824 drawing of Maiden Bradley Priory ruins (towards the left).

of God's supper on the Lord's table, and part of the stone of the manger in which was born Jesus in Bethlehem".

Some traces of the Abbey still survive at Priory Farm. These comprise a gatehouse range and a smaller structure projecting into the courtyard near the west end. Both buildings are of two stories and retain late-15th or early-16th C door and window openings; parts of the wall of the gatehouse may be older still. At the SW corner of the smaller building, a stone stair can be approached at ground-floor level by a doorway. The bases of the original boundary walls have suvived on the north and east sides of the enclosure, the latter forming part of the modern milking shed. At the west end of the gatehouse a run of masonry, 9ft from the ground, suggests the springing of a large stone arch.

The Dod Line then goes right through the summit of **Round Hill** and, a little further on, the road from Maiden Bradley weaves around the alignment for over two miles, crossing the axis four times. A milestone on the road (marked MS on the OS maps at grid ref: 862408) could not be found on a winter site visit.

Encountering King Arthur and Joseph of Arimathea

The next stop is the twinned hamlets of **Longbridge Deverill** and Hill Deverill, through which the Dod Line passes near the main crossroads, midway between the two churches (one of which is now redundant). The River Wylye runs through the area and the quality of the water has led to the establishment of watercress beds. There is plenty of evidence that the area was inhabited in ancient times, such as numerous tumuli on the surrounding hills, a henge site to the NE, and Iron Age settlements and dykes.

The parish church of St Peter and St Paul stands at the north end of the village, unusually sited on a steep slope that pitches down to the river. The church guidebook states that, *"a wattle church almost certainly stood previously upon the site, since the presence of a church is mentioned in the Domesday Book of 1086".* Our visit to the present Norman church was to prove one of the most memorable of all. We entered the churchyard gate, immediately finding two rough, craggy stones to our left, leaning

King Arthur kneeling before the Grail at Longbridge Deverill.

against the churchyard wall, next to some fragments of gravestones. The knobbled, undulating surfaces of the stones led us to suspect that they may be modified ancient megaliths, used later for gravestones. To our right, we found a thorn tree, which tradition says was planted here from a cutting taken from the Glastonbury Thorn. We thought this was interesting as we were following the Astrum line from the Abbey, where stands another Holy Thorn.

Inside the church, we found a profusion of esoteric symbolism, including further connections with Glastonbury, in the form of windows in the north aisle that depict both King Arthur and Joseph of Arimathea. The window may have been to celebrate the fact that Wulfhelm, who was the Saxon Archbishop of Canterbury in 926 AD, granted the manor of Longbridge Deverill to the Abbot of Glastonbury, an act certified by King Athelstan himself. One panel shows Joseph directing the building of the first wattle church at Glastonbury, whilst another depicts him holding his leafy staff in one hand, and the Grail in the other. Below his feet is a floor of black and white squares, typical Masonic symbolism. Above him, another panel shows Arthur kneeling before an angel, holding the Grail, from which golden rays emanate. The scene (see image above) is accompanied by the

Hexagram on the lectern at Longbridge Deverill.

89

words, *"Here is the vision King Arthur longed for to see"*. We were exhilarated to stand before this window, as we were on the Dod Line from Glastonbury. We soon found more links to Avalon here.

At the NE corner of the church is the Bath Chapel, extravagant and richly decorated, so named because Longleat House once stood within the parish of Longbridge; the chapel stands over the vault of the Thynnes family. We both felt that this powerful, yet peaceful chapel had once been the Lady Chapel. This seemed to be confirmed by our discovery behind the altar of a beautiful white memorial (obscured by a curtain) depicting Baroness Isobella, who died in 1830. Her features were beautifully carved in white stone, and this feminine figure would at one time have been the focus of worshippers. The stone altar was brought here from the church of Hill Deverill to the south (grid ref: 867403), which is now a private dwelling.

Magician with crystal ball at Longbridge Deverill.

More symbolism of interest to us was found elsewhere inside St Peter and St Paul. The wooden lectern was inscribed with a hexagram, the six-pointed star that was our primary focus. *"Well, that figures!"* was Peter's first thought. In a window in the south aisle we found the image of what we can only describe as a wizard or alchemist who, incredibly, is gazing into a crystal ball! Also in the south aisle, next to the font, another window depicts Jesus being baptised by John the Baptist, a figure highly regarded by the Knights Templar. His feast day is on June 24, during the old midsummer festivities. Behind the main altar, the central window shows Mary praying over her newborn son Jesus, whilst above her is the sacred Grail cup, radiating golden rays. What's more, the chalice is enclosed within a vesica piscis, the ancient symbol of the Divine Feminine, which we have encountered elsewhere on our Astrum journeys. Below the window are wooden reredos, which include St George slaying a dragon, Thomas à Becket and St Dunstan (Abbot of Glastonbury). The last figure gave us yet another connection with the holy town. The altar itself is noteworthy, as it is said that Thomas à Becket himself cut the five consecration crosses when he came to this quiet, isolated locale.

The alignment leaves Longbridge Deverill just north of the old Manor (now Manor Farm), opposite which we saw a raised earthen platform in the field. From here the line goes straight up the slopes of **Cow Down** and **Whiten Hill**, which loom over the River Wylye valley; with the same incredible precision that we had seen before, the centre of the Dod Line goes straight through the 206m trig point (grid ref: 887408). On the hill are Bronze Age tumuli and an ancient settlement, some of which can be seen from the stile at the end of the lane that runs SW-NE, north of Manor Farm. The line runs over the top of these hills, which are well seen from the Longbridge Deverill to Sutton Veney road. Whiten Hill can be ascended via a road south from Sutton Veney and the line crosses the road near a gate on the east side of the road, south of the ridge (grid ref: 897407). From here can be seen the rectangular wood lower down the slopes to the east, through which the Dod Line passes. On the skyline can be seen the woods on East Codford Down, on through which the line progresses. At the top of the Whiten Hill (another *Holy Hill*) we looked west to the broad summit of Cow Down, and to its right to the distinct outline of Cley Hill.

Whilst in the area, try to visit Old St Leonard's Church in **Sutton Veney** (grid ref: 908416). It is signposted from the main road by English Heritage. Ruins mark the main building, but there is a small chapel at the east end; keys can be obtained from a nearby cottage. The energies can be felt flowing down the axis of the church.

Tytherington and the Shaman

Beyond the aforementioned rectangular woods the line goes through Tytherington, the axis passing just south of the sharp bend and the large ponds. Tytherington is an ancient settlement, sheltered by a ring of hills just south of the River Wylye. Pottery from a Romano-British settlement was found on Tytherington Hill, near to a Bronze Age bowl barrow (grid ref: 910392). The barrow was opened by Sir Richard Colt Hoare who found a primary inhumation with flint arrowheads and a drinking cup.

The ponds can be accessed via a permitted path through the wrought-iron gates of Sutton Harbour House, just west of the bend. The place feels ancient and sacred, and the waters of the two large ponds, home to swans, are skirted by tall trees. Between the ponds, water issues via small waterfalls from sluices. It seemed fitting that these two bodies of water should be on the "feminine" Dod Line of the Chalice.

At the road junction in Tytherington stands the church of St James, perched on what looks suspiciously like an ancient mound. This small chapel is traditionally associated with the Empress

The chapel of St James at Tytherington.

Maud (or Matilda), daughter of Henry I, who in 1114 at the tender age of 12 was married to the Emperor Henry V of Germany. During her time at Heytesbury (1139-47) Maud endowed 28 acres of land at Tytherington, together with two chaplains to serve the chapel. It dates from the early 12th C and is one of the oldest churches in Wiltshire. The atmosphere inside is peaceful and sacred, which even the whitewashed walls (from the restoration of 1891-2) cannot diminish.

A *Methodist Chapel (Primitive)* is shown on the 1889 OS map, SW of St James', and may be one of the buildings set back from the road today. This chapel stood just yards

The ponds at Tytherington.

from the centre of the Dod Line, a phenomenon we encounter time and time again. The line then passes through the northern part of **Corton**. Old OS maps show two churches in the village, though none survive today. East of the pub (grid ref: 936945) the 1889 map shows All Saints Church, yet on the 1901 map this had been changed to *Mission Church*. The building survives today as a residential house just down the lane from the Dove Inn (which has a good atmosphere and fine food). The former chapel is half-hidden behind tall trees, but can be seen just east of a wishing well. We were surprised to see alpacas grazing in the field opposite.

At the north extremity of the village *Baptist Chapel (Particular)* is shown on old maps, next to a well and a burial ground (grid ref: 937408) on the east side of lane. It is just 100yds from the centre of the Dod Line. Again, the building survives as a residence, The Old Chapel, next to the entrance to Sundial Farm. A drain opposite was channelling the water from the well, which could be heard gushing below our feet. As at Tytherington and elsewhere, it is the more modern non-Conformist chapel that is closest to the Astrum Line, rather than the parish church.

Whilst in the area, take time to visit St Margaret's church at **Knook**, a charming church in a small hamlet. St Margaret is traditionally shown as a dragon slayer. Around the outside a circular rise can be seen, resembling the banks of a henge. Inside, notable features include a font full of fossils, windows depicting the animal icons of the Apostles, an old chair with two carved heads, and an ancient gravestone with a cross near the door. Back outside, above a blocked-off door is a carving of a dragon (on the left) and a panther (on the right), depicted with the Tree of Life.

The line then follows an old track east, crossing two footbridges (shown on older maps), which ford both the Wylye and a stream that served the former cloth factory.

Upton Lovell, the next village on the Dod Line, nestles midst an Area of Outstanding Natural Beauty in the Wylye Valley, just off the A36. The village overlooks water meadows and has the scarps of Salisbury Plain as a backdrop. The village pub, the Prince Leopold, is named in memory of the Prince, Duke of Albany, the youngest son of Queen Victoria, who lived at neighbouring Boyton Manor and who is said to have often drunk here.

The line comes into Upton Lovell via an ancient path from Corton, crossing the Wylye next to the Old Rectory. Standing on the footbridge (grid ref: 943409) we could trace the path following the alignment – Alfred Watkins would have appreciated this! It then passes by the site of the old cloth factory, before going through a huge tree, recently cropped back, and on through the large adjacent house. Just south of the line is the parish church of St Augustine (of Canterbury). There is parking at the adjacent village hall, on the wall of which is a plaque stating that the village was recorded in the Domesday Book. We were also greeted by

St Augustine's at Upton Lovell, with the Millennium Stone in the foreground.

a tall megalith, erected to commemorate the Millennium, carved with *AD 2000*.

Inside St Augustine's there is a window with a rare and delicate depiction of Saint Barbara. She is holding a miniature tower, symbolic of her captivity prior to her martyrdom in the 4th C. Next to the altar is a tomb with the effigy of a knight in armour, thought to be that of one of the Lovell's of Castle Cary. The manor was held by this family and from them the village takes its name. One of them was a participant in the Lambert Simnel rebellion, and managed to find sanctuary here. Unfortunately, he starved to death in a secret chamber in which he had hidden himself. The fine stone arch creates atmosphere and the energies felt ancient and gentle, one of those places that is difficult to leave.

On the hill north of the village is the famous Shaman Barrow (grid ref: 958427- unnamed on maps). This round barrow, officially listed as Upton Lovell G2a, dates from about 1500 BC, but is now less than 2ft high. It was excavated in 1802 by William Cunnington and again in 2000 by Dr C Shell. It covered one of the most unusual burials of the Early Bronze Age, regarded by many to be the grave of a shaman. A primary inhumation of a stout male was found, and with him a cloak into which had been sewn 36 bones and perforated boar teeth. He was also accompanied by axes of stone, flint and prestigious dolerite, a jet or lignite ring, biconical beads and a bronze awl, and a polished circular stone had also been placed on his chest (finds and displays are in Salisbury Museum). The association of so many bone pendants and the natural hollow flint nodules suggest that the burial was of a shaman, and/or a metal worker/goldsmith. Other tumuli and long barrows in the area have also yielded important finds, such as gold plate and amber, reaffirming that the area was held as very sacred in ancient times. It is thought that the Welsh Bluestones travelled passed here the en route for Stonehenge, just a few miles away now to the east.

The Dod Line then passes through the southern edge of **The Coniger**, which is situated at the east end of High Down (see map page 184). Officially, the earthworks are a medieval rabbit warren, but they partially enclose Winterbourne Stoke (West) Barrow Cemetery, which was surveyed in 1992. The earthworks form an irregular pentagonal enclosure, encircling an area of 1.5 hectares, defined by a bank and external ditch, which together have a maximum width of 9m. The enclosure is best preserved on the west side, where the bank still has a height of 0.5m above the interior and 1.3m above the shallow ditch. Several tracks traverse the enclosure perimeter, but there is no evidence of an original entrance.

There are around a dozen Bronze Age barrows in and near The Coniger. The banks cut into some of the barrows and therefore post-date them. Leslie Grinsell suggests that it is medieval, suggesting that the Normans designed the banks to be rabbit warrens, the earthen mounds being ideal for burrowing. The southern bank of The Coniger, however, aligns with the Astrum and points directly to Stonehenge, possibly suggesting a more ancient origin.

The line then passes straight through the **long barrow** west of Stonehenge (grid ref: 119422 – see map on page 184), which can be seen as a low rise from the north-south public track running just west of it. The county of Wiltshire alone contains 148 out of 260 of Britain's long barrows, and 16 of these are within a three mile radius of Stonehenge. This barrow is the nearest Neolithic mound to Stonehenge. The degraded mound does not show up well on Google Earth and has been ignored by most researchers of Stonehenge, which is strange considering its proximity to the henge.

The mound is officially Amesbury 10a and there has been some debate as to whether it is a true long barrow, because of the apparent lack of accompanying ditches. In his book *Stonehenge – the Secret of the Solstice,* Terence Meaden sums up the situation: *"... ditches have not been detected in air photographs; however, the barrow is shown on earlier maps as elongated with a self-orientation of 60° [pointing towards the Stonehenge Cursus]... even if it is not a ditched long barrow, this 'long mound' may have to be planned into the cursus barrow system".* The mound was excavated by Sir Richard Colt Hoare in the early 19th C, who found no burials. It is unusual but not unique for mounds to be devoid of internments; early archaeologists were frequently disappointed when their excavations revealed empty mounds. This would suggest that these mounds were for some other use, perhaps by the living for ritual, or as site lines as part of astronomical alignments. In his book, *Monuments of the British Neolithic,* archaeologist Miles Russell gives an example (on page 41) of such findings, referring to passage graves thus: *"Once again the term "grave" is somewhat of a misnomer, for it implies that the primary use of these structures was for human burial, a theory not fully supported by the archaeological evidence".*

The lack of burials in this mound, and its precise position on the Dod Line, leads us to conclude that the mound was at the very least utilised by the designers of the Wessex Astrum, and may possibly not be Neolithic at all, but contemporaneous with when the

Approaching Stonehenge from the same direction as the Dod Line alignment, which had originated many miles away in Glastonbury.

Astrum was envisaged.

Stonehenge stands proudly at the end of the Dod Line. The monument is described elsewhere in this book, concerning the sacred geometry and the other lines that converge on the monument. Countless works have been written over many years, so we need not elaborate too much at this point. Even today, dowsing confirms powerful earth energies in and around the monument. How powerful, we wonder, was Stonehenge when it was complete? The primary alignment is the direction of the summer solstice sunrise, on June 21/22 each year. In Book Two of, *The Measure of Albion,* John Michell informs us that if this summer solstice line is continued from Stonehenge, it eventually passes through Goring, on the Thames. The place name comes from *Gor-ting,* means *meeting place of choirs*. The exact spot is a house called The Temple. As well as the Dod Line, countless other ley lines, and numerous *energy grids*, have been connected in some way or another to Stonehenge. It is indeed *the* archetypal site to demonstrate that everything is connected to everything else, somewhat like a huge spider's web, a concept surely grasped by the monument's builders.

Chapter 10
The Chalice Defined

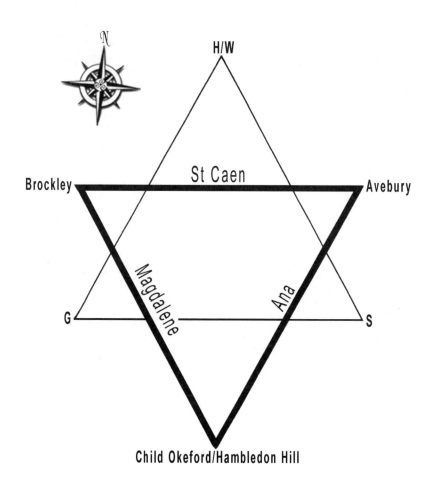

The Chalice is an equilateral triangle, with Brockley, Avebury and Hambledon Hill as the terminal points. At Hambledon Hill, especially, we were impressed that all five lines (the two Chalice lines, the Central Axis and the two hexagon lines) all converged within the Iron Age hillfort, within less than ½ mile from north to south, and ¼ mile from east to west (see map, page 117).

The inverted triangle is traditionally associated with the feminine, yin principle - the Goddess. It seems appropriate to us that the mighty ancient site of Avebury should be at one point and, as if to confirm the symbolism, that one of the Chalice lines goes through Silbury Hill, the huge ancient mound that symbolises the ripe tummy of the Earth Mother.

The inverted triangle has been associated with feminine fertility, as it resembles the pubic mound, as well as a woman's internal sexual organs. The Sumerians used the downward-pointing triangle to represent women, as people still do in China. In ancient Greece and Rome this triangle again symbolised women or the Goddess, and in India it still represents the Goddess Shakti today. In alchemical practice this triangle represents the element of water, its shape being the Chalice, holding the waters of the Goddess. In the Kabbalistic tradition, it symbolises the Seventh Sefirot of the Female (Nekuva). Ultimately, the inverted triangle is the sacred receptacle, the Grail no less. In our modern Quest for the Grail, we are actually seeking to reconnect with our Primal Mother.

To reiterate, we have named the Chalice Lines as follows:

The St Cain Line - Brockley to Avebury, after St. Cain, the 5th C saint.

The Magdalene Line - Brockley to Hambledon Hill, out of reverence for the biblical and archetypal wise woman, held in high regard by the Templars as the bride of Jesus.

The Ana Line - Hambledon Hill to Avebury, after the primeval British Mother Goddess; her sacred hill, Tan Hill, stands directly on this line.

We have thus named all three Chalice lines after three legendary women or deities. We do not advocate for one moment that these were ever the original names for these lines. Naming them, however, has enabled us to forge a closer, more personal relationship with the alignments, and their energies and spiritual dimensions. We also acknowledge that the naming of the Magdalene and the Ana lines, in particular, gave us the opportunity to pay homage to both an amazing historical heroine, and the Earth Mother respectively.

Chapter 11
The Chalice - Magdalene Line:
Brockley to Hambledon Hill

x Brockley
x Warren House
x Redhill

x Ubley
x The Wrangle

x Eaker Hill

x Whitnell Corner

x Maesbury Castle

x Downside

x Whitestone Hill

x Spargrove Manor Moat

x Bruton
x Redlynch

x Stoney Stoke
x Sunny Hill
x Stoke Trister

x Buckhorn Weston

x Fifehead Magdalen
x Todber/Thornton Moat

x Fontmell Parva
x Hambledon Hill

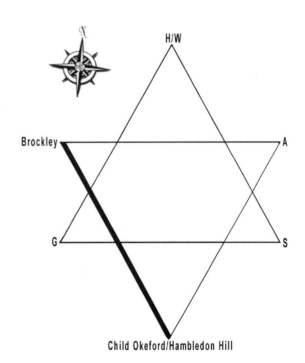

Brockley in Somerset marks the convergence of two lines of the Chalice, as well as the Samhain Line and two of the Astrum hexagons. Brockley Combe is just east of the village; the name arises from a rare co-joining of two Brythonic words. Combe means *'a small deep dry valley, easily defended'*, and Brock is either *'badger'* or, as some historians suggest, *"brook"*. In terms of the latter, the River Kenn has its source just 600m west of the church. Combe is sometimes spelt differently, such as *Coombe* and *Coomb*, but the meanings are the same.

Brockley Combe is a wooded gorge, a romantic glen nearly a mile in length, enclosed on each side by steep rugged rocks, rising to the height of nearly 300 feet. The combe cuts into the western edge of the Lulsgate Plateau, the Carboniferous limestone hills which form a northern outlier of the Mendips. Lead-ore was mined locally and there are also numerous basaltic columns, similar to those forming the Giant's Causeway.

Brockley Combe has folklore of ghosts, and a local informant told us of a ghost that is sometimes seen crossing the road that winds through the ravine. Underground tunnels are also said to exist, although these may be distant memories of the old limestone and lead mines that riddle the ravine. It is the Combe that seems to be the main focus for the Astrum lines, for only the Samhain Line terminates at Brockley church (see Chapter 23). Yorkhouse Cave, on the north side of the Combe, is the terminal point of the hexagon line from Glastonbury (see Chapter 20)

Just off the A370 is Brockley Hall, the Georgian manor house, latterly inhabited by the Piggott-Smyth family. In World War II it was occupied by American soldiers, who inscribed their names in trees and the large stone gate posts. The Magdalene Line commences at Brockley Hall, just a few hundred metres east of the church.

The Magdalene Line then heads off approximately SE and passes along Coombe Road, immediately below Yorkhouse Cave, crossing the hexagon line in the process. The next point of call is **Warren House**, a private dwelling hidden deep within Brockley Wood, and from there continues on to Redhill. Before then, however, a magical place this side of Redhill was awaiting us.

We discovered old records of a really interesting feature just 200yds east of the centre of the line, at the edge of Brockley Wood. The 1:25,000 OS map shows a water feature called Abspit Pond (grid ref: 486651) at the edge of the woods, and near the west end of the two airport runways. What attracted us to investigate further was a local tradition that, *"… a monolith, called the Bethel Stone,"* once stood at the pond, which was, *"…removed before the 19th Century"*.

We were excited enough about a megalith and a pond being so close to our line, but the name of the stone seemed incredible. The Bethel Stone is mentioned in the Book of Genesis as the stone that was erected to represent the "House of God". A search on the Internet soon revealed websites that discuss the stone further; many see it as having a direct relationship to the *Lia Fail*, the omphalos or *"Stone of Destiny"* of British and Irish folklore. Why was such a named stone standing near a lonely pond in rural Somerset? We had to investigate.

Above: Abspit Pond, once the site of the Bethel Stone. Right: planes landing at Bristol Airport fly over a row of stones near Abspit Pond.

We parked up in Brockley Combe at the car park at the entrance to Fountain Timber (grid ref: 483663), and made our way down the straight N-S bridleway that skirts the eastern end of Brockley Wood. The walk was pleasant in the autumn sunshine and the ground beneath was laid with old cobbles, which peeked through a carpet of newly fallen leaves. After around ten minutes we came to the pond on our left, although this was heavily overgrown and was only betrayed initially by a sign that proclaimed, "DEEP WATER". We could see water on the other side, next to an open field, so carried on along the path to find a way round. We soon came to a gate in front of us and, after crossing over it, turned sharp left and down the hill, where we found the pond in a hollow. A small stone lay nearby, and we noted others tracing the field boundary up the hill. It was a surreal experience, standing at this hallowed pond, once the site of the Bethel Stone, with aircraft skimming the treetops overhead. The 1888 OS map shows the pond on open ground, isolated, miles from anywhere; no airport then to shatter the silence of this holy place. The pond is now partly engulfed by reeds and lilies, adding to its charm and mystique. Of relevance to us is that it lies just 250m east of the axis of this Astrum line, marking the edge of the "corridor".

Next up on the line is **Redhill**. This village is perched on the slopes of a steep hill that overlooks the Yeo Valley. The ancient heritage of the area is borne out by the presence of a long barrow and a chambered tomb (both marked on OS maps) situated just north of the village, near the airport. Christ Church is the dedication of the pleasant parish church, which has nice gargoyles up the tower that gaze across the landscape below. We found the church unlocked, unlike many others in the area. Behind the altar was a magnificent window of Christ surrounded by a beautiful, flaming vesica, symbol of the Divine Feminine, and we found more vesicas on tiles near the intricately carved font. Once again, we felt strong energies in the Lady Chapel, to the right of the high altar.

Magdalene then follows the road down the hill through Lye Hole, where a Roman villa was discovered near the stream in 1876. A Romano-British settlement once

Above and left: the stone at Ubley, which is a shrine to the Madonna. The stone may be an ancient megalith.

existed at Scars Farm, right on the line, whilst Saxon homesteads were found at nearby Wulbikan Hill. The line then strikes through the meeting of four roads and tracks, next to Lyehole Farm, the latter of which also marks the alignment.

The next destination is **Ubley**, a charming small village in the Chew Valley, close to where the River Yeo flows into Blagdon Lake, and overshadowed by the steep wooded slopes of Cleeve Hill, the northern scarp of the Mendips. There is evidence of Neolithic burials locally and Ubley is listed in the Domesday Book as *Tumbeli*, meaning *'The rolling meadow'*. Another explanation is that it comes from *Ubba's leah* or *clearing*. There was once a weekly market here, as well as an annual fair on the feast day of St Bartholomew, in August. The small medieval church dates from the 13th C, with later additions, and is dedicated to St. Bartholomew.

Ubley cross and church, between which earth energies were dowsed.

The centre of the village, around the church, is idyllic, with quaint cottages and a village cross. On the base of the cross steps is a series of plaques dated 1992 to 2003, commemorating various awards such as Best Village and Best Small Village. Near the cross our attention

101

was drawn to Threeways Cottage, where we found a large stone to one side of the gate. It is around 4ft x 5ft, rough on the front yet with three rough steps cut into the back. Clearly it had been utilised at some time in the past for boarding coaches and horses. We had seen many such stones on our travels, but this one was not so precisely cut and purpose-built as the others, looking more like a rough, rounded boulder at the front. Was this an ancient stone marking the heart of the village (the omphalos), later used for another purpose? Amazingly, on the top of the stone stood a small statue of a praying lady with a crown on her head (presumably the Madonna), and in front of her were small vessels containing fresh-cut flowers. The stone was a shrine! Incredibly, the pendulum swung vigorously when held over the statuette and elsewhere over the top of the stone.

A beautiful depiction of Mary Magdalene, grieving at the foot of the cross, at Ubley church.

Peter then dowsed an energy flow that went from the stone, through a manhole cover (with the sound of gushing water beneath), through the cross and onwards across the road to the church. Toni dowsed two flows from the cross, one going into the church under a window depicting St Bartholemew, via a big old tree in the churchyard, the other going in through the porch. The two flows crossed paths in the middle of the church, midway between the two doors.

The church is elevated on raised ground, reminiscent of an ancient mound, partially shaded by huge yew trees and a large copper beech. The building stone is an attractive deep red and around the south side we found gargoyles, some of which were winged dragons. The inside is very atmospheric and dark (due to the proximity of the tall trees); the energy was palpable. It is notable also for a short, squat font and the fact that there are not fixed pews, only chairs, the latter of which were presented to the church in 1875. The lack of pews reminded Toni of ceremonies whereby people would precess around the stations of the cross – the church needed to be without pews. The floor of the approach to the altar is decorated with various designs, notably for us, three sets of six-petalled flowers. The altar itself is dominated by a window of the Crucifixion, with a tenderly depicted image of Mary Magdalene, holding Jesus' feet at the base of the cross.

The line goes through the site of the old Manor House, opposite the church, passing within yards of the stone and the village cross. The Methodist Chapel stands west of

Megalith at the top of the hill at The Wrangle, close to the Magdalene Line.

the line at the south end of the village, on the lower slopes of Cleeve Hill, and from the back of the chapel the hill can be seen beyond, over which the Magdalene Line proceeds.

After scaling **Cleeve Hill**, and crossing Compton Combe, the line then passes through a cluster of cottages on high ground known as **The Wrangle**. The vista from the top is incredible, with distant views north to Blagdon Lake and Chew Valley Lake. We intended to stop at the top of the hill, outside the gates of Holly Bush End, to look back and admire the view, but when we got there we were in for another surprise. For opposite the property, on the north side of the lane, stands a 5ft high standing stone! It is about 2ft wide at the base but tapers to around only 7ins wide at the top. Closer inspection revealed iron rivets, which shows that it had once been utilised as a gatepost. This stone, however, is not a nicely cut rectangle, the usual design, but is rough and slender, widening considerably near the base. Surely this is an ancient megalith, erected long ago at the very summit of the hill; it stands just yards south of the Magdalene Line! We dowsed an energy flow that ran across the lane from the stone, disappearing into the hedgerow at a nearby ivy-covered tree. OS maps show a Roman road emerging from Chew Valley Lake and ascending the hill to the Mendip plateau, an area rich in prehistoric sacred sites and Roman mines. The track must have passed very close to Stanton Drew to the NE. We were elated at our discovery, which is in fact the tallest "new" standing stone that we have found so far on our Quest.

Chew Valley Lake is framed by three of the Astrum Lines. Several farms and houses had to be vacated before the land was flooded, and old roads, hedgerows and tree stumps can reappear when dry summers cause water levels to drop. Prior to flooding, excavations were carried out by Philip Rahtz and Ernest Greenfield between 1953 to 1955. They found evidence of occupation from the Upper Palaeolithic right up until the Iron Age. Roman remains indicate agricultural and industrial activity from the 1st – 3rd C AD. Finds included a moderately large villa at Chew Park, where wooden writing tablets (the first in the UK) were found. Further excavations around the village of Moreton, which was listed in the Domesday Book but is now submerged, found evidence of a thriving community in medieval times, as well as the Nunnery of

Santa Cruz. The remains of the village cross from Moreton were moved to Chew Stoke parish church.

Magdalene then goes through the White Swan pub (grid ref: 546561), north of a crossroads, before passing through an old settlement to the SE (grid ref: 549555). It then follows the road briefly as it descends Smitham Hill, continuing on to the northern slopes of **Eaker Hill**, one of the defining spots of the Wessex Astrum. This hill marks the intersection of the Magdalene Line and the St Edmund Line. This occurs at a point marked on the 1891 OS map as *Soft Well*, just south of the road through Bendall's Grove (grid ref: 570527). The spot is atmospheric, with tall trees and crumbling, moss-covered stonewalls. On a site visit in May 2008, however, we failed to find any remains of a well or spring.

From there the line goes through Tor Hole (as featured in *A Mendip Tale*) and Bishop's Ponds, before going through Long Wrangle Plantation and on through the crossroads of **Whitnell Corner**. The Roman road to Midsomer Norton passes through the crossroads and several Bronze Age tumuli rise from the surrounding fields.

Magdalene then passes through the southern ramparts of **Maesbury Castle**, site of an Iron Age hillfort. The name derives from *maes*, meaning *field* or *plain* in Welsh, and *burh*, meaning *fort*. Its name was *Merksburi* in 705 AD, meaning *boundary fort*. This area was in fact a borderland between the West Saxons and the Romano-British Celts during 577-652 AD. The fort had a single rampart up to 6m high with an outer ditch, with entrances on the SE and NW sides, possibly astronomically aligned to solstice sunrises and sunsets. These entrances show up well on Google Earth, as does the outline of the whole monument. At a height of up to 292m (950ft), it affords spectacular views over the Somerset Levels to Glastonbury Tor and Brent Knoll. The hill is served by footpaths from both the north and the south.

The line then plunges down the slopes from the hillfort to lower ground at **Downside**. This small hamlet is huddled around a very busy crossroads, but is important in that crossroads is the crossing point of the Magdalene and the Beltaine Lines.

The Magdalene Line skirts the eastern side of Shepton Mallet, crossing the Roman Fosse Way and the River Sheppey. Two stones shown on the 1888 OS map north of the main road (grid refs: 637429 and 638429) lie right on the line! Neither have ever stood on a parish boundary. Just south of the road fork (at grid ref: 636427) old maps also show Egypt Farm, an unusual dedication.

The line then goes straight through Sleight Plantation (shown and named on older maps), and then crosses the east end of **Whitestone Hill**, *white* meaning *holy*, passing through the summit of the small rise (just east of the 217m spot height). From here it passes by a spring (grid ref: 651408) and crosses a prominent, yet unnamed, hill just below the summit. The hill marks the Evercreech-Doulting parish boundary and is also crossed by the Mary flow of the St Michael Line, as it passes from Maes Down to the earthworks and prehistoric mounds on Small Down Knoll to the east (see *The Sun and the Serpent,* page 160). The Magdalene Line then goes through Fosse Combe Cottage before crossing Fosse Combe Gully. From the entrance of the drive to the cottage, we could see Spargrove, the next location, in the valley below, to the left of the cottage. From here, we also looked back north along the line, where the hill from over which the line had just passed over could be seen, to the left of telegraph pole.

The alignment then goes through **Spargrove Manor Moat**, one of several moats we were to find on Astrum lines. The site nestles in a valley under the shadows of Creech Hill to the south, which is capped by a Roman temple site. It is a medieval moated site with a building of two stories in an L-shaped plan. A bridge dating from 1290 once spanned the moat. The 16th C Manor House was almost totally rebuilt in 1870. At Batcombe church (one mile east of here) are the remains of a font said to have, "...*come from Spargrove Church, now destroyed,*" evidence that a church stood in the vicinity. Parish records from the 18th–19th C record members of the Coward family of Spargrove, some of whom are buried at Batcombe church. In 1791 a record speaks of the estate and

Top: 1829 drawing of Spargrove by John Russell Bucker. The church to right of the manor house stood on the Magdalene Line. Bottom: Spargrove Moat, which dates back to medieval times.

manor of Spargrove belonging to Thomas Coward. A certain Thomas Moore came to the property in 1655, who appears to have been a Non-Conformist, for in 1662 he invited a man to stay who had been ejected from Oxford on religious grounds.

We visited the site in March 2008. The old barn north of the house has the estate crest (containing a stag) mounted on the east wall, and is dated 1749. The approach to the house crosses the best surviving section of the moat, and at the far end can be seen a three-arched bridge, also dating from the 18th C, where water issues from two statues. It was in this stretch of water that timbers were found dating back to medieval times, possibly from the original bridge. Built into the SW-NE run of the moat's bank is a prominent mound, of undetermined date, on which a solitary tree grows. The energies on this mound felt powerful. The estate manager showed us a drawing dated 1829 showing the original 16th C Manor House, prior to its complete rebuild in 1870 (see image above). What appears to be a church tower is visible towards the right, where we suspected it would have been, in the field east of the Manor House. East of the moat the 1888 OS map shows three stones in the fields, west of the road. These were all on the Magdalene line! These are thought by the owners to have belonged to the church in the field, which would have sited it right on the alignment. These tapered stones are now standing just west of Manor House.

Permission to enter this fine locality should be sought from Mr D Munark, at The Manor, Spargrove, Evercreech, Somerset BA4 6HQ.

The line then goes through **Carrot Hill Farm** (grid ref: 675375). Just south of it can be seen a very sharp and prominent hill, looking like a mound, capped by three witch hazel trees. An elderly local gentleman told Peter that it is thought by some that the mound was a tumulus. Incredibly, this landmark marks the Magdalene Line!

The alignment then goes through Higher Green's Combe Farm (shown on 1888 maps, but not named, grid ref: 679369). At this point the line is less than a mile from the major Roman Temple site at Lamyatt (grid ref: 670362). The line then traverses the steep slopes that channel Combe Brook. From where the road crosses Waddon Hill (grid ref: 685360) one can look down into Combe Brook, with Green's Combe Farm beyond. To the south, one can glimpse some houses on the outskirts of Bruton, although the rest of the town hides itself in the valley of the River Brue. Alfred's Tower, at Stourhead, can also be seen in the distance to the east. The line goes straight through Upper Marksdanes, shown on old maps, and crosses the River Brue at a weir (grid ref: 691351).

The mound on the hill at Carrot Hill Farm marks the Magdalene Line. The three trees are witch hazels.

Bruton is an ancient Saxon town, with many historic buildings including the medieval Packhorse Bridge, St Mary's Church, Sexey's Hospital and the Dovecote. The River Brue (from *briw,* meaning *vigour*, describing the fast flow of the waters) passes through the town and provides pleasant walks for townspeople and visitors. Prehistoric flint axes were found just to the north of the town near the site of the Iron Age fort, on the top of Creech hill. Bruton was certainly settled by the 7th C, as it is recorded that St. Aldhelm and King Ine visited. In 1985, during the building of the flood relief scheme about 1 mile East of Bruton, a Saxon sword, possibly dating from the 9th C, was found (now in Taunton museum, with a replica in Bruton museum). By King Canute's time we know that there was a royal mint here, and a market was in existence by the 12th

C. To the south of the town, a series of field and place names (such as Godminster and Holywell) suggest that there was a Saxon religious centre in the area.

Documentary evidence suggests that there were two 7th C churches at Bruton. William of Malmesbury mentioned a church in Bruton dedicated to St. Peter, which lay alongside a church dedicated to St. Mary, which had been founded by King Ine of Wessex. A Benedictine monastery was founded in the early 11th C, but Bruton Priory was founded by William de Mohun, Earl of Somerset, as an Augustian foundation in 1142, replacing the Benedictines. The Augustinians were technically not monks but Canons in Holy Orders. The foundation was raised to the status of an abbey in 1510 and in 1533 the convent received a licence for two annual fairs, one held on the eve and the day of St. George, the other on the eve and the day of the Nativity of St. Mary. At the Dissolution, the abbey was first leased and then sold to the Berkeley family, who converted the buildings into a manor house. The manor was damaged by fire in 1763 and eventually demolished in 1786. King's School at Bruton, which was re-founded in 1550, has been built partially on the site of the abbey. Unfortunately nothing of the main abbey buildings has survived but traces can be found in various buildings around the town. It is still noticeable on the modern map how the River Brue once formed a natural boundary between the townspeople (north of the river) and the various ecclesiastical properties (south of the river). Prior to 1900 there was effectively nothing by the way of houses to the south.

Hexagram in a window in Bruton Church.

Bruton parish church is dedicated to The Blessed Virgin Mary, a typical dedication for a site so close to a river, the Brue, which flows past just across the road. It was extensively rebuilt in the 14th C, with many modifications over the next 400 years. The present layout dates from about 1743 and it has been described as, *"One of the proudest churches of East Somerset"*. Built of Doulting stone, the church is aligned NW-SE – the winter solstice sunrise. In the late 15th C the splendid west tower was added, which is 102½ft high and crowned by pinnacles.

Inside, the east wall behind the altar is resplendent with white plaster and gold decoration – similar to that in some London churches. It has a spacious feel to it, and on the south side one of the windows displays a hexagram (see image above). Gargoyles decorate the tower, which has around the base a plaque showing where the floods of June 1917 came up to. On the south side of the church are two small mounds, the largest of which is mounted by a tomb. Peter dowsed earth energies flowing from the church to the larger mound.

Green Man and unicorn on the outside of Prior House, on the High Street in Bruton. Other carvings are of dragons.

A town trail (leaflet at tourist info on High St) takes you around the town's historical sites. Opposite the Sun Inn, on the High St, is Priory House, on the walls of which are mounted a Green Man, a unicorn and two dragons. Along the street is Sexy's Hostel, with its small chapel (open to public) and views to the south of the monastic dovecote on the hill.

Old records speak of a Lady's Well on Combe Hill, north of the town centre, where the waters were were referred to as, *"... a general tonic with curative properties".* The well was destroyed in 1914, the waters being diverted since then into pipes. The well dates from at least the late 15th C, as the initials WG were inscribed on a stone, which probably referred to William Gilbert, who was Prior at Bruton in 1498.

From Bruton, Magdalene passes just east of Discove Farm. Discove existed by Domesday, being named then as 'Dinescove' or 'Dignescove'. A Roman villa was found here in 1711, and included traces of a pavement.

The alignment then goes through **Redlynch**, running just east of the main cluster of houses, parallel with the road, and straight through the ancient crossroads. In the 18th C a Roman 'pig' of lead was discovered at Redlynch. It weighed some 50 pounds and was inscribed, "IMP DVOR AUG ANTONINI ET VERI ARMENIA CORUM", which translates as, *"The lead of the two joint rulers Antonius (Marcus Aurelius) and Verus called Armenian."* It is dated 164-169 AD.

Redlynch House was built in the 18th C and was once the largest mansion in the area. The original medieval church would appear to have been around 200-300yds west of the axis of the line – at the edge of our "corridor". It stood in the northern boundary woods know as The Plantation, and was approached by the surviving track on this side of wood. The church was demolished around 1750, to be replaced by the present church, built by Nathaniel Ireson, Master Builder to the Earl of Ilchester. It is north of the site of the original church and is dedicated to St Peter; it is not open to the public, except for services. In the 18th C Lord Ilchester introduced other features to Redlynch Park, such as a Temple, a great pond, a Chinese Seat and a gothic western entrance. He entertained George III here, during some of the King's visits to Weymouth.

Past the crossroads, the road continues to follow the line for a mile, until it reaches **Stoney Stoke**, going straight through the meeting of three roads at Round Hill. The village is recorded in the Domesday Book. It once had its own smithy and an inn called The Swan, both recorded in the 18th C. Just west of the axis is Lush's Farm, now a dairy and a collection of cottages, amongst which used to be a church (grid ref: 709321). It is shown on both the 1888 and 1904 OS maps, but no dedication is given. A site visit in March 2008 found the small chapel, the keys of which were obtained from the present owners at a nearby cottage. All the fittings have been removed but the energy inside is very peaceful. Some of the older villagers remember services being held here, and that it also once acted as the village school.

The line then proceeds to **Shalford**, a small hamlet recorded from the 13th C as

belonging to Stavordale Priory. From here can be seen **Sunny Hill**, over which the line next crosses. The summit can be accessed via footpaths, and across the busy A303 our next destination can be seen, Stoke Trister.

The megalith at Stoke Trister, now blocking a gate, is not of the local geology. An energy flow was dowsed from the stone to the altar area inside the church.

Church of the Serpents

The church of St Andrew at **Stoke Trister** stands at the east end of Coneygore Hill, one of the defining hills of the Astrum. The village is recorded from the 13th C, and Edward III visited it twice in November 1333. In 1784 it was recorded that the parish had its own performing Mummers. The church stands on a prominent raised area, with sweeping views to the NW and the NE. From the churchyard, Sunny Hill (named after a solar alignment?) can be seen on the left, with Arthur's Tower on the skyline to the right. Several years ago Peter had found a stone just west of the churchyard gate, which was blocking an old gate. The megalith is of sandstone and not of the local geology (which is limestone and clay) and is decidedly egg-shaped; about 4ft long, it is reminiscent of the shape of the Omphalos Stone in Glastonbury Abbey. Toni confirmed an energy flow previously dowsed by Peter, which flows from the megalith, into the churchyard, through the porch before wending its way eventually to the area just in front of the altar, where it spirals. Underfoot at this point a circle can be seen indenting the red carpet and, on rolling it back, we found an ancient, worn floor tomb monument with spiralled serpents on it! In addition to the serpents, there are mirrors, sun symbols, five wolves and a raised hand holding a sword. The name of the interred person has been worn away, as too the date.

Serpents on a floor monument at Stoke Trister mark where energy spirals were dowsed.

Elsewhere in the church is a stunning window showing John the Baptist baptising Jesus, dated 1887. It is in fact John who is holding a staff with a banner containing the words *Ecce Agnus Dei (Behold the Lamb of God)*. The Templars held John in very high esteem, of equal status to Jesus, and we wondered whom the words were actually referring to in this depiction. Other windows depict icons of the apostles, including Luke's winged bull and Mark's winged lion. Although the church is simple without and within, it demonstrates how power places are not defined by architectural finery. Stoke Trister is potent with energy – we knew we were on an ancient power centre.

The dragon in the Chalice at Buckhorn Western.

To the east of the church, down the hill, we found a spring gushing from a field north of Beech Lane (grid ref: 740387). The waters pour into a large stone basin from above and flow down the hill into ancient fishponds (named on 1: 25,000 maps at grid ref: 742287), with adjacent earthworks. The 1888 OS map shows *St Andrew's Church (site of)* immediately north of the modern buildings and pond, at grid ref: 742288). A small enclosure marks the site today.

110

The line then crosses the Somerset – Dorset border and passes through the summit of an unnamed hill, on the southern slopes of which **Buckhorn Weston** nestles. It was recorded in 1287 that Stavordale Priory claimed an advowson of Buckhorn Weston, and in 1345 Robert de Mandeville of Coker granted the Priory a rent on his land locally, for the support of a chaplain to say mass at St. Andrew's. From the $14^{th} - 19^{th}$ C an annual fair was held in the village on June 24th, which was revived in 1951. Marsh Court monastical community was situated a mile to the west.

The church is dedicated to John the Baptist and although parts of it date from the 13th C, it was restored and enlarged in 1870. We entered the churchyard through beautiful wrought iron gates embellished with seven-pointed stars, and could soon see unusual vesica decorations in the window arches. One striking window shows St John the Apostle holding a golden chalice from which is emerging a beautiful golden winged dragon (see image page 110), which we had seen elsewhere. Officially, it is said that the serpent rises from the "cup of sorrow", foretold by Jesus, or that it represents St John surviving a drink of poison from a cup. Interestingly, his Saint days are December 27 (during the old winter solstice festival) and May 8 (during the Beltaine festival). Esoterically, we see the image as the dragon representing the life force of the planet, rising from the chalice, itself a symbol of the Divine Feminine. Here, John is standing on a black and white chequered floor, associated with Masonic, Templar

and alchemical traditions. Behind the altar is a window showing the Crucifixion, with Mary Magdalene weeping at the foot of the cross. The scene is framed by two windows decorated with delicate interlocking four-pointed stars surrounding circles. Back outside, we found a small dragon decorating a window frame at the east end.

Hambledon Hill on the skyline, as seen from Fifehead Magdalen.

A Meeting with Mary Magdalene

Fifehead Magdalen is situated on a hilltop overlooking the Stour to the east and the River Cale to the west. The Biblical character gives her name to this whole alignment. The axis passes just west of the Manor and the church. Recorded in the Domesday Book as *Fifhide,* the land here was given by William the Conqueror to his sister's son Hugh, having been held previously by the Saxon Alnoth. The *Magdalen* element to the village first appeared in 1388. Fifehead House was built in 1807 and stood just 50yds SE of the church, until it was demolished in 1964. The site commands a good view of Hambledon Hill to the south (see image above), and, like the church, the house stood just yards from the centre of the Magdalene Line.

The church is of course dedicated to Mary Magdalene and is decorated with flowers on her feast day of July 22nd. First mention of the church is in records of the Abbey of St Augustine in Bristol in the mid-12th C. Some walls date back to the 14th and 17th C but most were rebuilt in 1870, and restored further in 1905. The church is shrouded by a tight circle of huge yew, beech and pine trees, and stands on a knoll that seems to betray an ancient site. We walked up a gently sloping path composed of large stone slabs and paused in front of the porch. The exterior was pleasing to the eye, composed of blocks of natural stone, and the tower was embellished with slit windows.

We could see a stone cross in the corner of the churchyard and felt drawn to it. The shaft and top were obviously modern but the octagonal base was much older and worn, and looked like the medieval cross bases we had encountered elsewhere. Two

Mary Magdalene drying the feet of Jesus, one of three paintings of the couple at Fifehead Magdalen. In all three paintings Mary is wearing blue rather than her traditional red.

shallow steps underpinned the whole structure and formed the shape of an eight-pointed star. How unusual was that - sacred geometry in a memorial, which was, according to words carved into one of the steps, dedicated in the last century to a certain Colonel Percival. What a wonderful coincidence that sacred geometry should be incorporated into a monument erected in memory of a namesake of one of the Grail Knights!

The top slab of a chest tomb that stands close to the porch further grabbed our attention. It is not a slab of finely cut stone, but is heavily pitted and roughly hewn; is this a modified megalith? Its many deep conical depressions bear a resemblance to the celebrated cup marks, which decorate rocks elsewhere in Britain. Is it possible that this is an ancient stone later customized for Christian burial? It would certainly lend weight to our suspicion that a sacred site was here prior to Christianity. We ran our hands over the stone, pushing fingers into the enigmatic depressions. There were no inscriptions on the tomb, only a diamond at each end, adding to the mystery.

The interior of the church of the Magdalene held further treasures. The old wooden door, dated 1637, creaked open and we found the interior to be as appealing as the outside, with naked stonework, a far cry from the monotonous Victorian whitewashing so often encountered. Behind the altar is a wooden screen decorated with three fine paintings, dating from 1904. On the left is Mary Magdalene anointing the feet of Jesus (see image above); she shows so much love and tenderness in her eyes and gestures. But why was she wearing a robe of pale blue, a colour usually reserved for the mother of the prophet? The central painting was a powerful depiction of the Crucifixion. Two middle-aged women stood to the left of the cross - the Holy Mother and Elizabeth. At the foot of the cross is the younger figure of Mary Magdalene, her face distraught with grief. She holds centre-stage with Jesus and looks like a wife in mourning. Again, she is wearing blue. The right-hand painting depicts Jesus' appearance to Mary Magdalene after his resurrection. Again, she is garbed in a pale blue garment. It made us wonder how many other images supposedly of Mary the Mother were actually Mary Magdalene! Projecting that further, how many images of Mary holding the infant Jesus might be that of Mary Magdalene holding Sarah, the child whom she allegedly bore by Jesus? Thought for the day!

To the left of the altar two wooden chairs attracted our attention. On the backrest of both is an inverted triangle, overlapping three circles. We were following a Chalice Line, and here was the symbol of the Chalice, overlaid on the three circles, the Divine Feminine. Incredibly, a shield containing a dragon embellishes the centre of one of the triangles. The Mortuary Chapel, next to the chairs, has an impressive 18th C monument to the Newman family.

Yards west of the church, at the edge of a field, we found a mound-like rise next to the road. Was this an ancient mound? Why had this field not been built on? The 1889 OS map shows that even back then it was an orchard, the "mound" being shown as enclosed by a fence.

At the northwest end of the village, on the road to Kingston Magna, can be seen the old Baptist chapel, shown on the 1889 OS map. It stands in isolation about 300yds west of the centre of the line.

The line then goes through Trill Bridge, with its two shapely arches, which was first named in 1791. Between Fifehead and Fontmell Parva the alignment impressively passes through no less than seven farmhouses, four of which have sizable ponds.

The line passes through the west side of the village of **Todber**, mentioned in the Domesday Book, and research has revealed that no less than three important localities stand exactly on the axis of the line! From north to south, the first is the high ground on Great Down Lane (grid ref: 793203). A gate on the north side of the lane gives access to a field where a large depression marks the former site of Great Down Quarry. It was here that quarrying operations exposed a Romano-British cemetery. Excavations between 1870 and 1892 revealed twenty skeletons and a Roman coffin, dated between 286-350 AD. From this ridge we could look in both directions along the line: north back to Fifehead Magdalen and south to Hambledon Hill.

The line then passes through the edge of Ashley Plantation to the next site. Allard's Quarry is still worked, but excavations in 1932-39 and 1944-5 found an early Iron Age village. Skeletons, pottery and 66 pits were exposed. This was once the original centre of Todber – and our line goes straight through the site! The last Todber site on the line is the old chapel, now Chapel Cottage, just west of road junction (grid ref: 798194). A worn plaque states that the chapel was opened in 1873 by James Hunt. We gazed up in awe at the decoration above the plaque – it was a six-pointed star! The style was slightly Celtic, with curved ends to the points, and a six-petalled flower at the centre.

St Andrew's at Todber, sited on a ley line that goes to Stonehenge.

The church at Todber is dedicated to St Andrew, and seems almost out of place midst the modern houses of the village. The church is usually locked but the keys can be obtained locally using the list posted in the porch. Parts of the present building date from the 15th C. It has rare fragments of a 9th C Saxon cross, discovered in 1879 when the church was rebuilt; the fragments are now remounted, and show fine vine and spiral designs. Also in the church is a medieval altar, as well as two windows both depicting Jesus who has a halo containing the red Knights Templar cross. In *Ancient Stones of Dorset,* Peter describes how Todber church stands on a ley that goes through Dorset all the way to Stonehenge (Fig 119). The church is small and plain but the locality is powerful. Toni dowsed several spirals on the path between the gate and the porch, that suggested former megaliths. There is a Temple's Cottage in Todber, but we are not sure if this indicates a distant memory of the Templars in the area. To the east of the churchyard we could also see low earthen banks in the field.

At **Thorton Farm** the centre of the line passes just east of another surviving medieval moat, still partially filled with water on two sides (grid ref: 804180). The farm buildings stand on the eastern section of this N-S orientated earthwork. There was certainly more to this site than meets the eye, for we found evidence that Thorton used to be an autonomous parish, with its own manor and chantry, and that the farm is on the site of the former church. Historian John Hutchins quotes an earlier record of 1464, recording a dedication of St Martin, and that the church was pulled down at the beginning of the 19th C. He states that some of it survived as a stable, later a barn. A site visit by us in early 2008 found the top arch of the holy water stoup preserved in one wall of the oldest barn, now a cattle shed.

The moat defines an 80x70yd island, with ridges up to 2ft high, which can be viewed from the western approach road to the farm. 13th-14th C pottery shards have been found here, but it is believed by many researchers that "medieval" moats may well have a more ancient origin. As we stood next to the moat, we could see Duncliffe Hill and Melbury Beacon, both Astrum localities, to the north and northeast respectively, with Shaftesbury sandwiched in between; Hambledon Hill rose to the south. Permission to enter the site should be sought from Mr. Mogridge at the farm.

Just east of the alignment is a large pond north of Thorton Farm, on the north side of White Way Lane (grid ref: 805184). On the north side of the pond we found 6 large, uncut megaliths, some partially submerged in the water. Were these cleared from the nearby fields, or from a mound next to the pond? The stones lie about 250yds from the centre of the Magdalene Line. The pond is shown on 1890 OS maps.

Manston Farm stands on the line; it once had a corn mill on the waters of Manston Brook. The next building of note on the alignment is Fontmell Parva House (grid ref: 827145), which dates back to the 17th C and was built by Edward St Loe of Knighton, who was buried at Child Okeford in 1686. The house was enlarged in the 19th C, although the original facade survives as window bays on the east front.

Magdalene then passes through the middle of **Porter's Hill** (81m spot height) and is then mirrored by Common Drove, a track shown on the 1891 OS map, which follows the line for almost half a mile. The line then climbs up the heady heights of Hambledon Hill, a fittingly outstanding site for where, incredibly, five Astrum lines converge in an area of less than half a mile (see map page 117).

Hambledon Hill rises from the Dorset landscape like a beached whale - steep, elongated, high and magnificent. The ridge rises to over 600ft above sea level and is an easily recognisable landmark, visible from miles around. It is a popular destination for ramblers, dog-walkers and those who conquer its demanding slopes simply to absorb the superlative views. The hill is home to two Neolithic long barrows (whose white mounds on the crests of the hill would have once been striking) and a Neolithic causewayed enclosure dating back to 3600-3300 BC. The most prominent features, however, are the massive banks and ditches of the northern spur that formed the defences of the Iron Age hillfort. The site is huge, covering over 12 acres of the northern end of the hill (where the Astrum lines converge). The Romans subdued local tribes and as late as 1645 it was the scene of a skirmish between ill-armed yokels and Cromwellian troops. A hundred years later Wolfe trained his troops on the hill in preparation for the capture of the Heights of Abraham at Quebec.

Folklore speaks of a yew forest being associated with the Druids, a haunting by a Roman centurion and that the hill protects local villages by supernatural forces (see *Sacred Dorset* by Peter Knight). The hill is linked with several ley lines, one of which is shown in *Sacred Dorset* (page 153) marking a midsummer alignment between Hambledon, Rawlesbury and Nettlecombe hillforts. At the foot of the hill is Markstone Cottage, which marks an ancient track up the hill from the southwest.

The Magdalene Line passes right through the 604ft spot height near the northern end of Hambledon Hill, where the Central Axis also terminates (see map, page 117). As we stood there we looked back down the line in the direction of Brockley, our starting point some 40 miles distant. Todber and West Orchard were difficult to make out in the lowlands before us, but we could see the trees that surround the church of Fifehead Magdalen, on a rise in the middle distance.

Bringing our attention back to Hambledon, we plotted the Magdalene Line directly through the long barrow that stands prominent on the spur. This Neolithic mound, which stands at over 620ft above sea level and is visible from miles around, is 6ft high and well over 200ft long. Gashes in its side bear witness to unsympathetic excavations in the past. It is orientated almost N-S (345°).

Hambledon Hill, the impressive focus for five of the Wessex Astrum alignments. The Iron Age ramparts can be seen on the slopes, and prehistoric mounds occupy the top of the hill.

We recalled how we had stood on the spur above Wotton, 52 miles to the north, on similar ancient mounds. The 360° views from this hallowed mound are breathtaking and we could well appreciate why our Neolithic ancestors chose this place. We both stood on top of the mound and sent out healing down all five lines that converge on Hambledon, and asked that the ancient wisdom encoded in the Astrum landscape be revealed to us. We truly believe that when one approaches sites with humility, as a humble student might approach a mentor or spiritual leader, then more can be accessed from these places. More than this, more is *given* by these places. Respect is the key.

We take the terminal point of the line as the large east-west embankment just south of the barrow, where the line converges with the Glastonbury to Hambledon hexagram line. This prominent bank (see image on page 168) stands well within the hillfort and appears to rest on an older platform, possibly indicating that something was here prior to it becoming an Iron Age defensive structure. This bank also marks the terminal point of one of the hexagon lines (see Chapter 15).

Child Okeford nestles below Hambledon, and is dealt with in some detail in Chapter 15, as it lies on the Hexagon line that comes to Dorset from Glastonbury.

Standing on the long barrow on top of the ridge at Hambledon
Hill, sending healing down the five lines of the Wessex

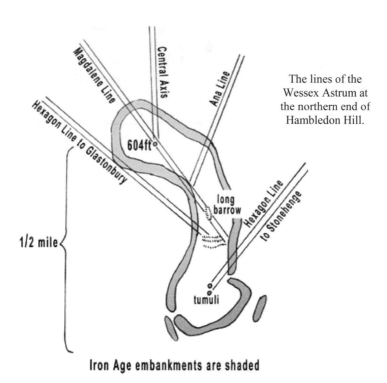

The lines of the
Wessex Astrum at
the northern end of
Hambledon Hill.

Magdalene Line

Central Axis

Ana Line

Hexagon Line to Glastonbury

604ft°

long
barrow

Hexagon Line
to Stonehenge

1/2 mile

tumuli

Iron Age embankments are shaded

117

Chapter 12
The Chalice
St Caen Line: Brockley to Avebury

x Brockley

x Dundry

x Whitchurch

x Keynsham

x Saltford (church)

x St Alphage's Well

x Little Solsbury Hillfort

x Northend
x The Mount

x Ashley
x Box

x Neston
x Monk's Park
x Gastard

x Lacock Abbey

x Clark's Hill
x Blackland Park

x Tumuli on Cherhill Down
x Cherhill White Horse
x Avebury Trusloe
x Avebury (church & henge)

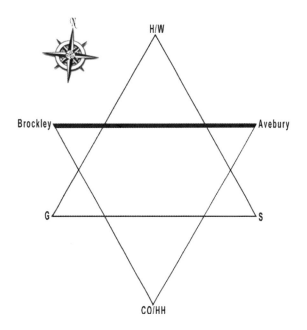

The St Caen Line, named after the female saint associated with Keynsham, begins at Brockley, in the vicinity of the church and Brockley Hall. The church is described in detail in Chapter 23, as it marks the terminal point of the Samhain Line.

The St Caen Line then passes through the woods to the north of Brockley Combe, and then along the north side of **Dundry**, a village situated 700ft above sea level, set midst the four-mile-long Dundry Hill. The lofty location affords spectacular views of

Left: the hexagram clock at Dundry. Right: the medieval cross and the Dole Stone in St Michael's churchyard, Dundry.

Bristol to the north, the Bristol Channel to the west, and Somerset to the south. The name comes from *Dun draegh,* the "Hill of Oaks", and local folklore speaks of fairies appearing out of Dundry Hill on Midsummer Eve. At the west end of the village is Elwell, the site of a sacred spring; the name El, and its variants Bel and Hel, refer to ancient solar deities. Dundry is famous for the local oolitic Dundry Stone, which has been quarried since Roman times. The quarries were later owned by the Church, and its stone was used in Cardiff Castle and for much of medieval Bristol, and large quantities were also exported to Ireland.

There is a record dated 1289 of a, *"...chapel of rest at Dundry".* The present church is dedicated to St Michael, appropriate for such an elevated location. The views from the northern part of the churchyard are spectacular, with panoramas of Bristol and both Severn bridges. It was rebuilt from local stone in 1861, although some of the original 13th C stonework survives. Long-standing subsidence in the churchyard, and

St Nicholas, Whitchurch, a beautiful church. It is a place of great peace and sanctity, and was built on the site of an ancient spring.

stories of tunnels, hint at possible caverns or springs in the rock below; this reminds us of folklore referring to tunnels under both the Tower of London and Glastonbury. The notable feature, however, is the 15th C tower which reaches a commanding height of 97½ft, and is built in the late-Gothic style. It was commissioned by local merchants as a landmark for Bristol Channel shipping. It originally housed a lantern, and five families were given land in return for tending the light. It is said that from the top fourteen counties can be seen on a clear day. Lower down the tower is a large clock, which is noticable for its hexagram design, which we thought relevant; we had seen another hexagram on the tower clock at Wotton (see image on page 215).

In Dundry churchyard there are two notable objects. The first is the large and fine medieval cross. The other is a huge block of stone, just yards to the south. This is the

famous Dole Stone, a rectangular block of oolitic limestone weighing over 10 tons. In the past it was used for giving alms to the poor, especially on New Year's Day, as well as for distributing bread to the needy at Christmas.

The line then proceeds to **Whitchurch**, where the church of St Nicholas stands just north of the axis. In *A Topographical History of England* (1831), Samuel Lewis has the dedication as St Gregory. The 1900 OS map shows it as the site of St Whyte's Chapel, with a well next to it. At

Whitchurch: St George is subduing this green dragon, which barely breathes fire from its mouth.

Whitchurch Canonicorum, in Dorset, the church is also dedicated to St Whyte (or *White,* meaning *Holy*). The crossroads is very busy and because of a confusing one-way system, it is best to park at the Maes Knoll Inn. The church is open 2.00-4.00pm on Wednesday in the summer, and 6.30-9.00pm on Tuesdays (all year). When locked, the keys can be obtained from the first house on the left past the church (Church House – No. 5). Debbie Fletcher is the key holder and is a knowledgable guide (tel. 01275 832730). She showed us around and confirmed that a spring still rises under the church, and that there is a well accessing the waters in her garden.

The statuette of Madonna and child at Whitchurch.

This ancient chapel has a short tower graced with gargoyles, and large yew trees offer shade. Inside the energy was powerfully felt, and "10 out of 10" was how Toni expressed it, one of her favourite Astrum sites. The energies were particularly powerful in the Vestry (formerly the Lady Chapel) and in front of the main altar. Exposed stone added to the atmosphere, and the whole feel of the church was that of a place of ancient sanctity. The main east window is of excellent quality and shows the Crucifixion, with Mary Magdalene expressively portrayed, grieving at the foot of the cross. Above Jesus' head are the sun and the moon. Next to a wooden lectern is a beautiful statue of Mary holding the child Christ (image left) and nearby is a fine window of St George subduing a green dragon, who is still alive and issuing fire (see image page 120). Debbie told us of the tradition of a tunnel, said to run from the church to Lions Court Farm, formerly the manorial residence of the influential Smythe family. The property (at grid ref: 608674) dates from the 13th C and is PRECISELY on the Chalice line!

The St Caen Line then strikes through the southern end of **Keynsham,** listed in the Domesday Book of 1086 as *Cainesham,* meaning St Keyne's home. The St Edmund Line also passes through the western side of the town, passing through the Roman villa site at the cemetery (see page 67). The town is located at the confluence of the River Chew and the Avon, an area with a prehistoric history. There is also a scattering of Roman sites, such as the villas at Somerdale and Durley Hill. The Saxons are thought to have had a minster here and the settlement, named after Saint Keyne, developed into a medieval market town, its growth prompted by the foundation of an influential and prosperous Augustinian abbey, founded around 1170. It survived until the Dissolution of the monasteries in 1539, when a house was built on the site. In the town there is a Temple Bridge, Temple St and Temple Court, reminding us of the former presence of the Knights Templar. The town was the site of a battle between royalist forces and the rebel Duke of Monmouth.

St. Keyne (c. AD 461- 505) has been adopted for the name of this alignment. She was a saintly lady with a number of popular epithets: St. Cain Wyry (*the Virgin*), Cain Breit (*the Bright*) or Ceinwen (*the Fair*) and *Caginus* in Latin. In Welsh, Caen variously means either **surface, spear** or **fair one**. She was the daughter of King Brychan or Brycheiniog of South Wales, and niece of St Cadoc. Keyne was the King's most distinguished and gifted child and many noble lords sought her hand.

Ammonites such as this are said to be serpents that were turned to stone by St Keyne.

Wishing to retain her virginity, the princess became a travelling missionary, crossing the Severn, travelling south and settling in *a wooded solitary abode*, where now stands Keynsham. It is said that she was warned by a local king that the area was swarming with serpents, making the area uninhabitable. St. Keyne, after praying to God, changed all the snakes into stone; a similar miracle is recorded of St. Hilda.

Today these are considered to be the fossilized remains of ammonites, which feature in the town's coat of arms, as well as symbols of local institutions. St Cadoc later persuaded Keyne to return to Wales, where she lived in isolation, *"... in a hillock at the roots of a certain great mountain,"* where caused a healing well to spring up. She had a strong cult in South Wales and Cornwall, with churches and wells named after her, and is said to have given magical powers to well water.

The manor and hundred of Keynsham was conferred to the Abbey, together with the church of St. Mary, St. Peter and St. Paul, and its dependent chapels of Brislington, Charlton, Whitchurch, Publow and Pensford. The Abbey was in use by the Augustinians from 1170 until being dissolved in 1539. Little now remains of the great building, as much of its stone was used in the 1634 restoration of the parish church. The site was excavated between 1961 and 1991, however, and some walls can be seen in the grounds of Keynsham Memorial Park. Access is via a path alongside the River Chew, under the by-pass, bearing left, where the remains will be seen near the road. Parts of the 12th C south transept of the Abbey Church, with adjoining parts of the south aisle, and some sections of the nave have also been left exposed. Many fragments from the Abbey are to be found in various parts of Keynsham, and others have been rescued and stored as museum pieces at the Town Hall.

The parish church is dedicated to John the Baptist, a figure much revered by the Knights Templar. Another church, at grid ref: 654677, is shown on the 1900 OS map as *The Lodge Isolation Hospital*. Keynsham has eight churches today, a sign of its deep spiritual heritage.

Left: the damaged heads on the font at Saltford; Right: St Michael and St George, both slaying dragons, flank Christ in this window at Saltford.

The next destination on the St Caen Line is the village of **Saltford**, on the River Avon. Initially, it appeared to us that most of Saltford lay well south of the line, but the 1890 OS map shows that the entire village once stood within the area bounded by the railway and the river, only later creeping south to the present main road and beyond. The main road traffic thunders through this modern part of the village, but as one approaches the church the scene changes to a prettier one of older houses and quiet narrower lanes. Parking for the church is in Queen Square.

The dedication is to St Mary, commonly found at churches near rivers and springs. It dates back to the 12th C, but may be of Saxon origin, and was fully restored in 1832. The tower may be partly Saxon, though it has been extensively repaired; the top ten feet and the pinnacles are Victorian. The font is Norman, or perhaps even Saxon, and has carved heads on its sides. It was removed from the church and had the heads defaced by Cromwell's soldiers after the Battle of Lansdown in 1643, and was subsequently found to be in use as a cattle trough. The frames of the two larger windows on the side of the nave are both of the 13th –14th C. Windows show St George slaying a green dragon (symbolic of the earth?) whilst St Michael slays a red dragon (the sun?). The Bible in the glass case dates to 1612. We felt powerful energies spiralling in front of the main altar.

From the churchyard we could see Lansdown Hill, with the tree-topped Kelston Round Hill to the right. They were linked by a lower, saddle-like ridge, and it was over this slightly lower ground that the St Caen Line ascends.

Saltford Manor, next to the church, is a rare survival of a Norman hall, contemporary with Horton Court in nearby Gloucestershire. The latter was a prebendal house and it can be assumed that Saltford had a direct association with Keynsham Abbey. The 1900 OS map shows a stone on the other side of the River Avon from the village (grid ref: 688675). We have not been able to confirm its survival or its age.

St Alphage, as shown in St Giles, London.
Viking longships pass by in the background.

Saltford Lock and its weirs are just north of the alignment, and it is a lovely spot to visit. Parking is at the Jolly Sailor (grid ref: 692679), and behind the pub one can walk along the river and witness the incredible power of the Avon as it thunders over the weirs on its way from Bath to Bristol, and to the sea beyond.

The St Caen Line then passes just south of **St Alphage's Well**, thought to be the only well dedicated to the saint in England. The well is near the top of a very steep slope (grid ref: 725681), and a valley channels the issuing waters down to the outskirts of Bath. A small lay-by is on the west side of the nearby road, at the crest of the hill. A steep tarmacked path leads down to the well, which recently replaced original ancient cobblestones. We could not find the source on a summer visit in 2008, but the waters issuing from it were seen flowing under the track at one point. By tradition, the waters once fell into a Roman coffin, said to have been brought from North Stoke to the NW. Chapel Farm, to the north, which was originally St Laurence's Hospice, was used by pilgrims on their way to Glastonbury. There was formerly another holy well nearby at Lansdown, known as St Winefrede's Well, where, *"...women with suspicious hopes of maternity"* took the waters. From the track by the well, we looked back along the alignment, to the saddle-like ridge and to Kelston Round Hill, now on the left.

St Alphage (originally *Aelfheah*, 953-1012 AD) was born in Weston-super-Mare, of a noble family, but in early life devoted himself purely to his faith. Having assumed the habit in the monastery of Deerhurst, he later went to Bath, where he became an anchorite and ultimately Abbot of Bath Abbey, distinguishing himself by his piety and austerity. In 984, he was appointed, through Dunstan's influence, Bishop of Winchester, where he built and enlarged the city churches. After a Viking raid in 994, he arranged a peace treaty with Olaf Tryggvason, whom he converted to Christianity. He was later appointed Archbishop of Canterbury, before being killed by the Danes in Greenwich in 1012. There is a ruined church dedicated to the saint in London, and he can be seen in a stained glass window in St Gile's (see image above).

The alignment then goes through **Little Solsbury Hill** (grid ref: 768679), commonly known as Solsbury Hill. The name probably derives from Sol or Sul, the pre-Roman sun god, from whom Bath (Aqua Sulis) was named. It is a small, triangular, flat-topped hill rising to 188m, overlooking the River Avon to the south. Immortalised by

Peter Gabriel in his song of the same name, the Iron Age hillfort covers 20 acres and was occupied between 300 and 100 BC. The ramparts were 12ft and 20ft wide with dry-stone walling. The huts were burnt down at the end of its use, perhaps during the Belgic invasion of Britain in the early part of the 1st C BC. It has been cited as one of the possible locations of Mount Badon, where Arthur defeated the Saxons. The axis of the St Caen alignment runs along the northern E-W embankments.

From Little Solsbury hillfort, the line passes through **Northend**, ascends the hill known as **The Mount** and then crosses into Wiltshire. **Ashley** is the next stop, and the old Manor House stands directly on the alignment. Next to the village green is Wormcliffe Lane, reminiscent of other British localities associated with worms; in these cases they were often large subterranean creatures, more akin to serpents and dragons. Close by is White Cottage, white meaning *holy*. From the lane that goes east from the green we looked down to the village of Box below.

This magnificent window at Box shows Jesus in a flaming vesica, and below him a pack of wolves, as well as a fallen caduceus with entwined serpents (below).

The village of **Box** is probably best known for the famous Box Tunnel, the underground railway passage nearly two miles in length, which is said to align with sunrise on April 9, Brunel's birthday. The Priory of St Mary Magdalene at Monkton Farleigh, east of Bath, held land and property around Box, and the church was given to the Priory in 1227, in an effort to aid its finances. The line approaches Box through the mortuary chapel in the cemetery, a phenomenon we have found elsewhere. This land was known as Great Lye Mead and lies in a hollow. Mesolithic and Neolithic finds have been found locally. The chapel is open during the day, and is ornately carved with foliated arch ends and praying angels.

The parish church of St Thomas à Becket, Box, is just yards north of the line, and stands near the site of a Roman villa, just to the north, which was expanded in 3-4th C to a large villa for a wealthy owner, containing one of the richest collections of mosaics yet found. Properties known as Roman Villas now stand on the spot. A fine Roman mosaic was also found in the churchyard. The church is approached via Church Lane, passing a group of Cottages called Springfield, alerting us to the possibility that the villa and the church are at a sacred spring. Waters from the spring issue from the ground at quite a rate next to the churchyard gate.

The church is open during the day and is entered via the north door, which does not have a porch and is not immediately obvious. The church has Norman walls and the church guidebook tells us that some of the stonework may possibly be from a simpler Saxon church. The inside of St Thomas' is a delight, with ancient stone walls and impressive monuments. One window shows St George subduing, but not killing, a green dragon, whilst another, in a side chapel, shows Jesus midst a radiant vesica piscis, with a pack of wolves laying down before him (see image page 125). Peter found this particularly pulling, as one of his totem animals is the wolf. Towards the bottom left of the window we noticed a fallen winged caduceus, with two entwined serpents, lying on the ground midst the wolves. The energies in front of the altar in this chapel were powerfully felt. Near the organ is a memorial on which are carved four griffins.

Four griffins adorn the Gothic fountain in Box.

In the centre of the village we found more interesting things. The Methodist Chapel is, ironically, opposite the Queen's Head pub, and next to the 1860 building is a green man set into the front of No 1, The Parade. Opposite is an area known as The Pound, which has a map of the historical monuments in the village. Where the roads divide stands the Victorian fountain, a grand structure built in the Gothic style, which has grand marble columns and, amazingly, four dragon-like griffins (image above). The line leaves Box by crossing Ley Lane and Upper Lay; Alfred Watkins would have loved this!

SE of Box, just south of the St Caen line, is Chapel Plaister (grid ref. 840678), a resting place for pilgrims journeying to the shrine of St Joseph of Arimathea in Glastonbury. Augustinian monks founded the chapel in the 13th C, but the present building dates from the 14th-15th C. At one time it was adjoined to a pub called the Bell Inn and antiquarian John Aubrey wrote that it was, *"...a place for pilgrim's entertainment"*. One of England's smallest churches, it is built of beautiful Cotswold Stone, and is still a place of pilgrimage today. Over the door is the pilgrim's scallop shell and pleasant meditative gardens can be accessed when the chapel is open (on Wednesdays between 2-4pm and on Sundays for services.)

The line then passes just to the north of Hazelbury Manor. The church guide book at Box states that the parish was, *"...originally served by its church (long-since demolished), this being located north of Hazelbury Manor"*. This may have stood right on the St Caen Line!

The line then goes just south of the Ebenezer Baptist Chapel at Moor Green, dated 1860 on the front, which is now a private residence. It then proceeds past the Country Inn at Neston, which is on Church Rise. The parish church of St Philip and St James is just south of here, open daily between 9.00am–4.00pm. It is a more recent 19th C building with a six-petalled window and has a *"living churchyard"* that is managed so as to encourage wildlife.

The quaint chapel at Monk's Park.

The line then passes just yards north of the Independent Chapel at **Monk's Park**. Built in 1622 by the Quakers, it was later owned in 1690 by the Independents, and still hosts Sunday services today. The churchyard is usually open, enabling inspection of the attractive chapel, built of Cotswold Stone and attractive old slates. Old cottages stand nearby and the locality is peaceful and quiet. At the southern end of Monk's Lane, to the south of the chapel, is a large pond, with water lilies and fallen tree trunks - a magical scene in a quiet locality.

The line then passes just north of the main crossroads at **Gastard**, at a point where three wells and *Silver Street* are marked on the 1889 OS map. A former chapel is recorded in Gastard from 1428, but in 1639 it was turned into cottages. The present parish church is dedicated to St John the Baptist – again! It was built in 1912 in the Gothic style, with a broad west tower. The church is usually open but the interior is plain, the only colourful feature being the east window, which shows a cross rising from the sea; a sign near the entrance explains the symbolism of the window. A tapestry shows Da Vinci's *The Last Supper*, with the person to Jesus' right again looking remarkably feminine! The pub at the crossroads is the Harp and Crown and is handy if visiting local sites, as it is open all day.

The line then enters the Lacock Estate, passing just north of **Lacock Abbey**. It was founded as an Augustinian nunnery in 1232 by Ela, Countess of Salisbury, whose husband, William Longespee was a powerful baron, present at the signing of the Magna Carta. It was completed around 1247, whilst a Lady Chapel was added in the 14th C. Henry III granted permission for an annual fair at Lacock and later a Tuesday market, and in 1257 the nuns were granted their own fair and market. Henry even gave a weekly cartload of wood from Melksham Forest for the Abbess's fire, and in 1260 he gave 40 acres of the forest to the nunnery. In 1300, the church at Lacock was appropriated by the Abbey, but by the 15th C the Abbey was exempted from taxes due to its poverty. The fine cloisters (with Green Man bosses), chapter house, sacristy and monastic rooms, are largely intact. The Abbey was turned into a country house in 1540, and is now managed by the National Trust (open Feb-Oct). The property has featured in TV and film productions, such as *Pride and Prejudice, Moll Flanders* and *Harry Potter.*

Left: the moon and hexagrams in Lacock church;
Above: Lacock Abbey.

The parish church is well worth a visit, and is actually closer to the line than the Abbey. It is open during the day and is approached via a lane of old quaint cottages, tearooms and a pub called *At the Sign of the Angel*. The church is dedicated to St Cyriac, an unusual dedication in this country but one that is common in Normandy; Cyriac was a 3-year-old child who was martyred by the Governor of Cilicia in 303 AD. As one enters there is a carving of a sun and moon overhead, and inside we found the Lady Chapel to be most powerful with energies; its ceiling retains ornate carvings and original paintwork; under the arch is a face with a crescent moon above, surrounded by hexagram stars! Nearby, behind the prayer candle stand, is a mythical head emerging from the bottom of the column, and a monument in the same chapel displays two opposing griffins. One window elsewhere shows Joseph of Arimathea, whilst another shows a female figure holding a sword and the scales of justice. The church is full of atmosphere and ornate carvings of tiny heads and foliage.

The charming church hidden away at Blackland.

The line continues on to **Clark's Hill**, then passes through Mile Elm and then on through the estate of **Blackland Park**. The line passes within yards of the little church of St Peter. In the 10th C or earlier the land which was to become the parish was part of the King's large estate of Calne, part of the land of Calstone (possibly *Calne's east tun*). By the late 12th C Blackland had separated from Calstone, and its church, and probably a manor house, had already been built. In 1194 the

128

land was called the Black Land of Calstone, and, later on, the manor, church, a farmstead and a mill all adopted the name Blackland. South of the church at Blackland Farm (which dates back to at least the 16th C) was a moated site, possibly from the mid-13th C. The moat enclosed a rectangle on which stood a house, apparently as grand as the manor house itself. The Quakers are recorded at Blackland in the 17th – 18th C.

The church of St Peter is signposted from the main road, and there is a small parking area. The small church is surrounded by tall trees, and in the porch is a memorial dating from 1675 to one of the Hungerford family, next to a list of rectors going back to 1583. On entering, one is struck by how dark the church is. The altar end is the darkest we have seen, small windows and large trees conspiring to block out much of the daylight. The atmosphere is wonderful and the main focus behind the altar is a scene of the Crucifixion, showing Mary Magdalene at the foot of the cross.

Back at the parking area we could see the Cherhill White Horse, the next destination on the St Caen Line. Before then, the line passes through a group of tumuli on Cherhill Down, to the west of the hill figure (grid ref: c. 039694). With amazing accuracy the alignment then passes right through the Cherhill White Horse. The gleaming figure can be seen from lay-bys on the A4, one of which has an information board (grid ref: 041701).

The Cherhill White Horse trots along the St Caen Line! The banks of Oldbury hillfort can be seen on the right.

The horse was cut in 1780, under the direction of Dr Christopher Allsup, who designed it to be elongated, to resemble the horses of the artist Stubbs. It measures 131ft long, 142ft high, and was restored in 2002 using 150 tons of graded chalk.

The alignment then passes through the northern embankments of Oldbury Castle, the Iron Age hillfort, which can be seen above the horse from the road below. It comprises 25 acres, enclosed by two banks and ditches with an entrance on the east side. Pottery dating 2nd – 3rd C BC has been found within the enclosure. The tall obelisk on the west bank can be seen from the stone avenue at Avebury, as well as from Bath.

The Mystical Landscape of Avebury

Hidden deep within the rolling hills and downs of Wiltshire is one of the wonders of the ancient world. The St Caen Line goes through Avebury Trusloe before passing through the Manor House and parish church in Avebury itself. As this is the first time we are describing a line converging on Avebury, a brief introduction would not go amiss.

Avebury is one of the six apex points of the Wessex Astrum (see map below). Incredibly, the five convergent lines pass variously through the henge, Silbury Hill, Avebury Church, West Kennet Long Barrow, Waden Hill, Tan Hill, Milk Hill or Windmill Hill, major manmade and prominent natural features in the area. Some Astrum lines go through more than one site. As at Stonehenge and Glastonbury, the main sacred sites appear to stand on converging Astrum alignments.

The Manor House was once the site of a Benedictine cell. The church has hexagrams in the floor tiles in front of the wooden vestry, similar to those we found at Wotton and by Toni around the altar at St Bartholomew's in London. The famous font in Avebury church displays two dragons at the feet of a bishop, taken by dowsers to represent the Mary and Michael flows of the St Michael Line. Outside, one of the buttresses on the NE side rests on a very rough stone, possibly an ancient megalith. The St Caen Line then goes into the henge and terminates in the centre, in the vicinity of The Cove, the Red Lion and the small chapel.

The village of Avebury stands within some of the finest achievements of the Neolithic Age. Within two miles of the Red Lion, in the centre of the village, (reportedly one of the most haunted pub in England), can be found the world's largest stone circle, Western Europe's highest Neolithic mound (Silbury Hill), as well as the vestiges of two stone avenues, numerous round barrows, long barrows, dolmens and stone circles. Several isolated standing stones (or megaliths) also guard this magical landscape, a place our distant ancestors held as sacred.

The five Astrum lines converging on the Avebury landscape.

Arguably Avebury's jewel in the crown is Silbury Hill, which rises majestically out of the land, having stood the test of time for nearly 5,000 years. The mound has never been a tomb, but was created

130

to be symbolic of the belly of the Earth Goddess. It was built around 2,700 BC, stands 130ft high and comprises an incredible 12 million cubic feet of chalk and earth. It is a true pyramid, built using cleverly interlocking blocks of chalk, arranged in steps 15-17ft high. The angle of its slopes is 30°, affording an extremely stable structure, ensuring that the hill had not slumped in over 4,500 years, until, that is, archaeologists started digging tunnels through it, believing it to be a tomb! Silbury stands on the Ana Chalice Line as it approaches Avebury (see Chapter 13 for more details).

The monuments of Avebury wonderfully demonstrate the spiritual beliefs of their builders. Its sacred sites were not built at random localities, but positioned very precisely and often with incredible subtlety; they are not just *on* the landscape, but are held *within* it. Line-of-sight effects were produced, the intervisiblity of monuments being of vital importance. The great megaliths themselves were chosen with great care regarding their size, shape and the symbolism. Anthropomorphs and simulacra abound at Avebury, the huge stones exhibiting lasting testaments to a spiritual driving force that revolved around the sun, the moon, and the Earth Mother/Goddess.

Aerial view of the henge at Avebury, with its huge bank and ditch enclosing massive megaliths. The field in the foreground contained a crop circle in 2008.

Avebury eloquently expresses many principles of the art of ancient sacred geomancy, the positioning of sites in relation to the landscape, as well as ley lines and earth energies. Dowsing around Avebury's huge megaliths can be a breathtaking experience, with many major currents of serpentine energy flowing through the landscape. The St Michael Line, the famous alignment that runs from Cornwall to East Anglia, cuts through the area and the male and female energy flows associated with it pass through several of the Avebury monuments.

The oldest monuments at Avebury are the long barrows, of which East and West Kennet long barrows are the largest and best known. West Kennet Long Barrow is

131

one of those "must visit" places for anyone interested in our prehistoric heritage, particularly from a spiritual point of view. The axis of the 330ft long earthen mound is aligned to the Equinox sunrise, one of the astronomical festivals of the year. It was in use for over a thousand years between 3,700-2,500 BC, ample proof of the sanctity of the site. It is thought that priests, priestesses and shamans would seek contact with the gods, the ancestors and the Earth Mother/Goddess to bring back important information for their tribe. Initiates may also have spent time here, sealed within the tomb's dark confines to meet the Spirits and contact their own inner nature and confront their inner demons. The mound and chambers stand just yards west of the Stonehenge to Avebury line, and the Mary current of the St Michael Line flows through its chambers. Every summer we take groups up to the monument to witness the full moon, to drum and chant within its candlelit chambers (see images page 181). Two avenues of stones formerly ran into the henge at Avebury, one from the south, the other from the west. The Adam and Eve stones are all that remain now of the latter. Some stretches of the southern avenue, however, have survived time and Man; West Kennet Avenue is arguably the finest megalithic avenue in Britain. It formerly comprised around 200 stones of which now, sadly, less than 30 survive today. One can walk up the mile long avenue, retracing our ancestors' footsteps, and dowse the earth energies of the Michael current that flow down its length. The avenue is sinuous as it twists and turns to follow the serpents of the land. Many of the megaliths display simulacra, such as heads, vulvae and phalluses. One can just imagine the torch-lit processions that wended their way up the avenue thousands of years ago, the images of the ancestors being animated by flickering flames.

The avenue proceeds north to the Neolithic henge at Avebury, where Astrum lines converge. The sheer scale of this construction can take one's breath away. A huge bank and ditch was constructed, and some 200 megaliths were raised in the enclosed

We never tire of taking groups around Avebury, to reveal its mysteries and power.

area. 100,000 tons of chalk and earth were moved (c. 3.2 million cubic feet) to create the ditch and banks, 60 times greater than at Stonehenge. This is in addition to the 4,000 tons of stone needed for the megaliths. It has been estimated that the whole ceremonial landscape may have taken centuries to complete, and has been dated between 2,700-2,200 BC. This was a truly immense undertaking by a culture in possession of nothing more than axe heads, antler picks and the human spirit!

The megaliths themselves are like an open art gallery - horses, human-like heads, vulva cavities, phalluses and other fantastic imagery leap out of timeless stone, inviting us into the world of the prehistoric shaman, a world of imagination and the Ancestors. We see this as one of the main differences between Avebury and Stonehenge. The latter is engineered, the stones are cut and crafted, the monument seeps masculine science and engineering. At Avebury, the stones are uncut; it is a shamanic landscape. One can study Stonehenge without the need for imagination, whereas at Avebury our imagination is an essential requirement.

Within an outer ring of megaliths two inner circles were erected and, within these, further megaliths of astronomical significance were positioned. In the northern inner circle there are two huge stones called The Cove. There was once a third stone nearby, together creating a sacred enclosed area. Terence Meaden suggests this was symbolic of the womb of the Earth Goddess. At summer solstice a shadow cast by another tall stone (recorded but now lost) just NE of the Cove would reach the *"womb"*, and a *"marriage/consummation of the Gods"* played out, through the dramatic use of light and shadow. It is interesting that both the male and female currents of the St Michael Line, after travelling their separate ways from Windmill Hill to the northeast, converge at the Cove.

It was in the southern inner circle that Avebury's tallest megalith, called the Obelisk, once stood. This phallic-shaped stone was a colossal 20ft high. During the festival of Beltaine (early May each year) the shadow cast by the huge phallus at sunrise stretched across the ground, the tip of it "penetrating" a very realistic vulva-shaped cavity on stone 106 nearby. Again, we have the *"Marriage of the Gods"* acted out with a fusion of stone, earth, the sun and Man. Paul Devereux further demonstrated another aspect of the Obelisk. He showed that the site of the stone (represented now by a large concrete marker) is the only place in the henge from where one can view Silbury Hill. The male/female currents of the St Michael Line remain merged around the Obelisk site, confirming the importance of the locality to its builders. Pendulums swing enthusiastically and rods twitch as we follow the meandering serpent currents through the henge, and they even swing when held over the pyramidal concrete markers, demonstrating that the energies will not be denied!

Many other sacred sites occur in the surrounding countryside, and the reader is urged to obtain some of the excellent guidebooks available. The Devil's Den dolmen and Swallowhead Spring (feeding the River Kennet) are particularly recommended. Both are places of powerful energies, yet also radiate peace and tranquility.

Although we go to Avebury on a weekly basis, guiding groups and individuals around on tours, we never tire of such excursions. Such is the pull and the magnificence of the area, a landscape steeped in magic and wonder.

We shall return to Avebury later, when we follow the four other Astrum lines as they converge on the area.

Chapter 13
The Chalice
Ana Line: Hambledon Hill to Avebury

X Hambledon Hill
x Sutton Waldron
x Fontmell Magna
x Compton Abbas
x Melbury Hill

X Higher Coombe (mounds/stones)

x Fonthill Abbey
x Fonthill Park (summit)
x Fonthill Bishop

x Stony Hill

x Sherrington (moat & tumuli)
x Codford St Peter

X Codford Down (tumuli)
x Breach Hill (tumuli)

x St Joan a Gore Farm
x Church Hill

x Urchfont Hill (tumuli)
x Urchfont

x All Cannings
x Tan Hill
x Tumuli

x Silbury Hill
x Avebury

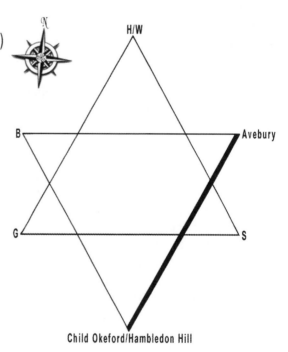

T**his** Chalice alignment is named after the ancient British Earth Goddess, Ana, for it passes through the prominent rise sacred to her, Tan Hill. The alignment commences on top of the dizzy heights of Hambledon Hill, about 150 yards north of the northern long barrow (grid ref: 844127 – see map on page 117). From this superb vantage point we looked straight down the line towards the next hill,

Melbury Beacon, which stood prominently just a few miles away. We could see the churches at Sutton Waldron and Fontmell Magna; the western sides of both villages are on the alignment. We took the time to stand at all five terminal points of the lines that diverge from Hambledon Hill, and we felt vindicated in our efforts - the Astrum really was for real; Hambledon Hill had played a key part in leading us to the hexagram.

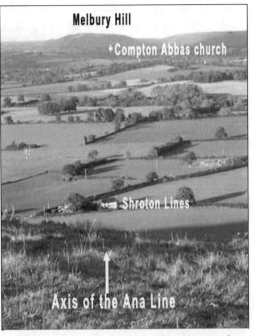

The Chalice Line plunges down the precipitous northern slopes and goes, incredibly, straight through a smallholding named Shroton Lines, two cottages that sit under the towering heights of Hambledon. Shroton Lines was the site where General Wolfe trained his troops prior to storming the Heights of Abraham in Canada. This tiny hamlet is named on Isaac Taylor's 1765 map of Dorset.

Looking down the Ana Line from the top of Hambledon Hill (west of long barrow). Shroton Lines, Compton Abbas church and Melbury Hill are in alignment.

The centre of the Ana axis then passes through the western side of **Sutton Waldron**, just under 500m west of the church of St Bartholomew. The first element of the name means *South Tun*, indicating that in Saxon times it was south of a well-known centre, probably Shaftesbury; *Waldron* is derived from *Waleran*, a huntsman who was given land here by William the Conqueror. Sutton's boundaries were clearly defined in a 932 AD charter by King Athelstan. In 980 AD the body of Edward the Martyr, murdered in Corfe Castle, was brought through the village on its way to Shaftesbury. The village is recorded in the Domesday Book.

The church is just within the limit of the Astrum "corridor" we had set ourselves, so we have included it here. But this is not the only reason, for the church's architecture yielded wonders very much associated with Astrum localities, plus the fact that it stands just yards from a sacred spring, another example of site evolution.

We visited St Bartholomew's on an overcast day in January 2008 and parked at the small car park alongside the churchyard. Little is known of the Saxon church that stood on the site but by the 19th C the Norman structure had deteriorated beyond repair. Canon Huxtable, a man of tremendous drive and wealth, built the new church at his own expense; it was consecrated in 1847. The fine spire is visible from miles around, and we had clearly seen it from the top of Hambledon Hill. As soon as we got to the gate we were met with sacred symbolism of relevance to our Quest. In front of us, the design of the west window was in the shape a large hexagram, carved from beautiful brown stone. We gazed with wonder at our discovery – we were obviously in the right place! To the right of the tower was another window with a six-petalled design at the top, each arm having a circle of inscribed glass. Above this was a small window, divided into three with a dove as the centre glass image. Walking around the

Sutton Waldron church. Left: hexagram in west window; Right: colourful and intricate Puginesque floor tiles.

south side of the church we could not only see the springhead and the pond it had birthed in the adjacent field, but could also appreciate how steep the slopes were to the east of the church.

As soon as we entered the church we knew we were somewhere special. Huxtable had designed and decorated the inside in a style very much influenced by Augustus Welby Pugin (1812-52), arguably the English leader of the Gothic revival movement. He believed the Gothic arch to be the true Christian form and attacked the Classical arch. He also used colour and hand-crafted tiles, resulting in an Eastern, almost Islamic, feel. As well as designing the Houses of Parliament, Pugin worked in Dorset, most famously at Rampisham Rectory, NW of Dorchester, which is also known as Pugin Hall, but his influence was widespread. Inside St Bartholomew, many columns and window supports are painted in shades of gold, black, red and blue, with delicate patterns running the length of them. We were also in awe of the beautifully crafted floor tiles near the altar, with their vivid colours, a Pugin trademark. We marvelled at a painted ceiling of golden *six-pointed* stars, set in a deep, rich sky, above our heads in the nave. The whole scene around us was more like a Byzantine cathedral than a small church in rural Dorset.

Marble carvings behind the altar depict the four apostles and we also noted a golden Templar cross on the pulpit. Peering over the organ, at the east end of the chancel, we could see a six-petalled design at the top of a window, as well as another hexagram, to complement the one we had seen from the outside. There seemed to be circles, triangles and hexagrams everywhere! As if this wasn't enough, we also felt powerful energies around the altar, particularly behind it.

We emerged into the daylight to let it all sink in, and to examine the exterior of the church further. We found a green man on the bottom of a window arch on the north side, and above this a round window frame that was divided into a three circled-clover leaf; within these were the points of an inverted triangle. We were following the Chalice and before us was the classic symbol of the feminine principle! From the east end of the church we could see Melbury Hill on the skyline, the next destination on the Ana line; the two sites were intervisible. We then descended the steep slope to the east end of the churchyard, through swathes of flowering snowdrops. At the bottom was a beautiful yew tree, which overlooked ancient, forgotten gravestones, creating a dark atmospheric locality. Next to it was an old archway, which formerly allowed access from the old manor house.

Oaks in the field next to St Bartholomew's mark where a spring issues from the ground. Inset: Toni's automatic drawing of the *Spring Sprite*, drawn at the spring (© T Perrott).

Back at the churchyard gate we turned left and went into the open field next to the church. We could see the pond beyond and soon found the fast-flowing spring that fed it. The spot is guarded by two huge oaks, elemental Guardians, one of which has fallen onto the other, splitting it open. Holly and ivy were also in attendance and the whole scene was magical and sacred. Surely, it seemed, fairies would jump out at any moment! We were joined by three shaggy, long-horned cattle, which followed us closely, periodically bellowing. To us they also seemed to be the guardians of the spring, checking out our intentions. Toni tuned into the consciousness of the site and did some automatic drawings, one of which is shown here; others can be seen on page 258 and 260.

The next destination is **Fontmell Magna**. The name derives from Font = *spring*, Mell = *bare hill*, and Magna, which is Latin for *Great*. The village is famous for the clear water that rises at the east end of the village, which collects in a large pond in the beautiful and healing gardens known as Springhead. Fontmell is named in the Saxon charters of 670-676 AD, and in 871 AD Alfred the Great granted land at *Funtamel* to the nunnery at Shaftesbury Abbey. The Domesday Book records a village with a large population and three water mills. There used to be a maypole erected on the site of the present war memorial, as well as a preaching cross, and a nearby *Cross Tree*. Alfred Pope, writing in 1906, recorded a stone cross that formerly stood in the centre of the village, near the stocks and the maypole (see *Ancient Stones of Dorset*, page 185).

Interestingly, the site of the new village hall is directly on the line! Locals certainly have a great spot for the new omphalos or moot of their community.

One of the fine dragons perched on the tower at Fontmell Magna.

The church of St Andrew is described as a, *"comely church"* by historian Arthur Mee in *The King's England – Dorset,* and a church here is mentioned in the Domesday Book. The lower parts of the tower date from the 15th C and the chancel, north vestry and north aisle are thought to be of medieval origin, rebuilt in 1862. Fine winged dragons adorn the tower, gazing out across the landscape. Notable features are the various reliefs, such as stags, sickles and other designs mounted on the north wall, dating from 1530. The Norman font with carved birds and entwined branches has been described as, *"exceptional".* One window depicts St George slaying a red dragon, whilst another shows St Michael vanquishing another, this time purple.

The Methodist chapel, opposite the war memorial, dates from 1831, this being an enlargement of a late 18th C building. It was said to be the oldest functioning Methodist chapel in Dorset prior to its closure in 2006. Whilst in the village, take a rest at the Crown Inn. It offers a friendly service and well-priced food. The waters from the spring flow beneath it, seen trickling under the small bridge that connects the pub buildings.

Leaving Fontmell, the Ana Line passes very close to Brookland Wood, a new Millennium initiative planted by local people. The centre of the line then passes within yards of Manor Farm, (grid ref: 869177) which dates from the 17th C, and still retains some original oak panelling.

Next stop on the line is **Compton Abbas.** It is recorded in 956 AD that Compton land was given to the nunnery at Shaftesbury, and the village is recorded in the Domesday Book. The old church of St Mary stood to the east of the present site and the 15th C tower and medieval stone cross can still be seen (See *Ancient Stones of Dorset,* page 184-5 for image; grid ref: 876188).

The new St Mary's was built on the main road in 1866 and marks the exact centre of the Ana Line. The interior is modest, one could say plain, after the unexpected delights of Sutton Waldron. It nevertheless felt peaceful and the energies were strongly felt in places. At the west end is a pleasing window depicting Jesus flanked by two angels, who have the sun and the moon above them. In the side chapel, a beautifully executed window shows the Annunciation, with Mary in gorgeous shades of purple and blue, and an angel with green wings.

Next to the bus shelter, opposite the church, stands a small stone, rising 18ins out of the ground, on a grassy bank. It is not a boundary stone and is too roughly shaped, we feel, to be a milestone. It stands on the pilgrimage route to Shaftesbury, but could be much older. The stone stands right on the axis of the Ana line!

The next site on the Ana Line is **Melbury Hill**, the spectacular and prominent landmark visible from many miles around, as it rises to 802ft above sea level. Folklore speaks of the hill being a weather indicator, in that if the top is covered in mist then rain is on its way. It was a beacon site, in use at the time of the Spanish Armada to give Wiltshire people warning of any Dorset landing by the Spanish. The beacon was used during an invasion scare in 1804, and again for the celebrations of 1897. The summit is just yards west of the very centre of the line, which crosses the hill at the gentler slopes. The hill is criss-crossed with ancient earthen dykes.

From here Ana descends Melbury and passes through Cann and Melbury Abbas village hall (as at Fontmell Magna), before following the road down to Melbury Abbas Mill and Barfoot Farm. At the bridge over the stream (grid ref: 878206) there is a picturesque pond on the west side, with attendant flocks of geese. A footpath can be followed around the south side to the mill, whose huge water wheel is visible (private property - to be viewed from the path). A spring rises from the slopes to the south of the mill, as the reeds and rushes testify; when we visited the locality the whole scene was idyllic. Back at the road is a gate, just to the north of the bridge, serving the pond. Through the gate we could see three large stones next to the water, all heavy and rough. On the road, outside the gate, we dowsed spiralling energies, as well as a line of energy that went through the gate to the stones. We wondered if the stones had formerly been part of a nearby sacred site.

Toni dowsing at the bridge at Melbury Abbas Mill. Beyond the gate large stones sit next to a pond.

Whilst in the area it is worth visiting the church of St Thomas in Melbury Abbas. Outside the churchyard gate is a large stone, now at ground level, which is probably a pre-Christian megalith. The exposed stone is decidedly heart-shaped.

The line then crosses the B3081 near Ponsonby Farm, and old maps show a Methodist chapel just south of here. It then goes through Cannfield Farm, where it passes through two great old trees and a pond, just south of the farmhouse. The pond is marked on the OS map of 1889.

Hidden Treasures in the Woods

Ana then passes from Dorset into Wiltshire and after crossing the Shaftesbury to Salisbury road, then descends to the quiet, sleepy hamlet that is **Higher Coombe**, where time seems to have stood still. Two large ponds nestle either side of a road that

139

soon turns into a sunken ancient track, which ascends the wooded slopes of Great Wincombe. We had found embankments and mounds on the 1:25,000 maps (grid ref: 888232), just west of both the track and the centre of the Ana Line, features also present on the 1891 OS map. Also on the old map is a grand house in the village named as *The Priory,* as well as *Knights Barn* to the south, and four wells. At Woodside Cottage (grid ref: 889231), as the tarmac gives way to gravel, the steep

This sunken way between two overgrown mounds is in woods at Higher Coombe, and is on the Ana Line.

slope on the left is strewn with about half a dozen large stones, which look as though they have been cast down from the top of the hill above. More stones have been incorporated into the rock garden of the cottage, at the foot of the slope.

Further on along the track, where a fence ends, a narrow ravine can be seen cut into the hill; we went to explore! More moss-covered stones were found and a narrow wooded gully was soon encountered –

the abode of fairies if ever there was one! At the end of it the slopes were ascended and two mounds were soon found, to the left (south) of a new wooden post. These two well-defined mounds were surely manmade and the energies were readily felt as we stood on them. Between the mounds, a wide ancient path led south to a level clearing, about 40ft across. This seemed to be where the large stones seen earlier had been cast down from.

All the windows at the former church of St Andrew's, Newtown, have six-pointed symmetry. Despite its isolation, the building stands directly on the Ana Line!

Beyond the clearing, we could see the ancient path continue down to the pond below (beyond the tennis court). Toni found a spot that was one of the most powerful she experienced on the Astrum, as well as having a delightful, transformative quality. As we stood in the clearing a large buzzard circled overhead, calling out several times before moving off; we felt truly blessed. The place was enchanted and surely it had been the location of sacred ritual in eons past. Although being consumed by rhododendrons, it was heart-warming that we had found unrecorded megaliths and mounds just yards from the axis of the Ana Line.

Three miles further on, Ana goes straight through the crossroads at **Newtown**, a small gathering of cottages west of Tisbury. We arrived at the spot in February 2008 and immediately saw a church, which turned out to be a private residence called St Andrew's House. We had found yet another former church exactly on an Astrum line! More than this, as we approached it we could see that each window was decorated with a six-pointed star. In fact there were eight all together – and every window had a hexagram! We were astounded and stood in wonder at this discovery and questioned what drove the patrons and architects to choose this design on a church whose patron saint is not associated with the symbol.

The line then goes straight through **Fonthill**, a 10,000-acre estate that occupies most of the land inside the area bounded by Chilmark, Hindon and Tisbury (see www.fonthill.co.uk for history and useful links).

Fonthill Abbey, also known as Beckford's Folly, was a large Gothic revival country house built at the turn of the 19th C. It was constructed SW of the site of Palladian House, later known as Fonthill Splendens, which was constructed by his father, Alderman William Beckford, plantation owner and Lord Mayor of London, who

Left: Rutter's 1823 drawing of the resplendent Fonthill Abbey, also known as Beckford's Folly.
Right: one of Beckford's grottos, in atmospheric woods north of the Beckford Arms at Fonthill.

bought the estate in 1740. The Splendens site is shown on 1889 maps and is directly on the axis of the Ana line.

But it is the old Fonthill Abbey (grid ref: 918309) that stands out in the annals of Fonthill. It was the brainchild of William Thomas Beckford, son of the wealthy William Beckford and a student of architect Sir William Chambers. In 1771, when Beckford was ten years old, he inherited £1,000,000 (the equivilent today of £320,000,000!). Newspapers of the time described him as, *"... the richest commoner in England"*.

After extensively travelling around Europe, this arch-romantic let his imagination run riot as he totally revamped his estate, erecting radical buildings, grottos, terraced walks and, most outlandishly, his very own Gothic cathedral. It was a grand structure, with a high tower and huge stained glass windows with beautiful gothic arches, as the drawing above testifies. The building had a St Michael's Gallery, a Sanctuary, and an observatory. Beckford lived alone here and used only one of its many bedrooms. Only once, in 1800, did he entertain guests, when Admiral Horatio Nelson and Lady

Hamilton visited. Not content with this architectural wonder, Beckford began to fill it with cultural treasures; 20,000 books in his own binding, and paintings by Rembrandt, Rubens and Canaletto, twenty of which now hang in the National Gallery, London. He also had a table from the Borghese Palace whose centre consisted of the largest onyx in the world (now in Charlecote Park, Avon) and the superb "Van Dieman", a black lacquer box that once belonged to Madame de Pompadour, which is now in the Victoria and Albert Museum.

Elsewhere on the estate his imagination led to the creation of a series of grottos (see below), a *Fairie's Lawn*, and even a replica megalithic dolmen next to the lake, all described by John Rutter in his 1823 book, *Delineations of Fonthill and its Abbey.* Beckford lived in the Abbey until 1822, when he was forced to sell it for £330,000. The main tower collapsed in 1825 and the rest of the building was later demolished. Only a gatehouse and a small remnant of the north wing remains to this day. William Beckford died in Bath in 1844.

Standing at the estate crossroads is the Beckford Arms, and just west of it is the Church of the Holy Trinity (Fonthill Gifford). There was a church recorded locally in 1299, thought to have been north of the present one. Beckford built a church here in

One of the dragons guarding the elaborate doorway of the Holy Trinity, Fonthill Gifford.

1748, dedicated to St Nicholas. Drawings show it as having a Romano-Greco frontage, more evidence of Beckford's wealth and his fascination with classical architecture. However, Rutter thought it, *"... a feeble attempt to produce the effect of a Grecian temple"*. It measured a perfect square internally, 34ft 4ins on each side, and was aligned to the NE, the midsummer sunrise.

The present church was built in 1866 by T.H. Wyatt for the Marquess of Westminster. Wyatt's version is bigger than its predecessor but is likewise aligned to the NE. It stands solid within a churchyard of fine yews and its octagonal spire rises between pyramidal pinnacles. The base of the tower serves as a porch and the entrance has short alabaster columns, each flanked by two dragon-like creatures. On both the north and south sides of the church large round windows contain six-pointed stars, each enclosing a smaller six-pointed star, angled at 45° to the outer one. In his book, *The Sacred Art of Geometry,* Nigel Pennick has laid two hexagrams onto the ground plan of St George in Bloomsbury, London, one of which is set 45° to the other, identical in design to these windows. In the same book, Pennick shows a 15th C illustration of two triangles, one inside the other, which are very unequal in size. Again, we found this design in another window in the Fonthill Gifford church, with the larger upright triangle enclosing a smaller inverted triangle. In the interior of the church (which is only open at weekends) are rich foliage carvings, a rib-vaulted chancel and a low arch. The semi-circular alabaster pulpit has carved heads of the four evangelists. The foundation stone from Beckford's church has been remounted into the vestry wall.

North of the church is a small wood (grid ref: 934315), through which the road to Fonthill Bishop passes. Beckford constructed five grottos out of solid rock, which are now SSSI sites because of bats that occupy them. Two of these follies are named as *"The Dark Walks"* and *"The Hermitage"*. We simply had to explore the woods to see if we could discover the caverns. To the west of the road two shafts can be seen (now covered with iron grills) and their depth can be appreciated when peering down into

them. It was on the east side of the road, however, that we found a magical place - a wood of ancient yews, which rose from a carpet of moss and ferns. We found two grotto entrances, which were barred, but into which we could see to a certain extent. Flash photography into the darkness of the largest grotto revealed carved features inside, which looked like a reclining, bearded figure, holding a pitcher. Access to this magical wood and its grottos is from either end of the low walls alongside the road, or via a path from the small lay-by to the

Fonthill Arch, built by Inigo Jones, stands on the Ana Line, and is decorated with four large Green Man carvings (inset).

north. Beckford had chosen these magical old yews as a backdrop to his grottos – it must have been a wonderful experience for him to spend time here, and the atmosphere today is still potent. More grottos were constructed east of the lake, but these are not open to the public.

To the north of the woods the road passes beneath the Fonthill Arch, also called the Great Gateway, reportedly built by Inigo Jones for Lord Cottington in the reign of Charles I. Intricate carvings of foliage decorate the arch and four large stone heads can be made out – each a huge Green Man. Incredibly, Ana passes right through the arch, just as the Central axis goes through a similar arch at Longleat!

Just north of the arch, the line goes straight through the Church of All Saints at **Fonthill Bishop**. A Saxon settlement was recorded here in 874 AD, when land was, *"... granted to the Bishops of Winchester"*. This is a pleasant hamlet with streams, weirs, a nice riverside tearoom, and the church just north of the bridge. It is a lovely small structure, the keys of which can be obtained from the house next to the church (go through the small gate next to the porch – four spaniels were found to be loud but friendly!). The present church was built in 1240, replacing an earlier one, with the porch and a south window dated 14th C. The chancel was rebuilt in 1879, but retains much of the original Norman stonework. Of interest is the fact that Christopher Wren's father, Dr Wren, was the rector here from 1620-1628.

North of the A303 the line goes straight through ancient field systems, marked as *British Village (site of)* on the 1889 OS map, before crossing the ancient banks and ditches of Grim's Ditch. The line then crosses through the summit of Stony Hill, passing the 196m spot height (grid ref: 951365) before descending to Sherrington, a place that was to hold more wonders for us.

Sherrington is a quintessentially English village, set midst peaceful rolling hills. It lies on the south side of the River Wylye. In 968 AD King Edgar granted land at Sherrington to Wilton Abbey, near Salisbury. The area was occupied, however, in earlier times, evidenced by local long barrows, tumuli and Roman remains. We found references to a mound and moat just north of the church, officially designated a Norman motte and bailey. We went to investigate.

We arrived on New Year's Eve, 2007, pulling up at the church. As we entered the churchyard we were immediately felt the sanctity of the locality. We went around the

The mound at Sherrington – a prehistoric legacy?

back to view the mound and moat, and stood in awe as we looked across the waters, which were host to two inquisitive swans. There may have been a timber stronghold on top of the mound, which is 48m across and 5.5m high. The ditch is 3.5m deep, which widens at the east end to a water-filled moat, which separates the mound from the church. The moat goes all the way round, but has been partly filled in at one side. The ancient mound was atmospheric and dark, covered in tall trees and tangled undergrowth. The sides were not steep and it looked more like a huge round barrow than a Norman motte. The whole scene convinced us that we were looking at a much older mound.

A lady of French descent, on whose land the mound stands, took us to the west end of the site, showing us the spot where a spring, which feeds the moat, emerges from the earth. She was gladdened by our interest and we struck up a deal that we would clear a way into the mound, in exchange for spending time exploring and dowsing this ancient earthwork.

Archaeologists surmise that the famous Bluestones of Stonehenge were brought from Preseli in South Wales via the Bristol Channel, the Somerset Avon and the River Wylye. If this mound were prehistoric in origin, then thousands of years ago people may well have stood on it, perhaps in awe, as rafts carrying the Welsh stones passed by. Perhaps the rafts may even have halted for a while at this sacred place, before journeying once more to the Temple on the Plain.

The inverted triangle of the Chalice, behind the organ at Sherrington church.

The church dates from the late 13th or 14th C and has the unusual dedication of St Cosmas and St Damian (one of only five such dedications in England). However, in *A Topographical Dictionary of England*, written by Samuel Lewis in 1848, the parish is described as *Sherrington St Michael,* which was for a while the church's dedication. Cosmas and Damien were martyred twin brothers who lived in 4th C Ayash or Aegea, in the Roman province of Syria. They have been described as students of science and both became doctors and surgeons, yet would never receive any money for their services; their healing was often said to be miraculous. They were martyred in AD 303 during Dioletian's persecution of Christians. Their festival day is on Sept 26, close to the Equinox, and they are the patron saints of medicine, surgeons and barbers. (Perhaps this place has a history as a place of healing.) As early as the 4th C their cult grew rapidly, with churches dedicated to them in Jerusalem and Egypt. The dedication here may come from the fact that Alexander Giffard was one of the few notable Crusaders who survived the Battle of Mansourah, in Egypt, of 1250. The myths of these saints take place at localities where the Knights Templar are recorded and the Templars were at their height of power in the mid-13th C, at the time of Giffard.

As we entered the church the atmosphere felt ancient. Almost immediately we saw a feature in the west window that seemed to confirm we were on a Chalice Line. Above and behind the organ is a window depicting an inverted triangle – the feminine chalice symbol! It is interlocked with three circles, the sum total of the symbolism being six - the hexagram. Why the chalice triangle, and not the blade? Surely, it was no coincidence (see image above). The east window, behind the altar, shows the Annunciation, with the

St George slaying a decidedly Eastern-looking red and green dragon, at Codford St Peter.

Archangels Raphael and Michael holding a spear and sword respectively. Behind the pulpit is a fascinating window dated 1549, containing a red Templar cross.

Back outside, we found a long tomb near the east end of the church, the capstone of which was very rough with large depressions on its upper surface, reminiscent of ancient cup-marks. Was this a remodelled megalith?

Ana then crosses the River Wylye close to a footbridge that connects Sherrington to our next destination, **Codford St Peter**. Opposite the church of St Peter, well-sited on top of a hill, runs a N-S track that mirrors the centre of the alignment, as if guiding it to the church. Fine gargoyles decorate the exterior, including winged dragons, a feature we had often found when following alignments. Above the entrance to the porch is carved a shield, showing a mason's set square and a dragon.

Inside, we experienced pleasant energy and were drawn to two adjoining windows opposite the door, each with powerful symbolism and beautifully executed. On the left is a stunning image of St Michael, the scales of justice and a staff bearing a flag with the red cross of the Templars emblazoned on it. On the right is a depiction of St George (above) who is slaying, with a spear, a dragon that has a red head and a purple body, with a decidedly Eastern appearance. On his chest St George sports his red cross that is, in reality, the Templar emblem. Once again we felt as if we were being given signs that we were being guided on our Quest.

The line then goes past tumuli on Codford Down before reaching the crossroads at **Breach Hill**. This spot marks the crossing point of the Ana Line and the Samhain Alignment (Chapter 23). The locality is lonely, bleak and is at the intersection of MOD roads and tank tracks. Seeing past these unwelcome distractions, we located a small mound that marks the southern end of ancient earthworks, marked on OS maps, which converges on the locality. We could see two rough tracks going away from us in either direction, each of which approximates with the Ana line.

Dowsing with a pendulum at the stone at St Joan à Gore.

The line crosses the main road at **St Joan à Gore Farm,** going straight through the cottages at the southern end (grid ref: 013502). We rolled up after visiting the deserted village of Imber, on Salisbury Plain (see page 255), parking just inside the gate of the grounds (this is private property – please seek permission). Even before we had alighted from our car we could see a large stone lying alongside the gravel path to the cottages. The boulder was a rounded sarsen stone, about 3½ x 3ft and it was shot through with mineral veins. Yet another unrecorded stone directly on an Astrum line! Toni dowsed the stone, the energies of which made her pendulum spin, and she also detected an energy line from here to the big tree next to the cottages.

The name was formerly St. John o' Gore, or St. John à Gore, and was so named from a small chapel that stood here in the 14th C. It was attached to a small settlement and dedicated to St. John. *Gore* was the name given to a wedge-shaped piece of land, on which the farmstead stood, just like Kensington Gore in London. At the time of Edward the Confessor, it was *"Gare"*, held by the Saxon Oswald. In 1274 it was recorded that fees were paid to a local knight Peter Delamare. In 1316 the land was held by John de Combe and the Abbess of Caen in Normandy. Excavations of the chapel in 1877 confirmed a tradition that it had been destroyed by fire. Grass was removed to expose the foundations of the ancient chapel, disclosing a nave 24 x 11½ft and a chancel of 19 x 12½ft. The site is in the field immediately behind the present buildings, near where the woods end. This is exactly on the Ana line!

The Wiltshire and Swindon Monument Records list an undated round barrow at St Joan à Gore farm, but they give no details of location. They also record an undated ring ditch, located somewhere NW of the farm. In his book *Wandering in Wessex*, Edric Holmes writes, *"... passing at its highest point, St. John a Gore Cross, where a chantry chapel once stood, a shrine where travellers might make their orisons before braving the terrors of the great waste."* Clearly, as late as Victorian times, Salisbury Plain was an inhospitable place through which to travel. It is not certain whether he refers to the chapel already mentioned, or if another existed at St John à Gore Cross itself, just half a mile to the north.

The alignment then crosses Church Hill and passes close to tumuli on Urchfont Hill, before going through the picturesque village of **Urchfont.** It was called *Ierches Fonte* in the Domesday Book, meaning *spring of the fawn.* Links to an Anglo-Saxon settlement are suggested by local field names. Jerusalem Well (grid ref: 040574) is north of the church and is thought by some to be this spring; the water flows into a rectangular stone structure situated beside the road. Two steps lead down to the water, which has a tradition of never running dry. Within living memory it was the main water source for the village, although there are several other wells dotted around the hamlet. The well isn't named on the 1901 OS map, but several paths are shown converging on the locality.

The church is dedicated to St Michael and All Angels, and stands west of the axis. Researchers of ley lines have commented on the frequency of St Michael dedications on leys, something we shall encounter in Chapter 22 when we look at the famous St Michael Line. Two stone heads either side of the door are thought to be King Alfred and his queen Ahlswith; around 900 AD the Manor of Urchfont was given by the King to the nunnery at Winchester, hence the connection. The font is Norman and other parts of the early church survive, such as the 15th C tower.

The line then goes through the parish of **All Cannings**, passing west of the church. Cannings is an interesting name, one of a small group (including Hastings) that originally referred not to a place, but to a tribe – here it is the *Followers of Cana.*

Such names originated during the colonization of southern Britain by Anglo-Saxon settlers in the 7-8th C. Cana's tribe settled around the marshy bowl that heads the Pewsey Vale, which became known as Cannings Marsh. The headquarters of a supposed Roman estate has not been discovered, although a Roman well was unearthed in 1913, west of All Cannings Cross Farm. The waters from two other local springs in All Cannings were good for eczema and brewing tea! About 500m NE of here lay an early iron-age village (c. 650–400 BC), excavated between 1911 and 1922, which has given its name, All Cannings Cross, to a type of early Iron Age pottery. A further 500m NE, on a spur of chalk, is Rybury Camp, an iron age hillfort on the site of a much earlier earthwork, a Neolithic enclosure or causewayed camp, dated at around 4,000–3,000 BC.

Sir Richard Colt Hoare's drawing of Tan Hill, showing pilgrims walking a track, a shepherd watching his sheep, and tumuli in the distance.

All Cannings Church is a large and impressive parish church of many architectural styles, from Norman to Victorian, and once dedicated to St Anne. Activities with pre-Christian origins continued in the village until the mid-19th C, in the shape of back-swording (a traditional duel using wooden swords), a maypole on the green, and Christmas mumming plays. The church clearly had competition from the remnants of pagan practices. This all took place on St Anne's day, 6th August, each year (around the Celtic Lughnasad or Lammas fire festival) on **Tan Hill** (a corruption of *St Anne's Hill*) on the downs above the village, until discontinued after 1932. Tan Hill and Milk Hill share the distinction of being the highest points (294m) in Wiltshire. Mesolithic and Neolithic axes have been found on the hill, as well as the site of a stone circle. A Romano-British torc was found just east of it, as well as a brooch. A Bronze Age bracelet, and a fragment of a Bronze Age gold torc, was also found in 1844.

One of the defining points of the Astrum, Tan Hill is traversed by the Ana Line and gives the alignment its name. The name of the hill has been connected with pre-Christian fire ceremonies and Celtic deities, St Anne being the Christianisation of the ancient British goddess Ana, Ane or Anu. She was the Mother of all Gods, the primeval Earth Mother. In some traditions, Ana was married to the solar deity Bel or Beli – the divine marriage of the Solar God and the Earth Mother. In their book, *The Lives of the British Saints,* Barrington, Gould and Fisher inform us that, *"St Anne stepped into the place of one of the Bonae Deae, the tutelary earth goddesses, themselves representing the Celtic or pre-Celtic Ane, Mother of the Gods".* In Brittany, locally discovered pagan images were revered as St Anne. The sister of

King Arthur is variously known as Anna or Morgana, depending on the tradition, and Anna was the name of both the mother and cousin of the Virgin Mary.

Tan Hill Fair was held in the late middle ages, the earliest record being that of 1499. It became one of the most celebrated of all downland sheep fairs, and played an important part in the agricultural and economic life of Wiltshire, impacting in turn on the pattern of tracks and paths leading to and across the parish. A remote and windy spot (one year the beer-tent blew down, which lingered long in locals' memories!), Tan Hill was nevertheless a kind of metropolis for Wiltshire shepherds, many of whom spent their working lives within sight of it. An 18th C map shows, *'A Building for the Receptacle of the Implements used at the Fair,'* on the site, alongside *'Devills Church',* which we haven't yet managed to decipher, but could possibly be a stone circle. There is also a tradition of ghosts being seen on the hill.

Leaving the summit of Tan Hill, the line then proceeds north to Allington Down, where two more tumuli (grid ref: 086654, not on 1:50,000 OS maps) are on the alignment. These can be accessed via the bridle way that runs across the downs.

Silbury Hill – Tummy of the Goddess

In a low-lying area immediately north of West Kennet stands **Silbury Hill**, through which the Ana Line passes. It was built around 2,700-2,6000 BC in three phases,

Silbury Hill from the air, seen by Peter when he was fortunate enough to fly over the Goddess mound.

stands 130ft high and was constructed using an incredible 12 million cubic feet of chalk and earth. It is a pyramid, built using cleverly interlocking blocks of chalk, arranged in steps 15-17ft deep, Recent geophysical work has shown that the steps were clearly intended as a processional way to the top. The angle of its slopes is 30°, affording an extremely stable structure, ensuring that the hill did not slumped in over 4,500 years! Excavations in 1968-70 tunnelled to the centre of Silbury and found grass that was still green, as well as insect remains, including flying ants. Poor back-filling by previous excavations resulted in the hill having to be repaired in 2007-8, which at least enabled further archaeology to be carried out. This included the discovery that Silbury had had three distinct stages of construction.

One feature of Silbury Hill is a ledge about 15ft below the summit. Paul Devereux was the first to demonstrate the importance of this precisely positioned platform. Standing on the summit at Lughnasad/Lammas (around the beginning of August), the sunrise is observed over the distant skyline to the east. If one then scrambles down to the ledge below, a few minutes later one will see the sun rise *again*, this time out of Waden Hill, east of Silbury: a double sunrise one of the sacred festivals.

Another feature of this ledge is that when Silbury Hill is viewed from several other sacred sites in the area, the distant skyline coincides with the ledge. Positioning the hill, and determining the height of it to enable such subtle line-of-sight effects, required incredible engineering and surveying knowledge. Devereux suggests that it is Silbury, with its intervisiblity with these other sites, and not the main henge, which is the hub of the ceremonial landscape. We are inclined to agree with him. Above all, Silbury was not built as some ego monument, perched high on a hill or plateau, like the Giza pyramids, but was placed in the lowest part of the landscape, with much humility. The symbolism of the hill is obvious and dramatic, the pregnant tummy of the Earth Mother/Goddess rising from the Land. The hill is not a burial mound, but a lasting epitaph to the Goddess, to whom the builders of Silbury had such a close affiliation. Michael Dames has produced two excellent books about the Goddess symbolism and archaeology of Silbury.

John Michell, in Part 2 of *The Measure of Albion*, finds sacred geometry and sacred number in the dimensions and positioning of Silbury. He finds the number 12 as significant and it crops up in several of the hill's statistics – 12 is of course the sum of two hexagrams. The measurements of the hill can be expressed exactly in both the Greek foot and the old Egyptian royal cubit, and can be extended out into the landscape, i.e., according to Michell, the figures relate not only to the distance from Silbury to Stonehenge, but also to both the polar and equatorial radii of the earth.

In *The Sun and the Serpent*, Miller and Broadhurst describe how it is the Mary flow of the St Michael Line that goes through Silbury, which seems fitting if it is regarded as the ripe tummy of the Goddess. Interestingly, they map the energy flowing from a node on the north side of Silbury to another focus just west of the trig point on Waden Hill; between these two points, this energy actually follows the course of the Ana Line to Avebury.

The axis of the Ana Line does not pass through the henge at Avebury (see map on page 130), although it certainly falls well within our "corridor". Rather, it terminates just a little to the east, at a Bronze Age round barrow (grid ref: 107701). Crop formations have regularly occurred in the field across the lane from here. We shall return to Avebury again soon, as it is at the apex of two of the hexagon lines.

Silbury Hill is silhouetted against the setting sun during one of our full moon drumming gatherings.

Chapter 14
The Hexagon Defined

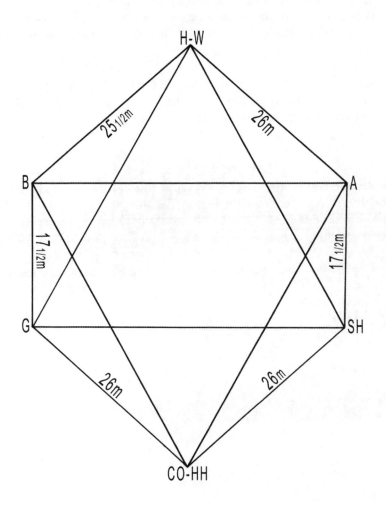

One of the consequences of a six-pointed hexagram is that the apex points can be joined to form a six-sided hexagon. These six alignments each connect two Wessex Astrum apexes, and they vary from 17½ miles in length for the side alignments, to around 26 miles for the four others. Considering that these hexagon lines were manifested as an indirect consequence of the formation of the hexagram, we were not expecting too many significant sites on them. The truth, however, was far from this, as we uncovered sacred sites aplenty. In fact the number of interesting and relevant locations occurred as frequently as we had found along the six lines of the hexagram itself. The Knights Templar preceptories at both Bristol and Templecombe are on or near hexagon lines.

Arguably, the most notable of the hexagon alignments is the Avebury to Stonehenge alignment (Chapter 17), which forms one side of the triangle involving those two sacred places and Glastonbury. This line was directly involved in our discovery of the Wessex Astrum.

We shall describe the hexagon lines in anticlockwise direction, beginning and ending at Glastonbury. We have not felt it necessary to name the six hexagon alignments, as we had been drawn to do with the lines of the Chalice and the Blade; perhaps more names would have only caused confusion.

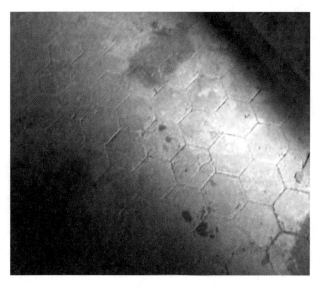

Hexagons at the entrance to the church at Pensford (see page 69).

Chapter 15
The Hexagon:
Glastonbury to
Child Okeford/Hambledon Hill

x St John's, Glastonbury
x Abbey (east end)
x Chalice Well

x Windmill Hill

x Ham Street

x Foss Wood

x Lovington (Brue Farm)

x Barrow Court

x Lower Woolston

x Maperton

x Horsington

x Abbas Combe/Templecombe

x Henstridge Marsh

x Philip's Hill/Pleck

x Manston

x Hammoon

x Child Okeford/Hambledon Hill

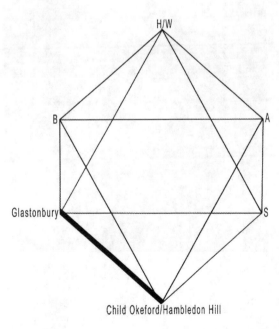

This hexagon line goes from Glastonbury to the prominent landmark of Hambledon Hill in Dorset, on a heading of approximately 127°, the direction of sunrise on both December 1-5 and January 1-5, either side of the midwinter solstice. The line is particularly notable as it goes through Templecombe, site of the Knights Templar preceptory. It is interesting that in an issue of the Cambridge publication *Arcana* (Aug 1973) we found the passage, *"Hambledon Hill is a notable centre for old tracks and lines of churches,"* and that, *"Hambledon Hill is in direct line with Glastonbury and passes by South Cadbury"*. Our line from Hambledon to Glastonbury does indeed pass just north of the ancient hillfort of Arthurian claim.

The alignment commences at the church of **St John the Baptist** on the High Street (see map on page 74), which is where it converges with the Glastonbury – Brockley line (see Chapter 20). John the Baptist was revered by the Knights Templar, and his feast day is on June 24, just after the midsummer solstice. The impressive 135ft high tower is the second tallest in Somerset and is a notable landmark. The earliest reference is from 1175 and stonework from that time survives in the north wall of the St Katherine Chapel. In 1987, the foundations of a smaller structure were found,

Joseph of Arimathea in St John's, Glastonbury.

possibly pre-Conquest; the rest of the church dates from the 15th C, built by Abbot Selwood.

In *The Sun and the Serpent,* Hamish Miller and Paul Broadhurst dowsed that the Michael flow of the St Michael Line went through the church. In his excellent booklet *The Glastonbury Chronicles*, Anthony Kennish has a diagram of the current running through the east side of the church, where carved stone dragons can be seen on the outside (see image at end of Chapter 20). His coloured maps, which are informative and accessible, are essential for following the various energy flows through Glastonbury.

Inside, the church contains several interesting relics, some of which have esoteric significance. In the St Katherine's Chapel (on the west side) can be found a beautiful window showing Joseph of Arimathea, resplendent in a purple cloak (image above) and in front of it is allegedly his tomb. Joseph is said to have brought to Glastonbury both the young Jesus and, later still, the Grail chalice. At one end of his tomb is a small caduceus, which esoterically represents the male and female serpentine flows of the energies that follow the St Michael Line, the Belinus Line and several other alignments. We had encountered this ancient symbol elsewhere on Astrum lines, such as at St Benedict's nearby and at Box. On the east side of the church is St George's Chapel, through which the flow of the Michael current can be readily experienced. It is a place of great peace and a wonderful window shows legendary figures such as St Michael and St George, the two dragon slayers, as well as the sun rising over the New Jerusalem.

The labyrinth in the churchyard of St John's, Glastonbury.

Back in the churchyard is the new labyrinth, opened and blessed at a ceremony in October 2007, which was witnessed by Toni. It is the vision of local geomancer, Sig Lonegren, who has designed and built labyrinths all around the world. It was built to mark Glastonbury's 300th anniversary of being granted a Royal Charter. Sig hopes it will *'heal energy rifts torn into the fabric of the town'* by unsavoury events in the past. Walking a labyrinth is an ancient practice; journeying into the centre of the labyrinth is a focus for going into the centre of oneself.

The alignment then crosses the High Street and goes through Glastonbury Abbey. This magnificent, ancient sacred site was described in more detail in Chapter 9, due to the fact that its axis aligns with the Dod Line, which extends all the way to Stonehenge. This hexagon line cuts through the east end of the Abbey, in the vicinity of the High Altar and the tomb of King Arthur. It is through this end that the Michael flow and the Mary flow of the St Michael Line converge, at the High Altar, a place where yin and yang energies are in perfect harmony. Dowsing by Toni indicated that a megalith may still be buried under the chained-off area of the High Altar; the energy is palpable and we spent some time lying on the ground at this magical place. It is here that Anthony Kennish shows an eight-pointed energy node, as he also does at the site of Arthur's tomb nearby.

The alignment then takes in the **Chalice Well Gardens**, in particular the central and southern parts, around the vesica piscis pool and the waterfall. Both the Michael and Mary flows of the St Michael Line pass through the gardens and it is a place that is both powerful and at the same time peaceful and liminal. This ancient holy place marks the terminal point of the Beltaine Alignment, as defined by us, and is therefore dealt with in some detail in Chapter 22.

The line then strikes through the 58m trig. point at the summit of **Windmill Hill** at Baltonsborough. Any windmills that may have stood on the hill had already gone by the time of the 1880's OS map. The hill is also on a ley shown on Palden Jenkins' map *The Ancient Landscape Around Glastonbury* (Gothic Image, 2005). His alignment goes from the Tor down to Spettisbury Rings in Dorset. From the hill, Glastonbury Tor can be seen to the northwest. The line then descends into **Ham Street**, a cluster of houses at the east end of Baltonsborough. The line passes through the crossroads and just west of this *Moravian Chapel* is marked on the 1889 OS map (grid ref: 549350). We found the former chapel on a visit in February 2008, as it was being converted into a dwelling. The unusual denomination seemed even stranger in this rural area of Somerset, so we looked into the Moravians.

The Moravian Church, or Herrnhuter Brüdergemeine, is a Protestant denomination whose religious heritage began in late 14th C Bohemia (now in the Czech Republic). Its official name is *Unitas Fratrum* meaning *Unity of the Brethren,* occasionally referred to as the Bohemian Brethren. It places a high premium on Christian unity, personal piety, missions and music. The movement was founded by Jan Hus, who objected to some of the practices of the Roman Catholic Church, and wanted to revert back the simpler rites of early Christianity. The movement gained royal support and a certain independence for a while, but was eventually subdued by Rome, and Hus was tried and burned at the stake. Within fifty years of Hus's martyrdom, however, his followers had become organized as the 'Bohemian Brethren', founded in 1457. These were some of the very earliest Protestants, rebelling against Rome more than a hundred years before Martin Luther. There are other local practicing Moravian chapels, at Kingswood (on one of the Astrum lines) and at Bath; their British HQ is in London.

We arrived at the chapel and found a carved and inscribed stone directly opposite, decorated with Celtic knotwork; it was

The memorial stone to St Dunstan at Ham Street.

dedicated to St Dunstan, Abbot of Glastonbury. The inscription reads:

Here stood the Beehive or Cobb Cottage
the traditional birthplace of
St Dunstan AD 909-988

We thought it incredible that such a quiet backwater should be associated with this major figure of the early Church, and that the stone be next to the former Moravian chapel.

The church itself, now Chapel House, is just that, a fully-blown stone church, and not some brick-built Methodist chapel, so often the object of such conversions. The builders kindly allowed us access and we explored and dowsed the interior. The original 19th C beams and window frames have survived, as well as the carved wooden pulpit. Toni dowsed the most powerful energies at the east end, where the altar would have been, and Peter also felt strong energies here.

Back outside, we found several gravestones at the west end of the graveyard. The oldest we could make out was dated 1857, the newest being 1966. Standing by these epitaphs we could make out Glastonbury Tor to the north, peeking through naked winter trees; the two sites are intervisible.

From here the line crosses the Fosse Way, passing through Park Cottages and then into **Fosse Wood.** We entered the wood and were amazed to discover that a wide track through the woods precisely followed the hexagram line! Standing at the beginning of the track, next to the road (grid ref: 579329), we could look back to Glastonbury Tor on the skyline.

Lovington church. We dowsed energy flowing between the huge yew and the church.

The line then proceeds to **Lovington**, where it passes through Brue Farm and the road junction next to the bend in the River Brue. Lovington is very strung out, for although the pub, mill and the main concentration of houses are at this northern end, the church stands half a mile to the south; the village has been virtually cut in two by the railway. The church is dedicated to St Thomas à Becket and is a pleasant place to visit, with a good vibe. The first recorded incumbent rector was installed in 1318, although the church may be older. The altar windows are delicately decorated in the style of Pugin, as we had seen elsewhere, complementing a beautiful light purple altar cover. Near the top of the window we were delighted to see three yellow six-pointed stars! By the altar is an old chair carved with the Tree of Life and on another chair we found carved an eight-sided design, more encoded sacred geometry. Toni dowsed a feminine energy current crossing in front of the altar, through the wall and into the small Lady Chapel on the north side. Here hangs a fine painting of the Madonna and child, full of tenderness. Back outside, Toni dowsed the feminine energy line coming out of the church and flowing to the large yew tree, which offered shade and atmosphere.

The pond at Barrow Court is on the hexagon line. The name would suggest an ancient mound once stood here.

The 1888 OS map shows *Providence Chapel,* north of the railway line (grid ref: 594315) and we located the building at a bend in the road. Now a private residence, The Old Chapel is orientated E-W and has a plaque which reads, "BIBLE CHRISTIAN CHAPEL 1896". To the north of the axis can be found the old mill, visible from the bridge, but which has unfortunately lost its waterwheel.

From Lovington, the line crosses Cary Moor before reaching **Barrow Court,** a modern property not shown the 1890 OS map. However, the large pond just to the NE, *is* shown (grid ref: 630290) and may be an ancient feature. The pond is now enclosed within the small wood north of the track leading to Barrow Court, but the old map shows it on open ground with a track leading around its northern edge. Possibly situated near the site of an ancient burial mound, it is the pond that stands on the hexagon line, not Barrow Court.

The line then goes straight over the summit of an unnamed hill that rises to 110m, and on to **Lower Woolston,** a small hamlet, before crossing a very steep and prominent ridge over which now passes the busy A303. Old maps show a crossroads at the spot, as well as two milestones (grid ref: 659267). The line then cuts through the small hamlet of **Maperton**, which has two large ponds and a fine manor house, viewed from the crossroads, where two stone eagles greet visitors at the gate. The fields east and north of the church are the site of a medieval castle and village, evidence that this quiet backwater was once a busier place. Overlooking the village is Stand Hill, which affords the village shelter. The line passes through the southern end of Maperton, via a small valley marked by two large ponds, both marked on 1886 maps.

The church of St Peter and St Paul at Maperton was one of the unexpected delights of our travels up and down the

The encircled hexagram behind the altar at Maperton.

Astrum lines. The church is set back from the road and is approached under a row of fine beeches, whose roots expose fossiliferous limestone. It is the site of a Saxon church and carvings from this period have been reset into the porch. Inside, the altar area is very elaborate, memories of busier and wealthier times; blue tiles surround images of the cross and animal icons of the apostles. Small stone arches above these have carved images, one of which is a small dove and another, to our delight, an intricate Star of David (see image above) – again the six-pointed star! The small Lady Chapel is very peaceful and on the walls hang two affectionate paintings of Mary the Mother. Behind the altar are two scenes showing Mary Magdalene, one showing her washing the feet of her husband (reputably), the other showing Jesus appearing to her after the Resurrection.

Horsington is the next stop on this hexagon line. Roman relics have been found locally, and tradition says that St Aldhelm preached here circa 705 AD. The village is mentioned in the Domesday Book as *Horstentone,* land held by William Fitz-Odo. It

was his descendants who were later to give Templecombe to the Knights Templar. On our visit, we approached the church of St John the Baptist via the old village cross, site of the medieval market, fairs and the stocks, and then alongside the long wall of Horsington House. The dedication of the church seemed appropriate, as we were only about one mile north of Templecombe, preceptory of the Knights Templar.

The church was rebuilt in 1886-7, although the lower parts of the tower date from the 15-16th C. The Baptist is duly depicted in a window, but it was another, on the north side next to the altar, that caught our eye. This shows St John the Apostle (otherwise known as John the Divine) holding a chalice from

Horsington. The beautiful window of St John holding a chalice, from which is emerging a turquoise, winged serpent.

which is emerging a beautiful blue dragon (see image above). Esoterically, it is the earth's vital forces emerging from the chalice of the Divine Feminine. Another chalice, the Grail no less, can be seen above. We certainly felt as if we were following our own personal Holy Grail - the Wessex Astrum.

Behind the altar we found St George and St Michael, and other windows show Jesus framed by a vesica, and a fine blue serpent hanging off the Tree of Life, which stands behind Adam and Eve. The church is a repository of ancient symbolism with esoteric

159

meanings. Outside, we saw fine winged dragon gargoyles on the south side of the church and, at the east end, a window in the shape of our guiding light - the six-pointed star! In the southeast corner of the churchyard stands a lone yew tree, which we found to be a powerful and nurturing spot.

Back on the main road is the former Baptist Chapel, closed in 1925. The location of this chapel, west of the A357, is right on the axis of this hexagon line (grid ref: 698237). Just to the west of here formerly stood the old mill, and down the road to the east, in the village, is the Half Moon pub. This dates from the 18th C and has an ancient well in the extensive cellars. As late as the 19th C it is recorded that Horsington children were given the day off school for St Thomas' Day on December 21 (the Winter Solstice) and were allowed to go begging, "... for an apple or a penny".

Place of the Knights Templar

One of the most well-known Templar locations in England is **Templecombe,** the only Knights Templar Preceptory in Somerset. Much has been written about these warrior monks and the esoteric knowledge they brought back with them from the Holy Land.

Founded in 1104 in the Champagne region of France, they were originally Cistercian monks who were released from their vows. They were powerful bankers and industrialists and the Order invented a system that developed into the modern banking systems; they lent money to Kings and Emperors. They learnt the secret of the pointed arch from the Sufis and developed it further into the Gothic style. They were also responsible for the red cross seen in

St Mary's at Templecombe. The village is the site of a major Knights Templar preceptory.

haloes of Jesus – it is the curved Templar cross. Templecombe was once two different parishes, Temple Combe and Abbas Combe, which are now combined. At the time of the Domesday records, the *Vill of Combe* came under the control of the Benedictine Nunnery of Shaftesbury, founded in 888 AD by Alfred the Great, of which his daughter, Ethelgeda, was the first Abbess. St. Mary's Church is believed to have been founded during this time. Interestingly, there is also a link between Shaftesbury Nunnery and Glastonbury Abbey, with a tradition that the monks and nuns would meeting halfway in procession, possibly to wash the Shaftesbury Byzant (a mace or wand) with the waters of the Chalice Well. For many centuries, Shaftesbury Abbey had the right of appointing the clergy at Templecombe. In 1185, the manor was held by Serlo Fitz Odo, but was later granted in that year to the Knights Templar, when it was known as Combe Templariorum. The Preceptor was responsible for managing the Templar estates in the West Country, admitting new members to the Order, and training men and horses for service in the Crusades. Poole (in Dorset) was a port much used by the knights in medieval times.

But King Philip IV of France was bankrupt, and owed money to Templars, and he conspired with the Pope to bring down the Order, leading to the suppression of the Templars in 1307. In England there was great unwillingness to accept the charges made against the Templars, but on 8 January 1309 most of the Templars were arrested, and by the autumn most had been collected in London. Many trials were held but the Templars were not tortured in England, by order of King Edward II. Nevertheless, the Order was suppressed and in 1313 Templar property was handed over to the Knights Hospitallers. William de Burton (Preceptor of Combe), John de Aley and Walter de Rokele, (two of the local knights), were committed to the Tower. Generally, those Templars who survived were assigned to various monastic houses to spend the rest of their days in confinement. In Bishop Drokensford's Register of 1315 there is an entry of payments made through him by the Sheriff to the Abbots of Glastonbury for maintenance of four local Templars.

In 1539, during the time of the Dissolution of the Monasteries by King Henry VIII, Templecombe had passed to Richard Duke, Esq. The major part of the Preceptory buildings were then taken down, and a substantial manor house built with the stone. In 1700, it was the seat of Sir William Wogan, who sold it to the owner of Stalbridge Park, Peter Walter. The property then passed to the Marquess of Anglesey in the early 19th C.

The naming of roads such as Templar Retreat, Templar Place, Templar View and Templars Barton are all reminders around the village today of the heritage of the Knights. The present day preceptory enjoys the patronage of members from a wide area, including Dorset, Devon and from around Bristol and Bath. Meeting every month, it has a long established rapport with the village, and assists with many local events and charities. Within the village, it regularly organises the village Winter Fair, where

The round platform on which the altar stands echoes the Round or Rotunda of many Templar churches in the past.

money is raised for charities.

Tower Hill, the road coming into Templecombe from the north, is called Tor Hill on 1889 OS maps, and at the top stands the church of St Mary's. The church is usually locked but a key can be obtained from the village shop. At one time the church would have commanded stunning views to the east and south. Today, only the tower, the nave roof, and transept, with piscina and font, are ancient. The tower probably rests on a Saxon foundation and the nave has a 500-year-old roof. Fine winged gargoyles decorate the tower and the Norman font of Purbeck Marble is one of the earliest features. Unfortunately, during WWII four bombs were dropped on the south side of the church, causing extensive damage.

The most intriguing feature in the church today is a panel painting of a bearded man, reputably Christ, on the wall next to the font. Believed by many to be a portrayal of the head of Jesus Christ, it was discovered in 1945 in the outhouse of a cottage in West Court, off the High Street. The keyhole and hinge marks on the panel suggest that it may well have been used as part of a door. This life-size painting, medieval in style, was carbon-dated at circa 1280 AD, when the Templars were at their height. It has been suggested that during the Crusades they obtained the prized possession of the Holy Shroud, brought it back to Europe, and from it painted copies. However, upon closer examination, its features do not match those of the Shroud of Turin, as the eyes and mouth are open. This has led some to believe that it is possibly the portrayal of a Templar Master, but it could just as easily be a copy of an image of

The intriguing 13th C painting inside St Mary's, Templecombe.

Christ on fabric known as the Mandylion (or the *Image of Edessa)*, an important relic of Christendom. When the English Templars were interrogated about the 'idols' they alledgedly worshipped, two of the knights, a Friar and one John de Dorrington, said there were four principal icons that the Templars held dear. One was kept in London, one in Lincolnshire, another in Yorkshire and a fourth in *Bristelham* (Bristol). We don't know exactly what these idols were. It is believed that William de la More (the last English Grandmaster) brought the four icons to England sometime before the French Templars were arrested. Could the Templecombe Head be one of these icons, brought here for safe-keeping? In *'Traces of the Templars'*, George Tull states that, *"It is not beyond the realms of possibility that the painting was imported into England, via Bristol, and thence brought to this remote Preceptory in Somerset"*

Other features in the church include the unusual rounded platform on which the altar stands, behind which are windows depicting Jesus, St Paul, John the Baptist, Mary and St Thomas. The small Lady Chapel has a lovely feel to it and behind the altar is a Faith, Hope and Charity window, depicting three women (the Christian adoption of the Triple Goddess). Next to the font are two iron grilles set into the floor and flash photography by us revealed a small chamber below. Back outside, just east of the church, an avenue of small sculptured yews channels a dowsable energy flow. At the back of the church there is what appears to be a sunken ancient 'green way'.

From the entrance to Manor Farm, at the south end of the village, one can look south and see Hambledon Hill rising out of the skyline – the destination of this line – proving that the Templars once had a good view of Hambledon. From this vantage point, Melbury Beacon and Duncliffe Hill (two more Astrum hills) could also be seen rising out of the lowlands of the Blackmore Vale.

The line then passes through **Henstridge Marsh**, now an industrial estate, although Marsh Farm reminds us of the original rural setting. The line crosses into Dorset and passes through Gibbs Marsh Industrial Estate, just north of Gibbs Marsh Farm. After the two unsightly estates, the line mercifully comes to a place of quiet and charm.

The Marnhull Ham Stones

The West Mill at Marnhull Ham once reaped the power of the River Cale, a swift-flowing river that feeds the Stour. It is reached via West Mill Lane and the mill can be accessed with permission from the site office of Colin Moore, in whose care the mill

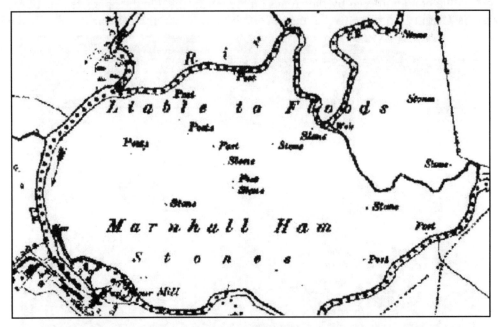

This old map shows several stones around an area known as *Marnhull Ham*. The hexagon line goes through the fields here.

is now entrusted. In the office is a collection of old photos of the mill. As well as a resident tabby cat, we found a rusting metal waterwheel still in situ, some of the mill machinery, and sluice gates over which the river still cascades. Marks and dates on one of the doors bear witness to former flood levels.

It was not the first time that an Astrum line has gone straight through, or passed close to, a mill. But the best was yet to come! On arriving home we checked old maps of the area online. On the very detailed 1890 OS map (1:10,560) we found that the river here marks the boundary between Stalbridge and Marnhull. More than that, the map shows no less than nine stones in the meadow east of the mill, on land bounded by the Cale and the Stour, inside a huge bend in the river known as Marnhull Ham. Nine stones in a tight area about 500m across, right on the hexagram line! The word *stones* is also shown under *Marnhull Ham* on the map, suggesting more stones now lost. The OS map of 1902 shows no stones at all – they had all been cleared or had become overgrown. On the 1890 map we looked further up and downstream from the mill, but could find no more stones – they really were very localised. Were we looking at a former prehistoric site?

The line then crosses the Stour and the vale formed on Kimmeridge Clay, before ascending the scarp of **Philip's Hill**, the southern end of the high ground on which Marnhull stands. This is formed of Jurassic limestone and rises to 300ft above sea level. The Knights Hospitallers preceptory at Friar Mayne owned land in Marnhull, named as *Manestone* in the Domesday Book, and there have at various times been five churches in the village. The view back from West View Cottage (grid ref: 771182) shows how high we have come from the low stretches of the Blackmore Vale. The line passes through the crossroads at Mounters (grid ref: 772182), a lovely spot with a pond bordered by flat stones on the north side. On the opposite side of the road is Chantry Farm (now having reverted back to its ancient name, after being

The six-fold design on Mary Magdalene's jar at Manston.

164

Pope's Farm since the 17th C), a beautiful old property with aged walls and window frames, and a well-tended garden. The name suggests a religious connection.

Just south of here along the lane is a garage; a stile nearby, opposite Bat Alley, takes you into a field, where a large pond can be approached (shown on the 1890 OS map). This is sunken and looks ancient. Further along the lane sits the Marnhull hamlet of **Pleck**, just south of the axis of the line, where two more large ponds can be located in the fields, again shown on older OS maps (as well as the modern 1:25,000).

The line passes just east of Hinton St Mary, where excavations of a Roman villa revealed a well-preserved mosaic (now in the British Museum). The line then goes through the western edge of **Manston**, which is mentioned in the Domesday Book; the church of St Nicholas stands 300yds east of the axis. Although the tower is 15th C, the rest of the church was completely restored in 1885. Fine gargoyles look down from the tower and in early spring the churchyard is carpeted in snowdrops. One fine monument near the porch has a skull and crossbones, wings and an hour glass at one end. Another has a very rough, barely-hewn surface, reminiscent of the 'megalith' we had seen at Fifehead Magdalen. Inside the church, the atmosphere is very pleasant, with bare stone walls and arches. Approaching the altar we noted floor tiles with the design of five Knights Templar crosses. The window behind the altar is of the Crucifixion, and shows Mary the Mother in a beautiful purple dress, and Mary

The church and the broken cross stump (left) at Hammoon.

Magdalene weeping at the foot of the cross (see image above). At her side is her famous alabaster anointing jar, which is, amazingly, decorated with a six-pointed star! Higher up, the sun and the moon float in the heavens, either side of Jesus.

The fine mortuary chapel (on the left as one approaches the churchyard gate) is usually open and has a fine heraldic window. The chapel was involved with the revival of cremation during the Victorian Era, partly brought on by the pressure for space in graveyards. There was also once a Wesleyan chapel in the village. Back at the main road, where the car had to be parked, we could see Hambledon Hill in the distance, with its long barrow on the top – we were once again closing in on the southern tip of the Wessex Astrum.

The hexagon line goes straight through the crossroads and church in the centre of the small hamlet of **Hammoon**, which nestles beside the River Stour midway between Sturminster Newton and Child Okeford. Mentioned in the Domesday Book, the

Knights Hospitallers preceptory at Friar Mayne owned land in Hammoon. We arrived on a bright November morning under blue skies, the sun bringing out the brown and orange hues of fallen horse chestnut leaves that carpeted the ground outside the church. The diminutive shaft and the surviving arm of the medieval cross, once the proud omphalos of the village, seemed to have barely survived time and Man. The alignment passes through the letterbox opposite, then through both the cross and the church, before carrying on through the 16-17th C manor house, now Manor Farm, which retains a grand porch.

The church of St Paul's stands behind the cross, and is entered via a south porch, where, over the door, are the words, *"Keep thy feet when thou goeth to the house of God"*. These words, from Eccles. VI, seemed appropriate to us, as we were quite literally walking in the footsteps of those who had been this way before us. St Paul's is a pleasant small church with a bellcote on the outside and a great atmosphere within. Some of the walls and window frames date from the 13th C, and there is a 14th C font, the base of which is said to be part of a Norman wayside cross. The east window is striking, depicting a variety of Old Testament heroes, as well as Jesus and Mary. In the churchyard behind the church, Toni found fragments of stone protruding from the grass, and we wondered whether these were ancient.

Child Okeford – the Home of King Harold

We had come along way since Glastonbury, but we were now within sight of the end of the line at Hambledon Hill. Before then, however, the alignment goes through the village of **Child Okeford**, which was to hold more wonders for us. In the Domesday Book of 1086 it was *Chyld Akford,* yet its present spelling was in use by 1600. It has been suggested that the first part of the name came from a child of noble birth. Harold Godwin, Earl of Wessex, held the *Manor of Chyldakford.* He was later to become King Harold, destined to be defeated near Hastings in 1066. We regard it as relevant that a Saxon king should be associated with an Astrum village.

The line passes along the northern slopes of the high ground of Gold Hill (just north of the street of that name), whose name suggests mystical, solar connotations. There used to be a Methodist chapel on Gold Hill, shown on the 1900 OS map which hangs on a wall in the Saxon Arms. This is now a residence known as Chapel House. The line passes through Nicholas's Copse (named on 19th C maps and formerly

The cross at the centre of Child Okeford. It replaced an ancient stone last recorded in 1906.

much larger than today).

The centre of Child Okeford, nearby, is a 'must visit' place, in respect to the Wessex Astrum. Near the church stands the modern cross, which replaced a small megalith seen here as late as the early part of the 20th C. In 1906, historian Alfred Pope saw, *"A huge block of green sandstone...34" square"*. He saw a basin-like depression on its upper surface, but no evidence that the stone had ever been part of a cross. This stone may well have been an ancient one, marking a sacred site prior to Christianity. The depression is reminiscent of the omphalos stone at Glastonbury. The village is at the hub of several ley lines that converge like the spokes of a wheel (see *Ancient Stones of Dorset* page 183-4). An old Victorian photo in, *Child Okeford – A Dorset Village* (ed. K George – 1999), shows what looks like the stone, as well as a large tree, at the locality. 250m north of the church there is Appletree Well, originally served by a track from the road going north out of the village. We found it as a small pool, with water trickling from it, in a thick hedgerow north of Yew Hedge House.

A Special Meeting with Mary Magdalene

It is thought that a Saxon church existed here and we know that a Norman one was built about 1250-70. The present church is dedicated to St Nicholas (4th C Bishop of Myra, in Turkey) and was rebuilt in the latter half of the 19th C, except for the tower, which dates from the late 15th- early 16th C. At the base of tower is a stone carving of a head that looks down one of the aforementioned leys, this one going down to Okeford Fitzpaine, Mappowder and beyond. The decorative marble walls of the nave

Child Okeford. Left: the magnificent tessellated and marbled hexagram.
Right: Mary Magdalene, resting her jar on her very pregnant tummy.

were completed in 1912 to commemorate the Coronation of George V. One of the large inlaid symbols is a hexagram, beautifully executed in marble and tessellated tiles. It is surrounded by a gold circle which itself is enclosed within a vesica piscis –

167

sacred symbol of the vulva of the Divine feminine. Behind the altar, the main window depicts Jesus standing within another vesica. Pride of place, however, is a window (dated 1879) in the Lady Chapel showing what we believe to be a very pregnant Mary Magdalene! The lady in question stands at Jesus' right hand and they are exchanging a tender, loving gaze. The present explanation of this window comes from a local newspaper of the 19th C, that describes it as showing Jesus, Martha and Mary at Lazarus' house, and that it is Martha carrying a wine goblet. It is clear to us that it is Mary Magdalene, holding her (handleless) alabaster jar on her inflated stomach, at Jesus' right hand. Other windows show King David with a sword, and St George and a dragon. Housed in a wooden case near the pulpit is the Bishop's Bible, published in 1568, the official edition prior to the King James Version.

A record of 1879 (*Dorset County Chronicle - Sept 25*) describes the old church prior to the rebuild as having, *"...a nave with a round roof..."* This may suggest either a semi-circular or circular structure, similar to many Templar-inspired churches, which often have a *Round* at one end. It goes on to say that the new church is, *"... now one of the prettiest fitted churches in the district... unostentatiously neat"*.

The hexagon line then climbs the steep slopes of Hambledon Hill, reaching its terminal point just yards south of the northern long barrow. The line also converges with the Magdalene Line, an amazing fact considering the two lines are both 40 miles long and each begins 40 miles from each other. This convergent point is marked by a very prominent embankment that crosses the hill, thought to be part of the Iron Age defences (see map page 117). Just yards away, the hexagon line arriving from Stonehenge also converges. From here, Hod Hill can be seen to the south, capped by the embankments of a Roman fort. There is folklore that both Hod and Hambledon are haunted by a Roman centurion, and that the yew wood, visible from here on the slopes below, was planted either by the Druids or the Devil, and is a place of ill-fortune. We found the wood to be a dark, magical place, with many of the trees displaying wonderful simulacra.

Two Astrum lines converge around this huge, prominent section of Iron Age embankment. Is it an enhancement of a more ancient mound or a natural rise?

Chapter 16
The Hexagon:
Hambledon Hill to Stonehenge

x Hambledon Hill

x Iwerne Minster

x Sutton Hill

x Long barrow

x Win Green

x Berwick St John (west end)

x Gallows Hill
x Meeting of tracks and dykes
x Tumulus/Sutton Down spur

x Fovant
x Fir Hill

x Baverstock

x Ebsbury
x Earthwork

x Stapleford Down Tumuli

x Druid's Lodge
x Normanton Down Tumuli
x Stonehenge

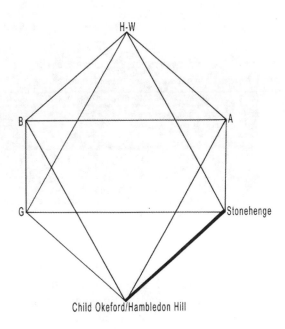

Magnificent Hambledon – the Druid's Hill

This line starts high up on Hambledon Hill, where four other lines converge. The terminal point of the line is about 150 yards NE of the entrance of the Iron Age hillfort, at the 623ft spot height. Three Bronze Age tumuli barely survive here, visible as low mounds that only rise about 1ft above the grassy slopes (marked tumuli on map, page 117). Grinsell numbers them Child Okeford 1,2 and 2a in his catalogue *Dorset Barrows*. Standing on the mounds we looked down into the valley below and could make out the church steeple at Iwerne Minster, which was to be our next destination. Beyond we could make out rolling hills and woods and, sticking out on the skyline, the tree clump at Win Green, also on the alignment. This line closely follows the northern major lunar standstill, the most northerly point

Hambledon Hill mirrors the huge landscape phallus seen at the opposite end of the Astrum at Wotton. The enormous Iron Age earthworks can be seen in this aerial view, and Neolithic monuments also grace the hill.

the moon can rise during its 18.61 year cycle. In *Stonehenge,* John North has this angle as 49°, but he takes it as the first glint of the moon on the horizon. The angle of the hexagon line is 47.5°, and this is the angle at which the moon finally clears the horizon, when the disc is fully visible. The difference arises from the fact that as the moon is rising it is moving constantly to the right. As we approached Stonehenge later, this alignment was to come into play again (see page 176).

The exact axis of the line actually follows a field boundary (shown on the 1891 OS map and Google Earth) that goes from the foot of Hambledon to New Field Lane. The line then passes just west of Bessells, and then proceeds just yards east of the site of an Iron Age settlement and Roman villa (grid ref: 856137). Pottery and coins proved a long period of occupation, from the pre-Roman period up to the 4th C AD. Both the 3rd and 4th C buildings were self-aligned with the Beltaine sunrise. Pitt-Rivers carried out the 1897 excavations, finds and models of which can be seen in Farnham Museum.

An Encounter with Boaz and Hermes

The line then enters **Iwerne Minster**, described by John Hutchins in the 18th C as one of the largest parishes in Dorset. The estate and village was purchased from the Bower family by George Glyn in 1876. Between 1857 and 1886 this wealthy gent was MP for Shaftesbury, Secretary to the Treasury and, ultimately, became Post Master General. The line strikes through the lake, already shown on older maps, within the grounds of Clayesmore School. The lake can be accessed via a public footpath from the main road. Passing east of the school chapel, the axis strikes through the war memorial on the main road. On the top of the memorial we found carvings of a woman holding a sword (Joan of Arc?) and a knight resting his sword on the ground; we felt the latter to be King Arthur. Leaving the memorial, we walked up Higher Street to the ancient water pump. Behind it is a shelter that has a fine carving of Hermes, the Greek God, etched in stone on a memorial shelter.

The parish church of St Mary nestles in the quieter part of the village, away from the busy main road. It is near a spring and a pond, and is a good example of a feminine dedication near water; in ancient times this would have been a place of the Goddess. The spring rises under *Divine House* and the resulting pond is not open to the public, but can be seen from Spring Cottage, after seeking permission. This part of the village is a pleasant collection of thatched cottages, old walls and babbling streams, and has an ancient feel.

The present church was built soon after 1100 AD, replacing an earlier Saxon place of worship. It once belonged to Shaftesbury Abbey and retains much of its original 12th C architecture, including fine columns with scalloped capitals, as well as later 13-15th C stonework; the church has one of the oldest Dorset spires.

From the moment we stepped inside we were greeted with fantastic symbolism. Next to the door, in the south aisle, are two magnificent memorials made of coloured tessellated tiles. One is a war memorial to a soldier who fell in 1915, the other being a private memorial dated 1930. The former is a beautifully crafted depiction of St George wielding a gold-hilted sword and wearing a golden cloak. Below him lies a fallen red dragon (see colour image on the front cover). The latter is a rare depiction of Boaz, an equally beautiful peace of artwork. Boaz was the Biblical grandfather of King David. According to the Jewish Talmud, Boaz was a just, pious, and learned judge. Boaz and Jachin were also the names of the two pillars in the porch of Solomon's Temple, the first Temple in Jerusalem, each being 6ft thick and decorated with brass. This symbolism can, of course, be linked to later Masonic traditions involving twin pillars, such as can be seen at Roslyn Chapel and elsewhere.

In the south chapel is a floor of black and white chequered tiles, a classic floor used by the Masons, and a window depicting Mary Magdalene, with a halo, at the feet of Jesus, the alabaster jar by her side. Jesus' halo shows the red cross of the Knights Templar. But it is the east window that left us in awe. It shows the Annunciation, with Mary the Mother shown praying, as the angels in a beautiful window appear overhead. Again, the black and white chequered floor is evident. This scene is flanked

on one side by a knight in armour (probably St George) slaying a green dragon with a spear, and on the other by St Michael holding scales, with beautifully-crafted iridescent purple and violet wings (see left, and the image on back cover of this book). Once again, a black and white floor supports the figure. As we stood in front of this east window, the low winter sun streamed in through the south windows, illuminating the wooden altar, bringing out its tones and textures. The whole scene was spellbinding, complementing the esoteric wisdom that had been incorporated into the church.

There is also a Methodist Chapel in the village, SW of the church. It has an interesting six-pointed flower window, each petal of which contains a six-pointed star. Around the corner is the church hall, formerly the Ebenezer (Baptist) Chapel, built in 1810 and enlarged in 1860. The lane linking these buildings to St Mary's is called *Hobgoblin,* inviting comparison with places elsewhere connected with supernatural folklore, funerary routes and death roads.

St Michael with sword and scales at Iwerne Minster. Note the Freemasonic floor.

Leaving Iwerne Minster, the line climbs up the slopes of **Sutton Hill**, and the edge of the line crosses the Higher Shaftesbury Road at Sutton Clump, a triangular copse that has the weird distinction of having an artificial pine tree rising from it – in reality a poorly disguised communications mast! Inside this wood we found what looked like a barely-surviving ancient bank, overgrown and enigmatic.

From there the line passes through the quiet glades of **Fontmell Wood**, with its pleasant bridle paths and cross dykes, before crossing the steep slopes of Boyne Bottom, and ascending the scenic heights of Ashmore Down. Much of the land around here is SSSI, protected chalk downland. Four roads meet in the vicinity of the line, the main north-south one being the old Roman road, which used to carry the legions from Badbury Rings north to Bath. This road marks the border of Dorset and Wiltshire, and on the Wiltshire side a **long barrow** can be seen in the field (grid ref: 696196), just opposite the turn off to Ashmore. This large elongated mound is closed to the public but is highly relevant as it lies on the Astrum line. It shows up well on Google Earth and mirrors the angle of the Astrum line. We noted that from here we could see Melbury Beacon to the west, one of the prominent hills on the Ana Line.

On the far side of the barrow, we could see the tops of the trees of a small wood (see image below), which turned out to be our next destination.

The Dizzy Heights of Win Green

From the long barrow the Hexagon line proceeds up to **Win Green**, the well-known landmark and viewpoint. Parking at the car park, we took the straight grassy path, which actually falls within the alignment, up to the trig point and beyond to the round clump on the summit. The height of the hill is 277m, or 909, 910 or 911 feet above sea level, depending on which book you read! The views from this lofty place are stunning in every direction. Standing at the trig point we looked south to the Isle of Wight and the Purbeck Hills, north to Shaftesbury, around to White Sheet Hill, and west to Melbury Beacon, Charlton Down, and the twinned wooded summits of Duncliffe Hill beyond. The clump of beech trees here at the summit is very circular and it is like stepping inside a small magical grove; we instantly felt its power, sacredness, antiquity, and great peace; it sent a shiver down the spine. We noticed what seemed to be a very pronounced rise at its heart. Was this once a prehistoric mound, positioned perfectly on the alignment? Surely our distant ancestors would have come to this place, to watch sunrises and sunsets over distant hills. Win Green is, we feel, one of the defining "fixing" places of the Wessex Astrum, along with similar predetermined natural and sacred hills. For Toni, it is one of her most special places of all those we visited. To the north we could see the western edge of Berwick

Left: the long barrow on Ashmore Down, and to its left Win Green in the distance.
Right: this track heads up to the clump at Win Green, a prominent landmark on the hexagon line.

St John, although most of the village was hidden by trees. This was to be our next stop on the Hexagon line.

The line goes through the west end of **Berwick St John**, about 300m west of the two churches. The parish church of St John the Baptist is worth spending time at. Records of a rector here go back to the 13th C, although the present church was built in the 15th C (with remodelling in 1861). Dedicated to a saint favoured by the Knights Templar, there is a magnificent window of St Michael, with sword and scales but minus a dragon, as one enters the church. At the very top of the window is a six-pointed star, and his halo has a circle of six-pointed stars. His cloak has a red apron full of oak leaves, and more decorate the frame of the scene. Behind the altar a window shows St John holding a chalice, out of which is emerging a small red dragon. There are also two effigies of 13th C knights.

The line is then "channelled" between the towering mass of Winklebury Hill (with its Iron Age hillfort) on the right, and White Sheet Hill (with its Neolithic causewayed enclosure) to the left. The line goes through a shallow valley, following a stream, running parallel with the lane to Woodlands, across the east slopes of **Gallows Hill** and up to the intersection of bridle paths with the Ansty to Alvediston road. The wide track follows the line, as does the ridge of the hill briefly, and there are fine views of the land below. Land and property at Ansty (a mile north of the line) was given to the Knights Hospitallers in 1210-1.

With pinpoint accuracy the line then goes directly through the small but prominent copse that encloses a tumulus on **Sutton Down** (grid ref: 984269). The hill can be accessed from good tracks from the west or south. The views from this vantage point make it well worth the steep ascent.

Left: a long metal sword is inlaid into the shaft of the war memorial in Fovant churchyard;
Above: a prone stone found in the centre of the village at Fovant.

The line descends from the spur and goes through **Fovant**. The name derives from *Fobba's Spring*, the waters of which flow through the area, supplying ponds in the heart of the village. There is thought to have been a Saxon settlement here following the Battle of Old Sarum in 552 AD. King Edward granted land to his minister Wihbroard in 901 AD, so there was presumably a wooden church here then. Fovant was owned by the wealthy Convent of Wilton in the Domesday Book. After the Dissolution of the Monasteries in 1539, the last Abbess was permitted to bring 31 of her nuns to live in the manor house at Fovant.

The hexagon line in fact goes right through the lower pond and the war memorial. South of the line is the United Reformed Chapel, set back from the road, and accessed by a bridge over a babbling stream. The door is usually unlocked during the day for, *"... prayer and quiet reflection".* Just south of the sign for the chapel we found a large megalith, 4ft long, by the side of the road, next to the entrance to Brook House. It was heavy and rough and may have been here since prehistory, marking some ancient site or ancient track. Once again we had found a large unrecorded stone very close to an Astrum line.

The parish church is dedicated to St George, dragon slayer and crusader. The church is now well north of the line, at the northern end of the village, but at one time there was a church in the centre of the village, and some traces in the surrounding fields survive, according to the guidebook in the church. As one enters the churchyard there is the war memorial, and fixed to the shaft is a huge, 6ft-long sword. It was as if Excalibur itself were guiding our way! Fine gargoyles decorate the tower and inside the atmosphere is good, despite the 1861 whitewashing that now covers the stonework. A window behind the font shows the four apostles and their animal icons, and a worn but fine window showing St George and a green dragon is near the altar. The main windows and focus behind the altar show the Crucifixion, with Jesus being flanked by his mother and Mary Magdalene, whom many would argue was his wife. The window is noteworthy for the richness of the colours, particularly the blue hues. Behind the pulpit is a banner on which St George is again displayed.

14th – 18th C graffiti has been carved into soft sandstone at the entrance to Baverstock church.

From Fovant the line then crosses another high point, **Fir Hill**, just east of the trig point. This can be accessed from a track leading from the road just north. There are fine views of the chalk scarps of Fovant Down, Compton Down to the south, as well as the famous Fovant Badges.

Baverstock, the next destination on this hexagon line, is a small hamlet with an ancient history. A Roman road passes the northern end of the parish, and a Saxon settlement was here prior to the Conquest. In the Domesday Book, *Babbastoke* belonged to Wilton Abbey, the name meaning *land belonging to Babba*, a local Saxon chief. Village earthworks lie in the field east of the church, and to the west an ancient enclosure survives, about 200m from the axis (grid ref: 025317), well-shown on Google Earth. The church is dedicated to St Edith of Wilton, a nun and the

175

illegitimate daughter of the Saxon King Edgar. The church stands directly on the axis of the line! It is a small church on raised ground, with views to the hills to the south and the alignment is about 15° north off due east. The church has its origins in Norman times, but was restored in 1861-3. Next to the porch is the base of a medieval cross, and the porch itself is interesting as it is daubed with ancient graffiti, with carved initials accompanied by dates such as 1329, 1612 and 1735. Someone has also carved a pentagram into the soft sandy stone. Behind the font are two beautifully crafted stained glass windows showing St George with a green dragon, and St Francis of Assisi. Either side of the altar are four ancient grave covers, carved with simple crosses. Behind these, in contrast, are decorative tiles, showing interlocking vesicas. The east windows show the animal icons of the apostles.

From Baverstock the line runs up to Grovely Lodge, crossing the Roman road along which the legions marched to Old Sarum and Salisbury. The ancient track can be followed through pleasant woodland for several miles. From here the line goes through the top of **Ebsbury Hill,** with its ancient earthworks and accompanying field systems. The line then descends into the valley of the Wylye, exactly following field boundaries, before crossing the road and running up a track that leads to a footbridge over the river (grid ref: 069362), west of Little Wishford. The field boundaries and track are exactly aligned with the axis of the line, and this too shows up on Google Earth. Rising out of the valley the line then strikes through a large wood, which contains two Bronze Age mounds and an ancient earthen enclosure.

The line then proceeds to **Druid's Lodge**, situated on the Salisbury to Devizes road. There was formerly an inn called *The Druid's Head* here, shown on the 1889 OS map, but which had ceased trading by the end of the 19th C. On modern 1:25,000 scale maps there is a boundary stone (*BS*) at grid ref: 098392, at the NE corner of the thin line of trees, north of the main buildings. On the 1889 map this is named the *Drinking Stone*, so it may be ancient and of some significance. East of the road, there is a mound marked next to the main road near the 126m spot height. Both features are on the hexagon line! On the OS map of 1901 the stone is no longer named, only shown as *BS*. An examination of the locality by us in January 2008 failed to find the stone. (There was another *Drinking Stone* on maps as early as 1773 next to Longbarrow Cross Roads, a mile north of here (grid ref: 100415), thought to have been a medieval cross base, and once known as *Long Barrow Cross*.) Druid's Lodge is now a training stable, a polo club, as well as a jousting school, where participants receive training in medieval foot and horse combat!

From Druid's Lodge the hexagon line convincingly follows tracks and bridleways all the way to Stonehenge, first skirting the Lake Group of tumuli, before going right through the famous **Normanton Down** barrow cemetery (see map on page 184). In his masterly work, *Stonehenge – Neolithic Man and the Cosmos,* Prof John North states that the track was, *"... almost certainly straighter in the past than now, but even now long sections are good enough for it to be claimed that it passes through the Aubrey Circle [the outer circle of pits at Stonehenge]"*. Fig. 130 in his book shows the alignment. North goes on to say that from a rise in the track around which the Normanton Cemetery is centred, the moon would have risen over Stonehenge at the northern standstill of the moon around 2700 BC. ***The track that follows the Astrum line is astronomically aligned with Stonehenge!***

North's line is 49°, whereas ours is around 48°, which is the difference between the moon's first glint on the horizon and the angle at which it has cleared the skyline, as whilst rising it is constantly moving to the right.

This track can be followed NE from the main road just north of Druid's Lodge. After ¾ mile, mounds will appear on the right, this side of the woods, which contain most of the mounds of the Lake Group. There are at least 16 barrows, including five rarer pound barrows and a disc-barrow with a diameter of 181ft. Some of these contained

Aerial shot of the Normanton Barrow Cemetery, and how the track on the left is aligned with the hexagon line as it approaches Stonehenge (compare to the map on page 184).

cremations and have been dated to around 1,700-1,400 BC.

Further along the track the Normanton Down cemetery becomes visible, mostly in the field to the east. Twenty-five mounds comprise what is regarded by many as the finest group of barrows in Britain. The mounds show up excellently on Google Earth, as the satellite image was taken when the mounds were in a field of pale crops. At one point two giant disc barrows rise either side of the track (grid ref: 115413), each of which are over 200ft in diameter. From here, Stonehenge can be seen, magnificent in the distance, less than a mile away. The world famous Bush Barrow rises to about 11ft (grid ref: 117413), and at one time covered one of the most powerful Wessex chiefs; excavations revealed a gold plate or "lozenge", a belt with a gold-plated hook and eye, three daggers, one of which had a handle inlaid with hundreds of tiny gold pins, and a bronze axe. We find it amazing that the axis of this hexagon line goes straight through Bush Barrow. In the distance other mounds can be seen, and these can be examined via another bridlepath that begins on the A303, just south of Stonehenge. The mounds are associated with the Stonehenge culture and were constructed 1,700-

1,400 BC. Also of note is that in recent years crop circles have appeared in these fields, some almost touching the tumuli.

Walking between these ancient mounds, along this ancient track, we really felt we were walking in the footsteps of our ancestors. Just to the west of Bush Barrow is an information plaque, headed Stonehenge Estate, with details and illustrations about the barrows. As you face the plaque, you can see the low banks of one of the barrows, and if you turn around at this point you will see Bush Barrow itself, on which stands a small tree. The plaque has a drawing of one of the incense cups found here, perhaps used by ancient shamans for the burning of hallucinogens. From this point one can

Left: the alignment of the track going through Normanton Down with Stonehenge (arrowed).
Right: Bush Barrow, inside which rich grave goods were found.

see how the track aligns with Stonehenge, which is now visible on the other side of the busy A303. A little further on is a signpost marking the boundary of the Stonehenge World Heritage Site, and here the path diverts to the left, leaving the alignment. However, on the full colour original of the aerial photo shown here can be seen marks continuing across the field in the direction of Stonehenge, suggesting that a track once continued straight to the monument.

The hexagon corridor takes in both the sarsens of Stonehenge and the large tumuli just east of it. This is the closest mound to the stone circle and the axis appears to go right through it. John North calculates that the track going through the Normanton Cemetery clips the eastern side of the Aubrey Circle of postholes, whereas we have the axis of the hexagon line a few yards further east; we really are splitting hairs! The aerial shot (above) also shows another straight track coming in from the right, and North also has this going into the centre of Stonehenge; Alfred Watkins would have appreciated this!

Chapter 17
The Hexagon:
Avebury To Stonehenge

x Avebury

x Waden Hill

x West Kennet Long Barrow

x Earthworks/Wain's Dyke

x Milk Hill/White Horse

x Ridgeway

x Alton Priors

x Woodborough

x Hilcott Hall

x Charlton

x Goddard's Cleeve/Rushall Hill

x Casterley Camp

x Hilltop trig point

x Aligned tumuli
x Cursus

x Stonehenge

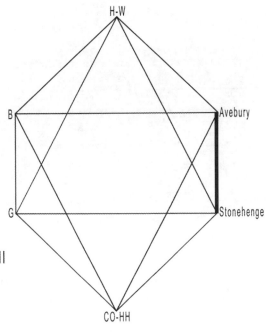

O f all the hexagon alignments associated with the Wessex Astrum, this one is perhaps the most vital, for it comprises the Stonehenge to Avebury line, which in turn is angled at around 90º from the Glastonbury-Stonehenge Dod Line. This hexagon also passes right through the centre of Casterley Camp, the important Iron Age-Romano temple site. Some researchers have extended the Avebury-Stonehenge line up to Arbor Low, a major henge site in Derbyshire (the setting for Chapter 1 of Peter's, *Thirteen Moons – Conversations with the Goddess.*)

Avebury – Temple of the Goddess

This alignment starts in the vicinity of the Obelisk and the SE quadrant of the mighty henge (see map on page 130). The Obelisk, the huge entrance stones (No. 1 and 98) and the southern entrance of the henge all stand within the "corridor" of the alignment. It is through this quadrant that the Michael and Mary currents of the St Michael Line pass during their passage through the henge, and the space between the two giant megaliths is particularly potent. Simulacra can be seen in several of the stones here, revealing an open art gallery of shamanic images and potential

Peter sitting on the seat of Stone No.1 at Avebury.

interaction. On the south side of Stone No.1, a seat can be seen, the "Devil's Chair", and above it a tube going vertically up through solid rock. Sitting here can be a powerful experience, despite the obtrusive traffic; who knows who sat here thousands of years ago, perhaps to witness and greet the torch-lit processions as they arrived after their walk down the avenue of stones to the south. Perhaps the "chimney" going up through the stone was channelling the shaman's soul on its way to meet the spirits of the Ancestors. The books of Michael Dames and Terence Meaden are essential for understanding Avebury (see Further Reading). The Henge Shop at Avebury has a good selection of books, as well as other related goods.

The alignment leaves the henge and passes through the solitary hawthorn tree in the fence, just where the Avenue takes a sharp turn. It then proceeds through the very field where two crop circles appeared in recent years. From here the line crosses Waden Hill, just yards from a Bronze Age tumulus and the 191m spot height. Close to here a crop circle appeared on June 21 in 2003, overlooking the entrance to the henge. It resembled a scallop shell, incorporating a yin-yang symbol. From here the alignment goes through the site of the West Kennet Palisade Enclosures. Discovered in the 1950's by aerial photography, both of these Neolithic enclosures were 200m in diameter, with earthen banks, and ditches up to 2m deep. There were close-set timbers which may have stood up to 8m tall, as well as megaliths, as at nearby Avebury. It has been suggested that these enclosures were feasting places, made of living trees, as opposed to the ancestral places of stone, which were for shamanic spirit journeys to contact the dead. The alignment goes directly through the site of the eastern enclosure.

The axis of the line passes within yards of the site of another 2007 crop circle and then within 50 yards of the megaliths of West Kennet Long Barrow, through which the Mary current of the St Michael Line passes. This Neolithic barrow is one of those "must visit" places for anyone interested in our prehistoric spiritual heritage. The axis of the 330ft long earthen mound is aligned to the Equinox sunrise, one of the astronomical festivals of the year. It was in use for over a thousand years between 3,700 - 2,500 BC, ample proof of the sanctity of the site. It is thought that priests,

West Kennet Long Barrow. Left: the main chamber is a powerful place in which to meditate and drum, as shamans did thousands of years ago. Right: the full moon rises at one of our gatherings.

priestesses and shamans would seek contact with the gods, the ancestors and the Earth Mother/Goddess, to bring back important information for the tribe. Initiates may also have spent time here, sealed within the tomb's dark confines to meet the Spirits, to contact their inner nature and to confront their own fears. Today, flickering candles illuminate faces in the stones. Of the 46 skeletons found in the chambers, only a handful were found in the main chamber (at the west end), implying that this space was not chiefly intended for the dead, but for the ritual activities and spirit journeys of the living. Where better to contact the ancestors than amongst their bones?

181

Megaliths lie under the floorboards of the church at Alton Priors.

We regularly take groups to the site to hold full moon drumming and meditation evenings, and on such occasions one can experience something of the energetic and spiritual potency of the site. Peter laid his father's ashes around the chambers in 2006, as told in, *Thirteen Moons – Conversations with the Goddess*. This place is now particularly sacred to him.

From here, one can also look north into the valley from which rises the magnificent Silbury Hill, which stands on the Ana Line (see Chapter 13).

The alignment then crosses **Wansdyke,** the Iron Age earthworks, before passing just west of the settlement of Eald Burh. From here it reaches the top of the scarp of **Milk Hill**, midway between the Alton Barnes White Horse and the Neolithic long barrow of Adam's Grave. The views from here are spectacular and one's spirits are uplifted to the heavens at this lofty, timeless place. The line then descends the steep scarp of Milk Hill and passes through the field where crop circles appeared in 2007 and 2008.

It then passes through **Alton Priors**, just 100yds east of All Saints Church (grid ref: 109622). An ancient ridgeway track runs through the village and the area may be the site of a bloody defeat of a Saxon army led by Caewlin in 592 AD. All Saints Church is Norman in origin although most of the surviving walls are late-medieval. The site is, however, generally regarded as being on the site of an earlier church. The chancel and nave are offset and may be a memory of this earlier structure. Brass and memorial date from 1528 and the tomb is 16th C. There is also a carved stone above the blocked doorway. The church is very atmospheric and the energies are

Ripples on the surface of the spring at Alton Priors.

powerfully felt and dowsed. One of the reasons for this is that the church is an excellent example of site continuity or site evolution. Two trap doors in the floorboards can be lifted, revealing two megaliths (see image above); the church was built on a prehistoric stone site on the ancient ridgeway track.

Back outside, a yew tree in the churchyard may be up to 2,000 years old, and within

This ancient yew tree stands in the churchyard of Alton Priors, a sacred place for meditation and reflection.

the hollowed interior a small "tree spirit" can be seen. Across the field, to the NW of the church, is Broad Well, one of the sources of the Avon. *'Bradewelle'* (meaning *'Wide Spring'*) is mentioned as early as 825 AD in the Saxon Charters. In fact, the name Alton probably derives from *'aewielle'* and *'tun'* meaning 'the farm by the spring'. Nestling in the corner of the field, beside fallen trees, the waters bubble up out of a gyrating sandy riverbed. The whole scene is straight out of Tolkien and one can easily imagine fairies sitting on the extensive complex of prostrate willows when no one is around. Tuning into the Elementals, Toni knew that the willows were the guardians of this source of the Avon, which was confirmed by our psychic friends, Caroline, Marie and Gary, who were with us.

Nearby is a modern standing stone, set up to commemorate the unusual crop circle pattern engraved on it. It is marked '1990', the year the formation appeared. It stands beside the gateway to the meadow immediately to the south of St. Mary's, the Saxon church at Alton Barnes. It was erected by a US crop circle enthusiast and regular visitor to Wiltshire. It is worth popping into the Barge Inn, at Honey Street, for the back room is where enthusiasts gather; the walls are covered in crop circle images.

The line then crosses the old ridgeway before proceeding to **Woodborough**. The parish church is dedicated to Mary Magdalene. From the churchyard the Alton Barnes White Horse can be seen. Inside, Mary is depicted at the Crucifixion, and above Jesus' head are images of the sun and the moon. From here the alignment passes through Bottlesford and then **Hilcott Hall.** A former chapel can be seen north of the road, just east of the axis (grid ref: 113583). **Charlton** is next on the line, where it passes just west of the Manor buildings, and then straight through the pub! The full name of the village is Charlton St Peter, and the church bears that dedication. The tower has masonry from the 12th C. The line then traverses **Goddard's Cleeve** and **Rushall Hill** before passing into the outer landscape of Stonehenge.

With incredible accuracy, the hexagon line passes directly through the centre of **Casterley Camp** (grid ref: 115535). This Iron Age enclosure has 5ft high earthworks, enclosing 68 acres, and there are three entrances, on the north, south and west sides.

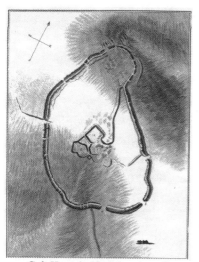

Colt Hoare's 1810 drawing of
Casterley Camp.

Excavations revealed archaeological evidence of temples at the centre of the site, as indicated by Sir Richard Colt Hoare's 1810 drawing, shown left. Roman occupation was proven by finds of Samian pottery and coins dating from Claudius to Constantine, plus pins and broaches. Folklore speaks of a golden chair buried within the ramparts, but which may be an ancient memory of shamanism and solar rituals. Four human burials were excavated and within the graves were found fourteen red deer antlers, which also ties in with the shamanic connection. The finds are now in Devizes Museum.

The line then traverses MOD land, passing just west of the hilltop trig point on Enford Down, before going through the army camp at Larkhill. Roads through the camp allow public access to the line and the adjacent public footpaths. Two long barrows can be visited (grid refs: 127453 and 124444), both of which lie just east of the axis. The line then passes by two tumuli west of Durrington Down Farm, the largest of which (grid ref: 122436) can be seen from the bridleway going south from Larkhill to Stonehenge. The line then passes directly through a group of three closely-packed tumuli nestling in the space between two plantations (grid ref: 122433); these low mounds can be seen from the same bridlepath as one walks south into open ground.

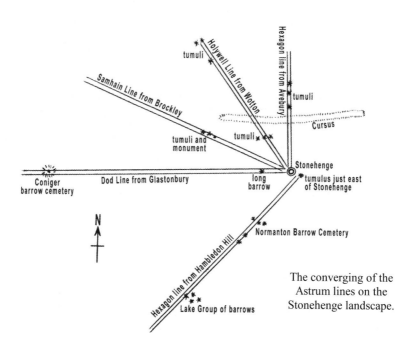

The converging of the
Astrum lines on the
Stonehenge landscape.

184

The alignment then crosses the **Greater Stonehenge Cursus**. The Neolithic monument is actually aligned with Gare Hill, which features in the Glastonbury to Stonehenge Blade line (Chapter 9). This ancient ceremonial way can be accessed via the bridleway heading north from the car park at Stonehenge. In the middle of the cursus, beside the track where it changes direction slightly, stands an information plaque about the monument (grid ref: 124430). The hexagon line crosses the cursus about 250m west of the track, cutting across almost at right angles. The cursus can be approached via stiles near the plaque. Not much is seen on the ground now, but the southern bank and ditch still show up at places, especially at the closest approach to the nearby barrows. We especially noted how Stonehenge is not visible from this section of the cursus, and only comes into view when the barrows are approached. Clearly, one's focus is meant to be in the here and now.

The centre of the line terminates within **Stonehenge**, taking in the west side of the stones, although the whole monument stands well within our "corridor". This is an incredibly accurate alignment, when one considers it starts right up at Wotton-under-Edge, passes through the temple site in the very centre of Casterley Camp, and ends within the famous stone circle.

We visited Stonehenge to honour the summer solstice of 2008. We arrived the day after the annual scrum involving the invasion of thousands of people on the beleaguered stones; for many it is just a funky rave site. To us this yearly invasion robs the stones of the little dignity they have left. As we stood outside the circle, held back by the security rope, we saw that a group of Druids, many in robes of white and cream, had been allowed access to the inner circle and were holding a ritual. Drums were banging and horns were being blown, and small children were in attendance, enthusiastically banging their own drums. Perhaps, we thought, there is hope for Stonehenge after all.

Chapter 18
The Hexagon:
Holywell to Avebury

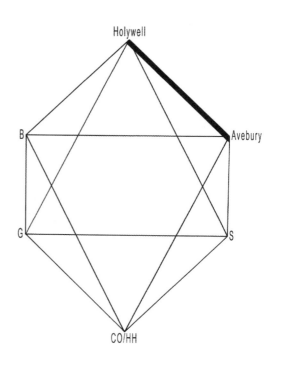

This alignment links the apex of the Blade, at Wotton-under-Edge, with the western point of the Chalice, at Avebury. The line commences on the gentler slopes near the top of Coombe Hill, where it intersects with both the Brockley-Wotton hexagon line and an extension of the Central Axis line (at grid ref: 760943), just south of the Old London Road. It then descends the precipitous slopes of Coombe Hill, via strip lynchets and an ancient path, down to the **Holywell** area. The *Holy Well* in question has already been described in detail on page 48, as it gives its name to the Holywell Line, the Wotton to Stonehenge alignment.

The hexagon line then ascends Blackquarries Hill, following the route of the road briefly, before striking directly through the heart of the **Blackquarries Hill Long Barrow** (grid ref: 775932). It shares high ground with a nearby wood, through which the line also passes. This Neolithic mound (officially Wotton-under-Edge I) may once have been a chambered tomb and is aligned close to both the midsummer sunrise and midwinter sunset (NE-SW). The mound is on private land and permission should be sought before entry. It can be viewed, however, from the bridleway that runs just north of it, where there are gaps in the hedgerow. Google Earth shows the NE-SW alignment well, and also confirms that the mound is wider, in proportion to its length, than the average long barrow.

From the mound and the woods the line passes the west end of the lake at Newark Park, and then along and down the slopes of a spur, crossing the river at **Ozleworth Bottom**. Whilst in the area, a short detour is recommended, to inspect the charming, and atmospheric church at Ozleworth Park (grid ref: 794933), which houses much esoteric symbolism and has a hexagonal tower.

The old river crossing at Pinkney is on the hexagon alignment.

The line passes just south of Holwell Farm and rises up the steep slopes of Hen Cliff, crossing just south of the hill summit (206m trig point), before running about 200yds to the north of a tumulus at **Stonehill**. The line goes through Avenue Farm at Knockdown, a fine old farm in Cotswold Stone, and then through ponds and a wood.

The next hamlet on the alignment is **Pinkney** or Sherston Parva. There was a small Saxon community here and *Sherston* is recorded in the Domesday Book. Just north of the line a Romano-British farm was found, on Vancelette's Farm. There is a local association with Rattlebone, a famed Saxon warrior who fought for King Edmund Ironside against the Dane Cnut, or Canute, in 1016. Pinkney Court, north of the village, is home to the prize-winning Pinkney Alpacas, which can be seen grazing in the fields.

The line goes through the road junction at Pinkney, across the bridge and past the site of the former pub (The Eagle), which was closed in 1998. Access to the bridge is down the lane marked *Unsuitable for long vehicles*. The old bridge is of Cotswold Stone and the River Avon flows beneath at this peaceful spot. The lane ascends, following the alignment, passing moss-covered drystone walls.

Pinkney House, south of the line, is shown on a map of 1773. John Aubrey in the 17th C records a certain John Tyvetot receiving a fee for being a Knight. Another record of 1660 speaks of Thomas Estcourt, a master in Chancery. Aubrey describes it as, *" a small Manor and parish. It belonged to the Priory of Kingston St Marie's…"* The latter was formerly St Mary's at Old Sarum. By the 13th C, the church at Pinkney was owned by Malmesbury Abbey.

The line then crosses the Fosse Way, one of the main Roman arterial routes. The modern road runs along the ancient one for a brief distance at this point. The alignment then goes through the site of the old windmill at Maidford, before going over a rise (300ft +) and crossing the A429. The line then passes close to Cleeve House at **Rodbourne Bottom**. Rodbourne is first mentioned in a charter that relates to a gift in AD 701; it refers to, "ten hides near the spring called Rodbourne", which were given to Malmesbury Abbey by King Ine of Wessex. A local site, Godwin's Meadow, revealed Romano-British, Saxon and medieval remains. Rodbourne was also owned by the Abbey at Malmesbury until the Dissolution. The line passes just west of Cleeve House, where several paths converge on a footbridge over a stream. The nearest cottage to the line is called Honeystones. The hexagon line then goes straight through the heart of Seagry Wood, which can be accessed via a bridle path.

Fine floor tiles at St Mary's, Seagry, showing lions, vesicas and fleur-de-lys.

Seagry is the next stop, and the line dissects the two centres of habitation. Seagry is unusual in that it has never had any kind of Lord of the Manor, and that free fishing has always been allowed on the Avon.

Lower Seagry has a Tithe Barn next to the church of St Mary the Virgin (grid ref: 958808). The archway is now used as the approach to Church Farm; old beams can still be seen underneath the arch. St Mary's itself is a little gem, and despite the whitewashing of the walls, the small church is full of atmosphere. The dedication to a female saint is typical of other examples of churches in the vicinity of rivers. Of note are the ancient floor tiles (image above), and the east window showing Jesus with

188

Mary Magdalene at his feet. On the south side, two wall memorials are dated 1678 and 1700, and both show a skull and an hourglass.

Upper Seagry has the vestiges of a moat (grid ref: 956806) in a field west of Manor Farm. Just west of the pub, at the main crossroads, stands the Methodist Chapel, dated 1825, and which is still in use.

The line passes midway between Upper and Lower Seagry and goes straight through the site of the old mill (by Mill House) and by the weir on the Avon (grid ref: 956803). Access is via a permitted track, and then on foot past cottages to the river. Along the track is an old, rotting footpath post, and in front of it we found two stones, barely visible now at ground level. Were these ancient markers, we thought? The weir over which the Avon flows is a noisy place, as the full force of the Avon surges beneath one's feet. To the south we could see Melsome Wood, to the right of the nearest pylon, through which the line next flows.

The line negotiates the M4, goes through Melsome Wood, before skirting the southern flanks of both Avon Grove Wood and Catcomb Wood. These can be seen from the road to the south, which in fact runs parallel with the alignment as it approaches **Catcomb**.

The prominent pines on the hilltop at Catcomb mark the hexagon line. There is a boundary stone at the edge of the wood, and the road seen above follows the alignment.

The alignment then goes along the top of Catcomb Brow, just south of Catcombe Farm and through the road junction, marked by tall pines that are a prominent landmark. Here (grid ref: 009766) the 1889 OS map shows the word *stone* at this spot. These tall trees, next to the junction, are known as Sheriff's Clump; it is right on the line! On a site visit we found the stone, a boundary marker that is dated 1876. It is easy to see why such a prominent spot, with views to the north and south, should have been chosen as a boundary.

The line then follows the road for about two miles. It passes the 112m spot height of **Beacon Hill,** a sharp prominent hill, especially so from the east. Incredibly, the same old OS map shows another *stone* about 50yds west of Beacon Hill Farm, in the small wood. Again, this stone is on the line! New developments mean that the hill is not now a right of way. The line then crosses the A3102 and the crossroads is the site of Whitcomb Mill, shown on 1889 maps. Standing on the bridge that crosses the river, we could see masonry, bricks and sluices on the west side, evidence that this place was once a hive of activity. Old maps show several buildings in the vicinity – all gone now. We saw an unmarked mound in the field next to the crossroads, and wondered at its antiquity.

Just south of the line is Hillmarton, a village containing the beautiful 12th C church of St. Laurence, a small Baptist Chapel and a Victorian inn called The Duke. The church is normally locked but a notice lists keyholders. Fine gargoyles decorate the tower, and there are several fine stained glass windows, including one showing St George slaying a poor dragon.

The line then goes on to **Highway**, which nestles below the steep chalk scarp of Highway Hill. The 1889 OS map shows the church of St Peter standing about 50yds from the centre of our line. Yet another example of a former church, that stood on or close to an Astrum line. It is now a private residence but can be seen from the road and the open ground to the west. Its simple spire is still capped with a cross.

Opposite the church, a tarred track, marked *bridle path*, ascends the scarp, and this in fact runs parallel with the alignment, which likewise ascends the hill in the field to the right. Parking at the top, we could look back to Beacon Hill and the tall pines of Catcomb beyond. The tarred track to the right is then followed southward briefly, before turning SE, exactly marking the course of this hexagon line! The track ascends further through a sunken way, the ground to the right plunging away into a woodland valley. Buzzards magically called above our heads and the place felt sacred; we truly felt we were walking an ancient way. At the top of the slope, the path continues past derelict farm buildings and off into the distance, following the alignment all the way. Unseen in the distance are Windmill Hill and Avebury. To the south can be seen the Monument above the Cherhill White Horse, another Astrum location.

For about three miles there are virtually no notable features on the maps, so it is even

Left: the former chapel at Highway stands just yards from the centre of the alignment.
Right: this sunken way marks the line as it climbs the scarp and heads towards Windmill Hill.

190

more astounding that the centre of the hexagon line goes straight through **Stert Pond** (grid ref: 068726). This feature appears on old maps and can be reached on foot from the south via bridleways from Yatesbury.

We were equally amazed that the hexagon line passes straight through **Windmill Hill**, one of the major sites of the Avebury landscape (see map on page 130). The huge earthworks are Neolithic and in fact pre-date Silbury Hill. During excavations in the 1930's several carved chalk phalluses and balls were found, as well as crude figurines and a lozenge with a depression in the centre, all suggesting that this was more than an occupation site; it was a place of ritual and ceremony.

To be precise, the centre of the line passes between the two Bronze Age mounds on

William Stukeley's fine 1723 sketch of Windmill Hill, crowned by tumuli, rising on the other side of Avebury henge.

the south side of the site, south of the boundary stone. The views from here were uplifting as we looked down to Avebury beyond, the terminal point of the line, one of the six apexes of the Wessex Astrum. On page 12 of his seminal book, *The Secrets of the Avebury Stones,* Terence Meaden has a map of the outlying stones he has found associated with fifteen "calendar stones" of Avebury's South Circle. Incredibly, he shows two stones (stone XV, and another unnamed stone which is shown on 1889 OS maps) that actually seem to define the southern edge and the very centre of the hexagon line! This seems to be more independent confirmation that the Astrum hexagon line is based on reality. Another of Meaden's stones marks the Beltaine Line (see page 245).

Windmill Hill is a major crossing point of the Mary and Michael flows of the St Michael Line, a node point occurring at the large tumulus on the north side. From here, the male flow follows the bridle path going east from the hill, whilst the Mary current flows up to St Mary's at Winterbourne Monkton; both serpents then wind their way down into the mighty henge at Avebury.

The axis of the hexagon line enters the henge through the north entrance, terminating, we would suggest, in the general area of the Cove and the northern circle (see map page 130). The Cove was once three stones, which formed a *"Chalice"*, a receptacle into which the shadow from a nearby stone formerly *"penetrated"* around midsummer. Terence Meaden's books are essential reading on the shadow phenomenon and the simulacra at Avebury (see Further Reading). The Cove is also important with respect to the St Michael Line, for it is at these stones that the Mary and Michael currents meet, before flowing through the henge - united. Concentric circles on the south side of the phallic member of the Cove often mark the centre of the flow. A pendulum will usually spin when placed in front of these markings.

The Cove at Avebury, where the hexagon line terminates. The stones are astronomically aligned, as well as marking the two main energy flows of the St Michael Line. Note the concentric circles on the phallic stone.

Chapter 19
The Hexagon:
Wotton to Brockley

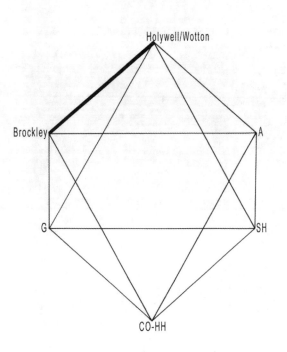

This alignment links the apex of the Blade, at Wotton/Holywell, with the western point of the Chalice at Brockley in Somerset. It is an important alignment, for it passes through Bristol, which has Knights Templar associations. The starting point is behind the steep slopes of the Cotswold Edge, north of Wotton, close to the Old London Road, the route of which continues the line onto the B4058. The line skirts the steep slopes of Wotton Hill at the Butts, and passes close to the Tabernacle (see page 60) with its hexagonal floor tiles, before leaving the town on its way to Merryford Farm. The line then continues to Grange Farm, before crossing three tributaries of the Little Avon, shown on 1:25,000 maps. More homesteads follow on the line, namely Charfield Hall Farm, Little Bristol Cottage and Newhouse Farm, before reaching the small and strung-out hamlet of Bagstone.

We thought the name **Bagstone** might reveal the presence or memory of a megalith, so we took a walk along its main street, which is a very fast stretch of the B4058. We peered over hedges and into gardens, and over walls into fields, but to no avail. We thought we *had* found a large stone at one point, but closer inspection revealed it to be an upturned rusty bath! On the way back to our car, however, just as rain began to fall, we passed a milestone (marked on OS maps, grid ref: 691871), whose worn inscriptions proclaim VII MILES TO WOTTON. We felt compelled to look at the back of the stone, as we knew from experience that ancient megaliths were sometimes later modified into wayside crosses or milestones. Our hunch paid off, for the rear of the stone is not smoothly carved at all, but heavily pitted and very rough. Is this the *Bag Stone,* or at least the remnant of a megalithic site that once stood in the vicinity?

The milestone at Bagstone is very rough on the other side; is this a modified megalith?

From Bagstone, the alignment is marked by a small bridge crossing a tributary of Laden Brook (ref: 684868) before running close to, and parallel with, a footpath and bridle way named Lock's Lane, running SSW from **Latteridge**. Also in the area, east of Latteridge, is Acton Court. In 1535, Henry VIII stayed here with his second wife, Anne Boleyn, whilst on a summer tour of the West Country. The owner, Nicholas Poyntz, wanted to impress his sovereign, so for Henry's pleasure built a magnificent new East Wing onto the moated manor house.

194

The line then crosses the B4427, passing through Gloucester Road Farm and straight through the **The Grange**, now a hotel. This is shown on old OS maps, and has been described as, *"...a 19th C building of architectural importance"*, but it had, in fact, replaced an even earlier house on the site. A certain George Bush lived at The Grange in the 17th C – presumably no relation! Old maps also show several stones just south of the Grange, alongside the B4427, just north of its junction with Trench Lane.

The line then crosses the M4 and goes through the lake at **Bradley Stoke**, before crossing Stoke Bridge, and the ancient crossing point over Stoke Brook (grid ref: 618805).

From here the next point of interest is **Filton**. Roman and Saxon remains have been found in the vicinity, including a mid-6th C Saxon cemetery south of the railway station. Older maps show Filton as a small village surrounded by open fields. In recent decades Filton has been swallowed up by Bristol, as well as being at the forefront of British aviation development; it was the birthplace of the recently retired Concorde.

The line passes through a residential area NE of Filton Church, but the 1881 OS map shows only one building of note here – Conygre House (grid ref: 607793). The building still stands in Conygre Road, which runs NE from the church; the alignment passes straight through the property! The parish church of St Peter stands just 100yds from the axis of the line and dates back to the 14th C. It was rebuilt of stone in 1845, with a green spire and has a collection of smiling gargoyles up the tower.

The 1889 map shows another former chapel 100yds east of the church – right on the axis! From the car park of St Peter's one can look down Gloucester Road and see the next church on the line, the impressive RC church of St Teresa.

Bristol – Giants, Romans and Hot Springs

We shall deal with the myths associated with the founding of Bristol shortly. In Saxon times, Bristol was known as *Brycg Stowe* (*Brycg* meaning *bridge* and *Stowe* being *holy place)*, and was centred on the area of today's modern city centre. It is recorded that St Augustine visited in 603 AD and Offa built a ditch and rampart around 790. Settlements are recorded in the Anglo-Saxon Chronicle of 1051 and there was a Saxon mint in the area, issuing coins for King Cnut and Aethelred. But there was probably not one single large settlement for, surprisingly, no mention of Bristol by name occurs in the Domesday Book, although other local places are referred to. The cathedral was founded in 1140, but was never known as Bristol Abbey, even when it was a monastery.

Throughout medieval times Bristol flourished, with a castle, market and several more churches being built, as well as a town wall with at least a dozen gates and a High Cross at the junction of Corn Street and Broad Street. It was also a great spiritual centre, and at various times had eleven separate monastic sites, including the Benedictine Priory and Augustinian Abbey. The Augustinian foundation was founded in 1313 by Simon de Montacute, who gave the friars a piece of land next to the town's Temple Gate.

Today, Bristol has not one, but two cathedrals and, incredibly, around 150 listed churches within the city boundary. And, as we have seen, several of these stand on or close to this hexagon line. Tracing the line through the NW suburbs of Bristol proved to be an enlightening experience, revealing an incredible number of sites of relevance and interest. The line goes straight through Southmead Hospital, whose chapel lies within yards of the centre of the line. It then passes through the **Stoke Bishop** and Sneyd Park areas of west Bristol where it runs through another substantial church at

the corner of Henleaze Road and Waterford Road (grid ref: 577766). This area was known as Golden Hill on older OS maps, suggesting past solar associations. The line then proceeds through the grounds of St Monica's, which has its own chapel, dedicated to St Augustine. We visited St Monica's (entrance in Cote Lane), which is now a large residential nursing trust. The main buildings and large church were built by the architect, Sir George

The sheer scale, and quality of carvings, of the so-called "chapel" at St Monica's took us by surprise.

Oatley, who is said to have wanted to create a chapel of Cathedral-like proportions. This he certainly did and we were stunned by what we found here in the grounds of the nursing home. Approaching the chapel from the entrance, we immediately noticed the height of it, the quality of the stonework, and the numerous finely-carved gargoyles around the outside. Inside, we found the commemorative stone, laid on St Monica's Day, August 27 1920. St Monica of Carthage (331-387 AD) is the patron saint of wives and abuse victims, and one of her sons later became St Augustine of Hippo. The chapel has fine wooden beams, a large rood screen and carved stone figures. The building was paid for by the Wills family, the tobacco giants, and we were soon to encounter their legacy again.

Nearby, on the 1889 OS map, on the opposite side of Westbury Road, the word *stone* is marked, near where the entrance to Henleaze Gardens is today. The stone was just yards from the centre of the axis.

From here the line crosses Parry's Road, where the OS map of 1888 shows interesting features. Just west of where the two branches of the B4054 converge, (grid ref: 569758) the old map shows ***Parry's Well***, as well as *stones* adjacent to it. The well is right on the axis and the stones are just yards from it! The ghost of a man named Parry is said to sit beside the well, where he cut his own throat. Being a suicide he was buried nearby, as he could not be buried in a churchyard. The well was later known as Paddy's Well, from its use by Irish drovers who watered their animals

Left: the rotund end of the chapel at Wills Hall, Bristol.
Right: the coat of arms at Wills Hall, showing the sun, griffins and a red Masonic hand.

there. We searched for the well inside the grounds of Wills Hall, but could find no trace of it. Toni dowsed where she felt the well had been, and outside the grounds, near a lamppost, we found crumbling masonry at this point, as if it had been weakened by the flow of water. Furthermore, there are more drainage holes on the walls here than elsewhere, surely to drain the water-sodden earth behind.

From the well the line passes through **Wills Hall** with its accompanying chapel, now part of Bristol University. This was again financed by the Wills family and its buildings within the grounds are lavish, with fine carvings and symbolism. Over the entrance to the hall are two golden griffins, a red Masonic hand and a golden sun (see image above). The French Romanesque-looking chapel itself is close by, and we were struck by the "round", the rotunda-like altar end of the church, a feature copied from

The 17th C entrance to Stoke House (now the Trinity Centre), Bristol, with "barley sugar" columns (left) and foliated heads (right).

197

Templar and Masonic foundations. It is called the Monica Wills Chapel and has fine rose windows. The interior is simple and the energies very peaceful.

The line then passes on to Churchill Hall, which shares its grounds with The Trinity Theological College, at Stoke House. On the 1888 OS map *Stoke House* is shown (grid ref: 564755), and was reportedly the best of the larger houses in the district. The mansion, which was built by Sir Robert Cann, originally stood in a 13-acre park; the property is just yards north of the centre of the line. We were impressed by the stunning porch of the main entrance (see images above), dated 1669, which has high quality stonework displaying the green man and a pair of spiralling columns, similar to the renowned Baroque "Barley Sugar" columns at St Mary the Virgin, Oxford. These columns are also known as the Solomonic Columns, deriving from the Biblical description of the pair that flanked the entrance to the Temple of Solomon in Jerusalem.

Less than half a mile to the west is Druid Stoke, where the remains of a long barrow survive in the garden of a house called Cromlech, on Druid Hill (grid ref: 561761). Just north of it is an area known as The Grove, suggesting more Druidic associations. *Stones* are again marked on the old map (grid refs: 560749 and 559748) as the line approaches Avon Gorge, next to buildings at the western edge of Clifton Down. Again, these stones stand almost directly on the axis!

We had initially been disappointed that the hexagon alignment did not go through the centre of Bristol, but rather through the west side and across Avon Gorge. But research soon revealed that, as well as the abundance of sites already described, it was this area that once was the ancient centre of Bristol, as well as a sacred place, and an

Statues of Belinus and Brennus can be seen on St John's Gate, at the bottom of Broad St.

area of Roman industry. The Avon Gorge was occupied as far back as the Palaeolithic, some 60,000 years ago, and large quantities of artefacts were found at Pill and Shirehampton, just a mile to the west of the hexagon axis. The Gorge also has links with Stonehenge, for it was along the Avon that the Bluestones were transported from the Preseli Mountains of Wales. It must have been an emotive site to see rafts carrying these megaliths through the Gorge at high tides.

Tradition speaks of King Molmutius (or Malmutius) founding Bristol c.450 BC. He called it Caer Odor, *Citadel of the Chasm,* suggesting that it was in the Gorge area. Molmutius was known as the pioneer of the law systems we use today, as well as a road-builder. The *Molmutine Laws* were translated into Latin by King Alfred, so they could be incorporated into Anglo-Saxon law. Molmutius had two sons; Belinus is said to have founded London, whilst Brennus is credited with enlarging Bristol. The Romans described Bristol as Caer Bren or the *City of Brennus*. Statues of the brothers can be seen at St John's Gate, at the bottom of Broad St, in the centre of Bristol. They are well worth a visit, and each one has a pair of dragon-like creatures beneath their feet. Built into the fine stone gate is the church of St John the Baptist, which is open on Thursdays, 10.00am - 1.00pm. At the other end of Broad St, the church of Christchurch and St Ewen has two Roman quarter-jacks, who strike bells every 15 minutes. The old medieval high cross of Bristol (the omphalos of the city no less) once stood close to this spot (shown on the Millerd map of 1673). This can now be seen in the grounds of Stourhead in Wiltshire.

All five of Bristol's Iron Age hillforts are west of the city centre, and all are within 1½ miles of the Gorge. Three of the encampments, Stokeleigh, Clifton Down and Borough Walls, are just south of the hexagon axis, all situated on promontories overlooking the Gorge and the River Avon below. Although on opposite sides of the river, all three hillforts are within 800yds of each other, and were occupied by the local Dobunni tribe. Clifton Down Camp is just north of the Suspension Bridge, whilst the other two are on the opposite bank. The degraded banks of Clifton Down Hillfort can be seen in the vicinity of the Observatory (grid ref: 566733, see below), whilst Borough Walls was virtually destroyed by the construction of the Suspension bridge. Stokeleigh Camp has faired the best; its double banks and ditches lie half-hidden midst the woods of

The magnificent setting of the Clifton Suspension Bridge, which spans Avon Gorge. The white arrow on the left marks where Giants Cave emerges from the cliff face. This is an ancient holy place.

the Avon Gorge Nature Reserve, overlooking Nightingale Valley. There is no evidence that the Romans took these settlements by force during their conquest in the 1st C AD.

When the Romans settled in the area they built a large town, Abona, at Sea Mills. It stood less than a mile NW of our line, on the east bank of the Avon where it emerges from the Gorge. Abona (the Latinisation of Avon) is recorded in the Antonine Itineraries of the early 3rd C AD and was a major settlement, which had its heyday in the 4th C, with street grids, temple, shops and a cemetery. A garrison housed legionnaires in transit from the port to South Wales and Caerleon-upon-Usk, once an Arch-Druidic site. Some foundations can be seen today at the junction of Roman Way and Portway (east of Sea Mills Station). Abona was linked to Bath via a road, which passed just north of the modern city centre, a major artery linking the port with the spa resort of Aqua Sulis. The hexagon line crosses the Roman road on Clifton Down, just north of Roman lead workings. At Sea Mills today there is Druid Stoke Avenue, Druid Road, Druid Hill, all within the vicinity of the old Roman town.

Directly north of the Suspension Bridge is an opening in the sheer limestone cliffs, about 250ft up on the east side of the gorge (see image on page 199). This natural karst cave, variously called Giants Cave, Ghyston Cave or Vincent's Cave, was named after giants of local folklore, two brothers named Goram and Vincent (or Ghyston). The giants were said to have both courted the same woman, Avona, who gave them the task of draining a local lake. Vincent triumphed over his brother and won the hand of the lady. He is said to have created Avon Gorge; Vincent Rocks, north of the bridge, is said to mark his burial. The views from the top of the cliffs at this point are breathtaking. Interestingly, the axis of the spired church to the NE of the cave is aligned with it.

The cave was used as a chapel in 305 AD and Romano-British pottery has been found. It was later known as St Vincent's Chapel, much of which fell away from the cliffs into the Gorge below. Fragments of carved masonry were also discovered in the cave from this period. This cave was a holy place in ancient times, and one that was both isolated and difficult to access. Entry is now via Clifton Observatory, from where a 2,000ft long tunnel, opened in 1837, goes down into the cavern. One side of the cave opens up to Avon Gorge, where one can look down to the Suspension Bridge and the Avon far below.

The Giants Cave, or St Vincent's Chapel, Avon Gorge. This is an ancient holy place, and its sacredness can be experienced today. The cave entrance opens up halfway up sheer cliffs.

We entered the cave site through the Observatory (with a small admission charge) and excitedly descended stone steps cut through solid rock. At times we had to crouch down to avoid low rocks, and the tunnel was quite claustrophobic in places. After a few minutes the cave opened up to us, illuminated by the sunlight that streamed in

Old drawing of the well houses that once served the hot spring at Hotwells.

through the original cave entrance. The view from the opening is incredible, and a little daunting as we peered through the metal grid below our feet to the bottom of the gorge! Opposite the cave we could see Nightingale Valley and to the right of it the higher ground occupied by the Stokeleigh Camp hillfort. At the rear of the cave there are more chambers leading off above our heads, but one side chamber is accessible towards the back of the cavern. We sat inside this dark, low area, which was ancient and sacred, and wondered who had sat in this energetic spot in the distant past. Every now and again, when we were alone, the sacredness of silence was felt.

Adding further to the sanctity of the Gorge, and no doubt attracting visitors from the earliest times, were two warm springs which rose from the mud at Hotwells, between low and high tides on the north side of the river. They emerged along the major fault line that extends from here all the way to the Bath area, and is responsible for the hot/warm springs at both localities. Donne's map of 1790 shows Hotwell House at the locality, at the height of the spa's fame (shown above). The 1990 OS map shows *Hot Well* at grid ref: 566728, just south of the bridge. In the Georgian era, Hotwells developed as a spa town, competing with nearby Bath. Grand buildings in Dowry Square catered for the needs of visitors.

The water was warm rather than hot, bubbling up at 23°C/76°F, flowing at a rate of 60 gallons a minute. It apparently had a fine taste, according to several accounts and was said to cure, *"... hot livers, feeble brains, old sores and diabetes."* Access was originally from above via a slippery zigzag path of nearly 200 steps cut into the rock; not until 1662 was a carriage road cut alongside the river. Methodist John Wesley was amongst visitors in 1754 and the lavish pump room attracted gentry from all over Britain. By the end of the 17th C, bottled water was being shipped all over the world. The well was found to be polluted in the 19th C, recorded as being highly radioactive, bringing to an end its use as a spa. Hotwell House was demolished in 1822 but locals continued to drink the waters from the foot of the cliffs until 1913, when further pollution made the water unpalatable. All that remains now is The Colonnade beside the river, built in 1786 as a shopping arcade for spa visitors. From the Suspension Bridge we could see old decaying wooden jetties, which once served the spa. A second spring was discovered further down river, a quieter locality favoured by Wesley, and this still feeds a drinking fountain on Portway.

The Knights Templar and Freemasons in Bristol
The Knights Templar once had great influence locally. It was Robert Earl of Gloucester who set up the Order of the Knights Templar in Bristol in 1145, where

their land was known as Temple Fee. As well as building their Temple, Sir Robert gave them land and here they also built a Priory for themselves. The Templars and the Hospitallers both had a preceptory in Temple Back (formerly Water Lane), just north of Temple Meads railway station. The land was not particularly good, being very marshy, as was much of the land outside the city walls. This land has long been built over, and on some of it stands Temple Meads railway station, *Mead* being an Old English word for *meadow*.

There seems to have been trouble between the Templars and the civic authorities from the onset. The problems arose from the fact that the civic authority had no jurisdiction in Temple Fee. The Order held their own courts, where they could execute murderers and enforce other privileges. Gradually, Temple Fee seems to have become a haven for those not willing to conform to the establishment, and it is said that when the local authorities tried to arrest some of these fugitives they, *"...would return bloodied and empty-handed"*.

Then came the persecution of the Templars across Europe in 1307. The English king at the time, Edward II, resisted this order for some time, but in 1312 gave in to pressure. The Order was abolished and their estates handed over to the Order of St John of Jerusalem, the Hospitallers. The Templars in Bristol were seized and thrown into the castle dungeons - some were killed, but the Knights of Saint John did manage to rescue a few. The Hospitallers demolished the old Temple and built in its place Temple Church. The ruins are well worth a visit as the foundations of the original round temple survive. Outside the energies can be readily dowsed. As well as the naming of the railway station, the Templar legacy is evident elsewhere in Bristol:

Left: Temple Church, Bristol, founded by the Knights Templar.
Right: hexagrams adorn the carpets in the Lodge of the Bristol Freemasons.

there is a Knights Templar pub at Temple Quay; and other street names include Temple Way, Temple Back, Temple Gate and Temple St. We dowsed an energy current that in fact followed Temple Back, went through a solitary horse chestnut tree, into the foundations of the original round in the church, and out the other side. Further dowsing by Toni found a current going through the south door, where smokers from a nearby office gather. We both felt the area just outside the east end marked a powerful flow that came out of the church through an alcove below the main window. This energy appeared to cross with the north-south flow that came in through the south door, crossing in the centre of the church.

Temple Church is closed to the public now, but can be viewed from just outside the ruins through arches and old windows. The tower leans markedly to one side and at the base of it is information and a plan. The axis of the church is slightly north of the E-W equinox line, in a similar manner to St Paul's Cathedral in London. Next to the road are the entrance gates, proclaiming above in stone that here is the *Temple or Holy Cross.*

In Bristol today, the Freemasons have over 2,500 members and the Freemasons Hall in Park Street is worth visiting on open days. Huge columns adorn the entrance and in the 1st and 3rd degree rooms blue carpets are covered in hexagrams. In the Royal Arch Lodge Room, the carpet is red and again covered in hexagrams enclosed within circles (see image above).

In June 2007, for the first time in 700 years, the Knights Templar (the modern order, that is) held an investiture service at the nearby St. Mary the Virgin, Redcliffe. This spectacular church has a 292ft high tower, the third highest in the country. The church contains several images of the Green Man amongst its 1,200 gilded roof bosses, as well as a fine foliated head at eye level in the small chapel to the right as one enters through the main porch. This very fine hexagonal porch is the oldest surviving part of the church, and dates to around 1185, the time of the Knights Templar. At its centre is a hexagon in the floor and on the exterior stonework we found wonderful carved dragons and other mythical beasts, including the Tree of Life issuing from a dragon's mouth. Inside the church are many fine windows, including those showing Mary Magdalene and St George, the latter subduing a fine lilac dragon. At the entrance to the choir area, there are three interlocking hexagrams in the floor (see image on page 15). The energies inside the church are wonderful and we recommend a visit to this ancient sacred site.

Green Man inside St Mary Redcliffe, Bristol.

Interestingly, the coat of arms of Bristol City Council, first recorded in 1569, shows relevant features. It has a banner of St George's/Knights Templar colours, and two flags of the Cross of St George flying from castle turrets. This is clearly an acknowledgement of Bristol's Templar heritage. Two arms come out of the top, one hand holding a snake, the other scales. Officially, the serpent represents wisdom and the scales are symbolic of justice, adopted perhaps because of the myth of King Molmutius, and his qualities of justice and the systems of law he introduced. Either side of the central shield are two unicorns, heraldically symbolising virtue of mind, purity of spirit and strength of body. In folklore, the horn was traditionally used for healing.

So we left Bristol, which had yielded so many wonders and surprises. Between Filton and Avon Gorge alone, in less than four miles, we had found evidence for a dozen sites either on or very close to this hexagon line. How many more had been lost without any record of their existence?

The line emerges from the splendid ruggedness of Avon Gorge midway between the Roman town of Abona and the Giant's Cave/Chapel, and goes through **Leigh Woods**, which hides the Stokeleigh Iron Age enclosure, south of the line. It passes through Lower Farm, just south of the centre of Abbot's Leigh, land once owned by the Bristol Augustinians. It was also one of the places where King Charles II took refuge on his way to France in 1651. It is interesting that on the 1888 OS map a field boundary (now gone) ran from Lower Farm to Leigh Woods –exactly following the axis of the line! The axis then passes through the crossroads at the east end of the modern hamlet of **Failand**, before going right through the monument (*Mon* on OS maps) in the grounds of **Belmont Estate**, a huge 230-acre property, the house of which dates to the 1750's. Now in the care of the National Trust, the grounds are open to the public all year, with an admission charge.

The next stop on the hexagon line is **Flax Bourton**, a village at the head of the Yeo-Kenn valley, which unfortunately suffers from being on the A370, the busy artery in and out of Bristol. The village has the distinction of being the scene of the first breathalyzation in Britain, in 1967. There was an Anglo-Saxon settlement here, and the church retains some features from this period. The centre of the line passes through Priory Farm, which is recorded in the 16th C, and the church of St Michael and All Angels stands on the main road 250yds to the south. It is a perpendicular church with fine gargoyles around the tower, and a clock dated 1897. The church is usually locked except for Sunday, but in the porch the fine Norman doorway can be seen, with banded pillars. Inside are images of St Michael slaying a poor dragon on a Norman tympanum.

The line then proceeds to **Backwell**, which straddles the A370 at its junction with the Nailsea road. The area has long

The peaceful Rodney Chapel in Backwell Church.

been inhabited, proven by the discovery of eighteen Romano-British and Iron Age skeletons in Backwell Cave. The older part of the parish is called Church Town, and sits under the steeper slopes of Backwell Hill. The hamlet was named as *Bacoile* in the Domesday Book, meaning *Well, back on the hill*. The church of St Andrew (grid ref: 493683) is significant as it stands directly on the axis of this hexagon alignment. Church Lane runs past the church and in fact follows the exact centre of the line for around 500 yards. Entering the churchyard we were confronted by a magnificent 15th

C cross. We then noted a fine foliated gargoyle on the east side of the porch, a Green Man no less, and up the west side of the tower strange symbols that we did not recognise. There is a tradition that locals climb to the top of the tower to see the sunrise on Ascension Day (40 days after Easter).

The church is usually locked and a local key holder called Elena (tel: 01275 462435) kindly let us in and showed us around. The church displays Norman stonework, but when it was renovated in 1980, a 7ft by 2ft stone was found under the floorboards, which historians took as a foundation stone of the original Saxon church. We wondered if this was another example of a large prehistoric megalith, later modified and incorporated into the fabric of a church. The energy inside the church's beautiful arched Rodney Chapel (named after the foremost local family from the 12th C onwards) was powerful, yet peaceful and we felt that this might be the equivalent of a Lady Chapel elsewhere. In front of the chapel is the tomb and effigy of a fully-armoured knight, thought to be Sir Walter Rodney, who died in 1466.

The line continues into Brockley Wood, where it passes through the eastern embankments of Chelvey Batch, the Iron Age settlement. The line's termination is in Brockley Combe, where it intersects with the other four alignments of the Astrum in the space of just 500yds. The centre of this hexagon line passes within 250yds of Yorkhouse Cave, a hermit's retreat of folklore and the terminal point of the Brockley to Glastonbury hexagon line, described in detail in the following chapter.

Chapter 20
The Hexagon:
Brockley to Glastonbury

X Brockley Combe (Yorkhouse Cave)

X Goblin Coombe

X Hill summit (166m spot height)

X Perry Bridge

X Burrington/Rickford
X Burrington Coombe

X Beacon Batch (325M) & tumuli

X Gorsey Bigbury Henge
X Long Wood

X Cheddar Gorge (east end)

X Tumulus

X Big Stoke Wood

X Lodge Hill
X Chalcroft Hill

X Henton

X St John's Church
X Glastonbury Abbey

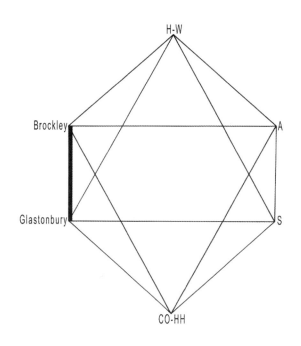

This hexagon line runs from Brockley Combe to Glastonbury. The alignment could perhaps be subtitled *Line of the Four Gorges* – for it passes through the ravines of Burrington, Goblin and Brockley, as well as Cheddar Gorge. Of interest is that Palden Jenkins, in his map, *The Ancient Landscape Around Glastonbury,* plots an alignment that closely mirrors this line, running a course just ¼ mile east of it, and which also passes close to Gorsey Bigsbury Henge and Beacon Batch. Jenkins' line continues north of Brockley to Cadbury Camp; the ley is detailed in the archives of The Society of Ley Hunter's website (www.leyhunter.org).

This 17½ mile alignment begins at one of the most magical places of the entire Astrum, Yorkhouse Cave; it is easily the most isolated and inaccessible of the six

---

Yorkhouse Cave

GPS: 51° 23′ 46.48″ N, 2° 45′ 10.16″ W   Grid ref: 47742.66631

Directions: Park at entrance to Fountain Timber, and walk east along Combe road for 150yds and then take the cobbled bridle path north into the woods. Ignore the signposted track to the right, and take the path going into woods soon encountered on the left, which then skirts a clearing on the right. Where five tracks converge take the one straight ahead of you (the one heading due west on 1: 25,000 maps). After about 300yds the path bends left and from here look out for a stone resting on a tree stump, to the left of the path, which cavers have left to mark the spot. Walk south into the woods behind the stone and look out for a large oak tree in front of you, the one with two large fallen branches either side of it, near the precipice beyond. The right-hand (western) branch in fact points the way. Go to where it is pointing and a steep rocky cliff is soon encountered. There is a way down, via natural steps and you will see two yew trees to your right, which have wrapped themselves around the rock face. Walk towards these and the cave entrance will soon be seen beyond. If you can't find the cave, dowse for it!

---

apex points. This little-known cavern is perched high above the road that winds through Brockley Combe. The Combe has folklore of a spectral hunchback crone and of secret tunnels, and it is said that a hermit once lived in the cave. As well as being the exact terminal point of this hexagon line, the Samhain Alignment also crosses the road just to the west of the cave, as it comes from Brockley church (see pages 247-249). Because it is difficult to find, being well-hidden amongst woods at the top of the ravine, we provide very precise co-ordinates, as well as detailed directions, above.

As we walked through the woods in search of the cave we felt the magic of the place and could appreciate why the cave had been chosen, hidden away from the outside world. As we scrambled down the rough rocky steps we could see several huge yew trees before us, some twisting around rock outcrops. We approached the cave entrance and felt humbled, thinking of those who had come here before us, seeking solace and solitude, at the end of the Astrum.

The cave entrance is around 9ft high by 3ft wide, tapering up to a point, giving the appearance of a vulva; we were entering the womb of the Earth Mother, symbolism surely not lost on our ancestors. We left bright autumn sunshine and stepped into the half-light of the cavern. The main chamber is 12ft square, rising to 10ft high, clearly a natural cleft later enhanced by human effort. A shaft goes up through the rock, following a natural fault, and an opening around 18ins wide lets in light from above. Opposite the entrance, on the left, is a narrower chamber at the back, about 6ft wide, which terminates with a crack in the rock. From this protrudes a clitoris-like projection, stained red (the blood of the Goddess?), which Toni only found after feeling drawn into this dark area. The sanctity of the cave was palpable and we could sense the presence of the hunchback crone or the hermit sitting here, perhaps mixing ancient herbal potions. Peter reflected on the fact that Brockley Combe was called *Wolf Combe* by the Saxons; the wolf is one of his totem animals!

We had been puzzled originally about Brockley being the apex of five alignments of the Astrum. But now, sitting inside this sacred orifice, we felt vindicated and truly humbled that we had been chosen to reveal its ancient wisdom. We stood together on a powerful feminine energy spiral that Toni had dowsed, near the centre of the cavern, and together we sent healing down the five lines that diverge from the area,

Yorkhouse Cave, Brockley, the terminal point of the hexagon line. Secluded in woods at the top of steep limestone cliffs, the cave is sacred and energetically charged, and said to have once been the abode of a hermit.

whilst we chimed small Tibetan symbols; the high tones echoed and resonated around the cave. The moment was sacred and we felt connected, free and alive.

The alignment then crosses the Combe, passing through Warren House, and then the eastern end of **Goblin Coombe**, and on through a hill summit to the monument in Barley Wood. It then descends to the lower ground either side of the Yeo, crossing the river at **Perry Bridge**. The bridge is marked on John Ogilby's semi-pictorial map of the London-Bristol-Huntspill coach road of 1675, and repairs to it were noted in Manorial Court Papers of 1733-1757. The name suggests that this crossing may be much older still: *perry* may either be a corruption of the French *pierre* (stone), a stone bridge, or it may indicate that a stone once stood in the vicinity.

From here the line crosses two junctions between **Burrington** and Rickford, where five roads converge. It then climbs the steep slopes of Burrington Ham and crosses the east end of **Burrington Coombe** – the line going right through a cave known as Toad Hole (marked on 1:25,000 scale). The Coombe has an ancient history of habitation in limestone caves, such as in Aveline's Hole, which yielded evidence of human activity back to the Mesolithic. Legend says that Augustus Montague Toplady was inspired to write the hymn *Rock of Ages* while sheltering from a thunderstorm here in the late 18th C.

The line then ascends the spectacular heights of **Beacon Batch**, one of the defining hills of the Astrum. It is one of the Mendips highest and most prominent hills, rising to 1,066ft at the trig point. Archaeologist Leslie Grinsell recorded ten Bronze Age tumuli in the vicinity of the summit, although several are now badly damaged and difficult to make out. A ring of five well-defined mounds still encircles the summit and is shown on 1:25,000 maps, most above the 1,000ft contour. The views from this lofty place are stunning; to the north can be seen the impressive vertical limestone faces of Burrington Combe, and beyond rise the towers of the two suspension bridges that cross the Bristol Channel. Brean Down, Steep Holm and the Welsh mountains can be seen to the west.

The view from Beacon Batch, looking towards Steep Holm, Brean Down, and the Welsh mountains (far right).

The line then crosses a Roman road and then onwards to Long Wood, where it follows a stream along a valley bottom, going through Lower Farm and then Swallow Hole. Just 200yds west of the centre of the line, overlooking the valley, is **Gorsey Bigbury Henge** (grid ref: 484558). It is a circular Neolithic site, defined by a ditch, up to 9ft deep, with a bank on the *outside*, and a single causeway leading north. Over 4,000 flint flakes were found here, together with pottery, charcoal and hearths, dating back to 1900-1700 BC. The henge had been founded as a ritual site in Neolithic times, but was subsequently used in the Beaker Period for domestic purposes, revealed by charcoal, hearths and large quantities of animal bones. 'Portal posts' at Gorsey Bigbury were held in place with pieces of red sandstone, which is not a local stone, evidence of the selectivity of stone at an early stage in the megalithic age. The feature stands in a cultivated field but little is to be seen today except a slightly raised ring of rough ground. Gorsey Bigbury is one of the sites on the other previously mentioned ley going from Brockley to Butleigh Church, via Glastonbury Tor.

The hexagon line then proceeds to the east end of **Cheddar Gorge**, passing over the path going east from near Black Rock. The line then goes over Ram's Cliff, a small but prominent limestone precipice. There is a tumulus just west of the axis, before the line crosses through a place where four fields meet (grid ref: 489524) and where, amazingly, the 1891 OS map shows the word *stone,* exactly on the line! This is not the first time we have found this. The land is private property so we have not been able to confirm the stone's survival; it was certainly not a parish boundary stone.

The alignment crosses an airfield before passing close to an ancient settlement, and skirting the west end of **Big Stoke Wood**. An old track called Wind Lane (a public footpath) mirrors the line, just west of it. The line then descends the slopes of the Mendips to Wedmore Moor, a northern extension of the Somerset Levels. It was very gratifying to us that the line then goes through two prominent hills that rise out of the low ground, namely **Lodge Hill** and **Chalcroft Hill** (the latter of which was once Chequer Hill). The woods on the top of Lodge Hill are shown on older maps and the line goes through the summit of Chalcroft Hill, just above the 100ft spot height.

The line then ascends from the Somerset Levels and passes just 200m east of the church of Christ Church at **Henton**. This village is mentioned in the 14th C in records by the Bishop of Bath and Wells, where mention is made of, *"… the prior and monks of Henton of the Carthusian Order…"* The present church is a sizeable 1847 construction, comprising a nave, chancel, south porch and a west bellcote. The main east window is a scene of Christ in Majesty, with disciples and harp-playing angels in attendance. On this site once stood the more ancient chapel of St Thomas, *"long destroyed"* according to local records; we could find no further records of it. From here the line goes straight through the 75m high summit of Yarley Hill, before passing near the Lake Village as it enters the ancient Isle of Avalon.

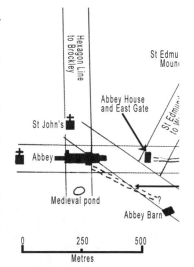

Close-up of the route of the hexagon line through Glastonbury.

Glastonbury

The alignment passes through St John's Church on the High St, dealt with in detail in Chapter 15 (pages 154-155). It is through the southern edge of St John's that the Michael flow of the St Michael Line passes (marked by dragons on external stonework), through the St George Chapel, which is on that side. The church also contains the alleged tomb of Joseph of Arimathea, with a small caduceus (with serpents) at one end, and next to it the beautiful window of Joseph, resplendent in a purple robe (image, page 154). The newly conceived labyrinth in the churchyard also marks the alignment and pilgrims are invited to walk this winding healing way for themselves. Opposite the church is

Labyrinth Books, which also stands on the alignment, where a green man can be seen carved on the outside.

The alignment then terminates at Glastonbury Abbey, covered in detail previously in Chapter 9, when it was shown how the Dod Line goes along the axis. The hexagon line goes through the west end of the Abbey, in the vicinity of the Lady Chapel, north Porch and the two former western towers. This is an area of powerful energy nodes. The flow of the Mary current of the St Michael Line, which runs along the axis of the Abbey, usually splits into several thinner "streams". Anthony Kennish has produced an excellent guide, *The Glastonbury Chronicles,* containing coloured maps that are both informative and indispensable for following the dowsable energy flows through Glastonbury.

The hexagon line continues a short distance to the westernmost pond, which archaeologists believe was in existence in medieval times. Nearby, an ancient megalith can be found behind the Bishop's Kitchen (see image on page 75). Glastonbury Abbey is a classic example of site evolution/continuity, as it was a sacred place long before Christian missionaries arrived here.

St George slaying the dragon at St John's, Glastonbury.

Chapter 21
The Central Axis

X Wotton-under-Edge

X Long barrow
X Hawkesbury (church)

X Birch Hill

X Hill summit trig point

X Marshfield
X Bathford (church)

X Farleigh Hungerford
X Tellisford (church)
X Rode
X Beckington

X Berkeley Marsh

X Longleat
X Horningsham

X Round Hill
X Brimsdown Hill (tumulus)
X Rodmead Hill (tumuli)
X Burton/Holwell
X White Hill (church)

X King's Court Wood

X Duncliffe Hill
X Hartgrove
X Farrington
X Hambledon Hill

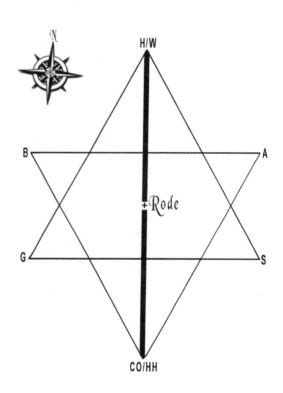

The 52-mile-long Central Axis is the longest alignment of the Wessex Astrum. The line is just a few degrees off north-south, with the northern apex at Holywell/Wotton-under-Edge, and a southern extremity at Hambledon Hill. The midway point is the village of Rode, where the line also converges with both the Samhain and the Beltaine (St Michael Line) alignments. We started our Quest at the northern end of this long axis, working south, and we will describe the line in that order here.

The alignment begins high on Coombe Hill, one of the towering scarps of the Cotswold Edge, and one that overlooks Wotton-under-Edge, which we described in some detail earlier (see page 46 onwards). We ascended the hill to see for ourselves if we could find any features where the Central Axis and the two Blade lines converge. The axis goes along the prominent spur that overshadows Wotton, close to a group of

Up on the heights of Coombe Hill, Wotton, where Astrum Lines converge. Left: dowsing the elongated mound near the reservoir. Right: the round mound with a sunken centre near the end of the spur. Both mounds mark the Central Axis alignment!

pillow mounds, before plunging down into the town. We approached the spur via a woodland footpath from the Old London Road. The scene then opened up at a grassed-over reservoir and, after crossing a stile, we turned right and marvelled at the panoramic views before us. Almost immediately we saw a low, elongated mound to the south of the reservoir, not on any maps. It is right on the Central Axis line and very close to the convergence; our spirits were elated at this revelation.

But there was more to come. We walked south along the high windswept spur, which to us seemed like a huge phallus reaching out into the landscape below. Just as the ground began to fall away we spotted another mound, this time circular with a noticeable depression at its centre (grid ref: 761938). The mound shows up clearly on Google Earth, to the right of a prominent, elongated pillar mound. It had the appearance of a tumulus that had been hollowed out by excavation. We both sat midst this sacred mound and spent time sending healing down all the Astrum lines as they diverged away from us. This was one of the first places we visited on our Quest, and we visualised the lines spreading out across the land, asking that we might be shown further secrets in the months to follow. And as we did so the wind suddenly dropped, falling from strong gusts to a breeze that gently caressed our cheeks. It was as if our prayers had been acknowledged.

The six-pointed star in the clock up the tower of St Mary's.

We came down from Coombe Hill via Adey's Lane, a sunken green way that descends steeply through woods and which is crossed in turn by three Astrum lines. Near the bottom of the lane is an almshouse and on the main street stands Berkeley House, which is on the alignment, and houses a famous carving of the *Genii Loci*, the triple Goddess, found in the Chettles area. The Central Axis passes through Wotton just east of St Mary's church, crossing Valley Road, a quiet lane with sleepy cottages that leads from the church to Holywell. We visited the church one late autumn afternoon, approaching it from the War Memorial. The tower was golden brown, the rays of a low sun illuminating glowing Cotswold Stone. Toni had dowsed a "male" energy current, flowing from the Old Town Meeting House through the War Memorial (see image on page 59), past the Surgery and on to St Mary's. As we approached the church we could see that the tower clock had a six-pointed star design! The original church dates from Saxon times, the present building from 1283. It is a large church, being 120ft long and 72ft wide and its claim to fame is that Mozart once played on its organ. The inside was light and airy and a low sun streamed through stained glass windows. Toni had a feeling that the site might have once been a stone circle and having dowsed the centre of the circle she looked up, to find the largest roof boss was immediately above her! We paused in the St Catherine's Chapel, a side chapel dating from medieval times. It felt a special place, one of great peace, with beautiful windows showing St Catherine, St Agnes and Mary the Mother.

The Central Axis leaves Wotton just yards east of the milestone west of Little Tor Hill (grid ref: 763922). It then runs parallel with the road linking the villages of Worley and Hillesley, crossing fields and rolling hills about ⅓ mile west of it. Near Lovetts Wood Farm, the alignment passes midway between an ancient moat and Abbot's Well, before uncannily following steep scarps either side of Hawkesbury. We were struck by the alignment of Hawkesbury Knoll, Hawkesbury church, and the summits of both Broad Hill and Birch Hill, all within a single mile.

Hawkesbury Knoll Long Barrow stands within 100yds of the centre of the alignment and commands splendid views over the Vale of Berkeley to the River Severn, with the Forest of Dean and the Welsh mountains beyond. The mound is a couple of metres high and we were struck by how it is aligned with (or very close to) the Central Axis!

Hawkesbury is recorded in the Domesday Book, the name deriving literally from *a place where hawks fly*. Evidence exists that the village was the site of a monastic grange and subsequently a medieval manor, and the remains of great fishponds survive behind Church Farm. The original church of St Mary was probably founded in the 7th C, when the manor belonged to Pershore Abbey. The alignment comes down off the Knoll and goes exactly through the church, which is dedicated to St Mary the Virgin. It was recorded back in the 12th C and is on the site of the earlier Saxon church. Most of the present building is 14-15th C and the height of the tower is striking. Next to it, also on the line, is Hawkesbury Manor. The naming of nearby Inglestone Common suggests that at least one standing stone may have once stood in the area.

Left: Hawkesbury church, with the well in the foreground. Right: esoteric symbolism inside the church, including six-pointed stars and a Templar cross.

When we arrived at the church it had just rained, and thick black clouds hung overhead. But as we got out of our car the sun burst through and a double rainbow came out over Hawkesbury Knoll – a truly magical moment. A stream ran by, and it seemed typical that the dedication should be to Mary, as we had often found before at places next to water sources. Varying textures and materials in the walls and bricked-up windows betrayed a long history of modification. The church is normally locked but we met a charming American lady called Ricia, who turned out to be into alternative spirituality and shamanism! She got the keys to the church from a neighbour and showed us around. This was yet another of those magical "chance" meetings during our journey with the Astrum. The interior displays natural stone, which had not been whitewashed as in so many churches. One window shows St Michael slaying a red dragon and on a memorial to Madeline Jenkinson, dated 1922, a shield has two six-pointed stars, a crescent moon, a Masonic hand, and a Templar cross!

Megalith at Culverslade, close to the Central Axis.

Ricia told us that the long barrow was not open to the public as the landowner was not too happy with people walking across his land. It was a bit of a disappointment, but she did tell us that locals thought that the site of the former manor house was in the field to the north, between the long barrow and the church; this would place it exactly on the alignment!

South of Hawkesbury the alignment runs along the summits of both Birch Hill and Broad Hill. Parking up by the roadside north of Upper Chalkley Farm (at grid ref: 767861) we could see both hills; a path to the top can be followed from the road here. Less than a mile south of Birch Hill the line passes straight through a 205m trig point (ref: 771846), which can be accessed from the crossroads to the north. The footpath follows the line for the next half a mile to the A46. Even after this, the track continues to run parallel, be it slightly further to the east. Nearby, to the west, is Horton Court, managed by the National Trust (with restricted openings), with its Norman hall and, reportedly, the oldest rectory in England.

Heading along the Tormarton to Marshfield Road, we passed **Culverslade**, just east of the Axis, and as we did so Toni shouted out, *"There's a megalith by the road!"* Peter turned the car around and we went back to investigate. Sure enough, on the west side of the road, next to the entrance to the property, was a standing stone (grid ref: 784747), about 3ft tall, squarish in shape and about 2ft wide. It had a depression in the top, possibly indicating use as a wayside cross or, still further back in time, as an altar. It also had a "feminine" crack down the side facing away from the road. It stands only ¼ mile east of the very centre of the axis and we were ecstatic at unexpectedly finding this unrecorded stone so close to the line. Toni dowsed a female energy flow which she felt came from the church at Tormarton and ran to the church at Marshfield, our next destination.

Marshfield is a pleasant town, with pubs, tearooms and a plaque on the main street stating, "103 miles to Hyde Park Corner". Marshfield land was a source of income for Lacock Abbey in the 13-14th C. At the Sweet Apples Tea Room we found two framed pictures and info on the Marshfield Mummers, who still perform here on Boxing Day, a continuance of an ancient tradition. The axis line takes in both the modern cross, where three roads meet, the old marketplace and the church, which is dedicated to St Mary the Virgin. The churchyard had been lovingly decorated with flowerbeds on our

Bathford. Left: the church and megalith in the foreground.
Right: gnarled, perforated megaliths under a tree next to the porch.

visit, and we noted winged dragon gargoyles adorning the tower. To the right of the porch we found a curious stone grave cover, which was heavily cup-marked, with a head carved out of one end. Was this a modified megalith? The energy around this stone was readily felt. Inside, the church had a "big" feeling, with a high roof, old exposed stonework and 18th C floor monuments.

The journey from Marshfield to the next site, Bathford, can be undertaken via the minor road south that winds through a river valley which runs parallel with the axis, passing through St Catherine and Northend. Folklore speaks of a sacred well at St Catherine. It was a pleasant wooded drive and to the east we could see the ridge along which the Axis runs. The line then goes through the eastern end of Batheaston, where a record of 1917 speaks of a warm spring with curative properties in the vicinity, giving the village its name. The nearby City of Bath of course developed into a major spa resort due to its hot springs.

More New Megaliths Revealed

Bathford is a pleasant village of Cotswold Stone cottages and hanging baskets, just east of Bath. The church is dedicated to St Swithun and is entered via an ornately carved lychgate. As we approached the porch we immediately noticed a group of small stones, up to 3ft long, nestling under a holy tree to our left. They were of gnarled Cotswold stone and some were perforated with holes. We were very excited by this, and saw it as evidence that the site had been sacred prior to the arrival of the Church. Inside we found not one, but three windows depicting St George and the dragon, with the red Templar cross emblazoned on his armour. Another red dragon was found as a wooden carving behind the piano and, amazingly, the church was carpeted throughout with a red carpet bearing the engrailed cross, another sign of the Templars. More treasures were soon revealed to us. Toni shouted out, "Take a look at this then, you're not going to believe it." She was pointing at a large window at the east end (above and beyond a locked area) that is in the shape of a six-pointed star! The energy of the whole church is powerful, particularly so in the Lady Chapel, home of two of the St George windows.

Back outside, we found three strange stone heads and a Templar cross on the outside wall of the Lady Chapel. From higher up the sloping churchyard we could see The Mount, the hill to the north along which the Axis had crossed. We were also struck by the intervisibility of the church with nearby Little Solsbury Hill (see page 124). But the greatest revelation was left until the end. We crossed over the road from the church to the corner of Ostlings Lane, which marks the alignment as it heads north from the church. There at the corner stood a small standing stone, about 2½ft tall, proudly guarding the wall next to which it stood. We were amazed, for it stood on the axis, and marked the start of Ostlings Lane, which soon turned north, following the Central Axis. Toni dowsed an energy flow that went from the stone, leading her to a half-buried stone to the left of the lychgate (which we had not noticed earlier) and on through the megaliths next to the porch. A male flow from the Ostlings Lane standing stone went through the lychgate (pausing to spiral beneath it) before passing through the tall war memorial cross (phallic symbolism) and subsequently entering the church through the porch. All in all, what a magical place it is.

From Bathford, the Central Axis heads south, crossing the Avon four times; it passes

Farleigh Hungerford Castle.

through the bridge over the river at Claverton, past the mast at Conkwell, skirts Winsley (just west of church) and crosses the Avon twice more before reaching **Farleigh Hungerford**. During the Roman occupation, Fairleigh Hungerford stood within the catchment area of Bath (known as Aqua Sulis) and supplied the food, fruit and wine for the Roman legions on leave in the sophisticated recreational town. To the east of the Castle ruins, the field is terraced and this may be the site of vineyards. In 1822, the foundations of a villa, *"... of considerable dimensions"*, was excavated in a field just NW of the Castle; it included a bath, a number of apartments and a quantity of Roman coins.

Farleigh Hungerford is noted for its Castle, now a ruin, which played a significant part in the English Civil War. The castle was begun in the 1370s by Sir Thomas Hungerford, Speaker of the Commons, on the site of a former Norman manor overlooking the River Frome. It was extended in the 15th C by his son, Sir Walter Hungerford, an Agincourt veteran and distinguished medieval statesman. The remains of their fortress includes two tall corner towers, along with a walled outer court incorporating the castle chapel of St Leonard, once the only church in the village. Crowded with fine family monuments and bedecked with wall-paintings, the chapel stands above a crypt containing lead coffins of 16th - 17th C Hungerfords. These have 'death masks' of the deceased, said to be the best examples of their type in Britain. The castle is now in the care of English Heritage, and has limited opening times. Even if closed, one can view the castle through the entrance and from the car park of the nearby Hungerford Arms.

St Leonard's Church, west of the castle, stands exactly on the axis. The church is situated just north of the brow of a hill, overlooking the Frome valley. It is usually locked and the keys are held at the Castle nearby (which is open most days in summer, but only weekends in winter). The church was built in 1407 but not consecrated until 1443.

It is worth noting that the master dowser Guy Underwood visited the village. In his 1969 classic, *The Pattern of the Past,* he tells how an apple tree damaged by lightening had a twisted trunk, indicative of an earth energy node or flow. He noted how the new growth of the upper branches continued to grow in a twisting manner even though they were growing at right angles to the trunk. He associated this unidentified site with an underground water line.

Mary Magdalene is the primary focus of the congregation, in this east window at Tellisford.

Mary Magdalene Centre Stage

The next destination on the line is **Tellisford,** a village four miles NE of Frome, and one that inspired 1930's author Arthur Mee to write, *"We do not remember a more charming place in all our journeyings".* It is located on the River Frome, which is spanned by the medieval Pack Horse Bridge. The parish church of All Saints stands within yards of the axis, at the west end of the hamlet, and dates back to the 12th C. Built of Doulting Stone, the same as was used at Wells Cathedral, the church was remoulded in the 13-14th C and restored in 1854. The approach to the church is a long, enclosed passageway and we both dowsed an energy current, which ran down the passage in a very serpentine manner. We visited the church in November 2007 and it was nice to find that the church was open from dawn to dusk. We arrived just after a wedding, to find confetti strewn on the floor outside and flowers bedecking the interior. Approaching the church we saw a carving of three interlocking sickles up the 15th C tower, which is the escutcheon of the Hungerford family. We saw, however, that the interlocking blades actually form a vesica!

The arch over the door is the original late-Norman stonework and on entering the interior our attention was drawn to the main window behind the altar; the central character was Mary Magdalene, bedecked in red and kneeling in front of two angels, her jar at her feet. Jesus had been "relegated" to a window at the west end of the church, and it was clear that the congregation's focus should be the image of Mary Magdalene. Two small mats also caught our attention, as they each depicted four converging vesicas, surrounded by five-pointed flowers. Excavations at the church had uncovered a *"Maltese Cross"* (symbol of the Knights Templar) on the underside of one of the paving stones in the porch. It was now clear to us why Mary Magdalene was centre stage in the church.

Back outside, Toni found a 6ft long stone incorporated in the eastern wall of the churchyard. We wondered if this had formerly been a megalith from somewhere in the area. At the crossroads nearby, a milepost told us that Rode, our next destination, was only one mile to the south. The sign stands on a slight mound with some large stones protruding from it. Were these further evidence that either megaliths or a wayside cross had once stood at this ancient crossroads?

Rode – Hub of the Astrum

The town of Rode is located where the Central, Samhain and Beltaine alignments of the Astrum converge; the Central Axis skirts the west end of the town, the Samhain axis enters the town via the northern bridge over the Frome whilst, in a likewise manner, the Beltaine alignment crosses the southern bridge. The first mention of Rode appears in the Domesday Book, whilst in *Somerset Folklore,* Ruth Tongue records a *Puck Well* in Rode, which people resorted to for eye troubles. The old

A green dragon and other symbolism graces this monument to Elizabeth I in the church at Beckington.

village centre (formerly known as Rode Major) was around St Lawrence church on the main road. Formerly a market town, Rode rose to prominence as a trading centre on the borders of Wiltshire and Somerset. In 1822 Colt Hoare wrote about a monastic foundation in the vale NE of Rode, founded by King Stephen, the hospital of which treated women and priests with leprosy.

The parish church of St Lawrence suffers from its close proximity to the busy A361. The church dates from the late 14th and 15th C and was restored in 1874. The tower has a railed battlement at one corner, called the King's Chair, from a tradition that Charles II mounted it for reconnoitering after the Battle of Worcester. Folklore says of the church that it is haunted by a dark-clad monk, who walks towards the altar prior to disappearing. In *The Sun and the Serpent,* Miller and Broadhurst followed the Michael current of the St Michael Line from the church to the nearby Neolithic site called The Devil's Bed and Bolster (grid ref: 815533), which is well worth a visit. We shall return to Rode soon, in Chapter 22, to describe Christ Church and the megalith we found next to it, for they stand on the Beltaine Line.

Next down the Central Axis is **Beckington**. The origin of the name is probably *Becca's people*, who were possibly the English who arrived following Rome's withdrawl from Britain. It is mentioned in the Domesday Book as "Beckintone", and that the land was owned by Roger Arundel. Beckington Abbey (which never was an Abbey but rather a hostelry for Augustinian canons), was built about 1156 and a 12th C record speaks of this land and property being given to *"The Order of St John of Jerusalem"*, the Knights Hospitallers. In 1347 it was converted to a college for priests and it may later have been an Abbey Grange, connected with Wells. Beckington prospered in the Middle Ages as a result of the wool trade and by the 15th C mills were established along the banks of the River Frome and the cottage industries of spinning and weaving were thriving. Charles II is reputed to have spent a night in the village after his defeat at the Battle of Worcester. As well as the parish church of St George, there is also a Baptist chapel, built in 1786 and a Methodist chapel, built in the Gothic style in 1871. The 1891 map shows a nunnery to the west of the village crossroads, just west of the axis.

The church of St George, Beckington, stands just 150yds west of the centre of the axis. The dedication is likely to be an ancient one, as a St George's Day fair was granted to the village in 1318. The church is "wide", almost box-like, a style we had found in other churches north of Bristol. Entering via the north porch, we turned left to the altar of the Chapel of John the Baptist, who is portrayed in two windows, and here the energies were powerfully felt. This saint is of course closely associated with the Knights Templar. A striking feature of the chapel is two stone lions, whose heads are turned to face the onlooker. Elsewhere in the church, stained glass windows depicting St George and St Catherine are notable, in particular the wonderful depiction of Catherine's

The Longleat Estate stands on the Central Axis.

flaming wheel. Other points of interest are a stone green man and the painted coat of arms of Elizabeth I, with its green dragon (image above).

From Beckington, the Central Axis runs just east of St George's Cross and on to **Berkley Marsh**, where it passes through both Fairoak Farm and Berkley Cross. The line crosses the A362 before passing right through a property named on the 1891 maps at *Stonenge* (*Stonehenge* minus the *"he"*).The line goes through High House Farm, which on old maps is called Mad Doctor's or Martock's Farm, before entering the Longleat Estate.

The *Sacred Cradle* of Longleat

For us, one of our greatest finds is that the Central Axis goes right through **Longleat**, the centre of the axis passing just east of the house, running more-or-less parallel with the N-S orientated lakes, which the axis crosses. These water features are enhancements of an ancient river flowing north from Horningsham. The estate marks the Somerset-Wiltshire border and has been a sacred area for millenia. Cley Hill rises just east of here and the village of Temple nearby suggests the Knights Templar settled hereabouts. Interestingly, a line can be drawn from Gare Hill (on the Dod Line), through Longleat House and on to the church at Temple.

The present Marquess of Bath, Alexander Thynn, has written a series of books about Longleat and his family history, entitled *Strictly Private to Public Exposure*. In *Book 1: The Early Years* (pub. 2002) he considers that, *"...Longleat has always been a holy site. They would say that Wessex abounds in such sites, and that Glastonbury, Stonehenge and Avebury are the prominent examples. Yet strategically, at the centre of this triangle stands Longleat, which may have been the holiest of them all. They speculate that long before the priory there was an even holier place. They point to the saucer-shaped cradle of the park..."*. He continues about the association of the area with UFOs, and memories flood back of the nearby Warminster Triangle UFO sightings.

As with several other Astrum sites, Longleat was the site of a medieval religious foundation. Longleat Priory stood on the site of the present house in the 13th C, and was dedicated to St Radegund. It was occupied by the *"Black Canons of the*

The Central Axis follows the N-S lakes that pass just east of Longleat House.

Order of Augustine". By all accounts, the Augustinian priory was always a small and poor establishment, which failed as a going concern, even throughout the pilgrimage-obsessed Middle Ages. In 1324 land at Horningsham and Longbridge Deverill was given to the Priory to help raise income, but in 1529 it was eventually supressed. The Monks' fishponds still survive today, and, according to, *A History of Wiltshire* (1956, Ed. R B Pugh), *"...the remains of the priory must now be sought in the cellars of Longleat House"*. In 1530 the property became a manor or grange, belonging to the Carthusian monks of Hinton Charterhouse. Following the Dissolution, Sir John Thynne bought the estate from the Crown in 1540, including the ruins of the priory, and it has been in the Thynne family ever since. Some years later, his great wealth gave rise to rumours that he had found buried treasure on the estate. He had been making changes to the old priory over several years, but in 1567 it was burnt down and he started work on the present house, which was completed 12 years later. Henry VIII liked the new Italian architectural influence and Longleat was one of the first English houses to be built wholly in this style. Elizabeth I rested at Longleat in 1574, on her way to Bristol, and Charles II and Queen Catherine stayed there on their way to Bath, where it was hoped that the water might help the Queen produce an heir.

Spectral apparitions have also occurred at the house; one corridor is named after the apparition of a green lady, and the spirit of Cardinal Wolsey has also been reported. Black Dog Hill at Longleat is named from a spectral dog said to haunt it.

On our visit to Longleat we stood alongside the lakes, looking to where the axis passed large trees, and through the waterfall; it then crosses the lakes, leaving the grounds through the arch of the southern gatehouse. We went down into the cellars below the House, which now serve as the café and a gift shop. Large, worn flagstones lay underfoot, possible remnants of the priory, reused in later times. Some whitewashed walls in both the café and the corridors were clearly of rough stone, contrasting with the walls and arches of brick above them. The energies in these underground passages and rooms was stongly felt by both of us, and were also palpable in front of the house, at the bottom of the stone steps.

Next to the east end of the house are the Sun Maze and the Lunar Labyrinth, made from 10,000 box plants, and a plaque tells the story of their planting and the mythology they represent. They reminded us of the male and female, yin and yang, solar and lunar nature of the two interlocking triangles of the Wessex Astrum. From the plaque we could look to the eastern banks of the lake, along which the Central Axis line proceeded.

Also in the grounds of Longleat is Dod Pool, named on 1:25,000 maps. The head guide at Longleat did not know the origin of the name, but to us it was a reminder of the Dod Line and Dod Lane, both of which we had encountered previously. From this pond (grid ref: 827434) we looked down across the bowl that is Longleat, with the grand house nestling in the bottom.

The line then leaves the grounds of Longleat, passing through the south arch, and goes through **Horningsham**. Six tracks diverge on the village centre – all shown on old maps. The main road linking the parish church and the centre of village is called White Lane, which the line crosses. The village is mentioned in the Domesday Book and has always been closely associated with Longleat House. A stream called

Redford Water rises in the village and feeds the lakes of Longleat. One source of this stream is Town Well, found near the top of Water Lane, close to the War Memorial cross (grid ref: 817412). It was called the Cross Well on 1891 maps, suggesting that an older cross may have preceded the WWI monument. Water issues from the ground, some of which is channelled through a small stone shelter, with an angled roof which bears what looks like a worn hexagram! The water is cold and fresh, with a slight irony taste. The flow can be followed downhill, to where it feeds the Mill Pond.

Horningsham, on the Longleat Estate. Left: the well at the top of Watery Lane.
Right: the hexagram inside the church of St John the Baptist.

Just east of here, at the top of the hill, stands the parish church of St John the Baptist. When Sir Robert de Vernon, Lord of Horningsham, built this church in 1154 he picked a beautiful setting. The views to the south are stunning, and the lakes and the south gatehouse can be seen below, marking the course of the Central Axis. The church was extensively rebuilt in 1783 and 1843 and only parts of the medieval tower survive. The population in 1841 was 1290, so the old church was too small; the new church accommodated 700 people. This was important, as at this time all Lord Bath's tenants and workers were required to attend church every Sunday. The main east window shows the Crucifixion, with a grief-stricken Mary Magdalene at the foot of the cross. The narrow window to the left (north side) of the altar shows various Biblical scenes, but our attention was drawn to a hexagram at the top. Behind the organ another window has beautiful, multi-coloured, sacred geometrical designs, incorporating four and eight-fold (grounding) symbolism. A window at the west end shows Zacharias, Elizabeth (mother of John the Baptist) and John himself. Back outside, we found a finely carved hexagram next to a door in the south wall of the chancel. Above it is carved THIS IS MY REST FOREVER HERE WILL I DWELL.

Around the other side, the north porch is decorated with two fine, female foliated heads. Periodically, Morris dancers still perform at the church.

The centre of the line passes just east of the chapel (next to the post office), built for Presbyterian Scottish stonemasons employed in rebuilding Longleat House; the area around the Pub is still known as Scotland. This beautiful thatched building is dated 1566 and the atmosphere inside is peaceful. Now known as the Old Meeting House, it is said to be oldest of its type still in use for worship. The chapel was enlarged in 1754 and 1860, and is approached down a gently descending cobbled path.

The line leaves Horningsham via Pottle Street, where a map of 1773 shows a collection of houses known as Little Horningsham. It then runs up to the top of **Round Hill**, where it crosses the Glastonbury-Stonehenge Dod Line, precisely at the 165m spot height. From here it crosses to **Brimsdown Hill**, where the line goes straight through a Bronze Age tumulus (grid ref: 816392), which is situated where the hill narrows to a ridge. Three footpaths enable inspection of the mound. From here, the line passes just west of Newmead Farm, before rising to the top of **Rodmead Hill**. The summit of this hill is a 229m spot height (grid ref: 819360), and to the east are two tumuli (only shown on 1:25,000 maps) that are located precisely on the alignment! Another tumuli and an earthen enclosure (at grid ref: 819366) are just yards east of the line, and yet another mound stands to the south (at grid ref: 821349) - exactly on the line! Likewise, neither of these three monuments are on 1:50,000 scale maps. We thought it amazing that four tumuli and an enclosure, not shown on smaller scale maps, should all be on or very close to the line, which also goes through the summit of the hill.

The line then decends the chalk scarp and goes along Chetcombe Bottom, between two prominent spurs. The axis does not go through the centre of Mere, but instead passes through the west end of **Burton**, only yards to the east of **Holwell** (not named

on the 1:50,000 scale maps). The name indicates yet another sacred well or spring close to or on an Astrum line. In 1495, a spring associated with St Osmund was documented, but we have not been able to trace its exact locality. Burton is a charming hamlet, with mill ponds, a waterwheel and a lovely riverside path that follows the swift-flowing Ashfield Water, crossing the Central Axis line

The huge mound at Mere. Tumuli on the nearby ridge indicate that the hill was sacred prior to the arrival of the Normans. The views from here are glorious.

350yds west of the mill. A tumulus can be accessed (grid ref: 826325) in the field to the east of the mill, immediately north of an ancient sunken green lane that continues east as a public footpath. As we approached the ancient mound a large buzzard circled overhead, as if leading the way. The mound is peppered with the holes of a rabbit warren, and the energies felt powerful.

The centre of Mere warrants a visit, in particular the huge chalk knoll which overshadows the town, and which we had long been drawn to, even before the current book arose. Ducal Castle was built on the summit, although the prominent hill was used for ritual purposes prior to this, as four tumuli west of the castle testify. The natural slopes of the hill, circled with beech trees, give way to the enhanced Norman mound at the top. The climb is worth the effort, with fine views in every direction. The tree-covered slopes of Duncliffe Hill can be seen to the south (also on the Central Line), obscuring Hambledon Hill, the line's termination, beyond. Below is the fine church of St Michael, described by Colt Hoare in 1822 as, *"...amongst the best structures in South Wiltshire"*. The Willoughby family of Mere had a heraldic shield displaying engrailed crosses, so prominent at Roslyn Chapel. Also of interest is a document of 1650 stating that the Abbot of Scone, in Scotland, was given the responsibility for the custody of Richard de Chiseldon, who was held at Mere castle.

From Ashfield Water the line continues south to **White Hill** (= *Holy Hill*), and the redundant church of St Matthew, which stands just yards west of the axis (grid ref: 824307). The present building was built in 1882 as a "mission" church. When we visited in February 2007, the vacant building was on the market as a private residence, so we could not examine the interior. We saw that the east end of the church was built to a semi-circular design, so often favoured by the Templars, and so often copied since. We could make out stained glass windows and one was dated 1914. A sad epitaph to the church was its final list of services, still posted on the notice board, dated May 2004.

South of the church the line follows the road briefly, crossing from Wiltshire into Dorset at White Hill Common, before passing right through the middle of King's Court Wood, east of Gillingham. This wood is the largest surviving piece of the Royal Estate of Gillingham Forest, a huge forest in which stood King's Court Palace, the Royal hunting lodge ½ mile west of the Central Line axis. The Palace site (grid ref: 818263) can be accessed via King's Court Road and a footpath. Earthen banks enclose a 300ft x 170ft interior, with an entrance at the SW corner, and during wet weather the moat still partially fills with water. It is possible that timber structures may have been present here as early as the reign of William II. King John held a *feast for the poor* here in 1203 and fortified the site between 1204 and 1211, when a chapel was built. A second chapel was erected 1249, and yet more buildings were erected by Henry III in 1252-5. In these times the forest occupied nearly all the land between King's Court Wood and White Hill, the previous Central Axis site. In 1369 Edward III ordered the demolition of all the buildings, although the last remaining stones were not removed until the late 18th C for the construction of the Shaftesbury-Gillingham road. We felt strong energies at the east end of the site, where dowsing revealed spirals, suggesting the position of a chapel. From here a strong energy flow left the

Duncliffe Hill from the north, as the Central Axis approaches the hill. Its tree-covered, double summits are a local landmark. There may have been a Roman temple on the higher summit.

site where the bank is lower, going east towards the woods. To the south, can be seen both Melbury Beacon and Duncliffe Hill (two Astrum hills) on the skyline.

The axis then runs along the east slopes of **Duncliffe Hill**, the prominent tree-covered Greensand outlier that rises to 690ft out of the meadows of the Blackmore Vale. The presence of a Romano-British temple on the hill was implied by votive offerings found in the 1980s, which may be associated with a *circular entrenchment* recorded by John Hutchins, and then by Charles Warne in the 19th C. Nothing has been shown on any OS maps, however, and further research is hampered by the thick woodland that now carpets the hill. From the west and east, the hill can be seen to have two summits, the highest being the northern one, reminding us of other twinned hill sites that are thought to represent the breasts of the Earth Mother. There is a local saying, *"As old as Duncliffe"*, to express something or someone being particularly aged, and Thomas Hardy featured the hill in *Jude the Obscure*. The following local verse concerns the appearance of the hill with regards foretelling the weather:

"If Duncliffe Wood be fair and clear,
You Stour Boys need have no fear,
But if Duncliffe Wood do wear its cap,
You Marnhull folk look out for that."

The line leaves Duncliffe following the track to Jadewood Farm (grid ref: 833221) and next up along the axis is **Hartgrove,** a small village which first appears on documents in 1254. On a 1748 map of Dorset by Thomas and John Osborne, *Hargrave* is the only village marked between Shaftesbury and Sturminster Newton. In the 18th C, historian John Hutchins described it as *Hargrove* and that it was, *"..anciently a manor, now a hamlet and a farm"*. He also described a chapel, built in the early English style with a 42x 21ft nave, and a west bell turret. Nothing is present on modern OS maps, but we found it marked on one dated 1811 (at grid ref: 837182). This site is just yards east of the centre of the alignment! Church Lane goes south from the main village road near this spot, but no remains of this building appear to have survived. Interestingly, the lane mirrors the course of the Astrum line for half a mile. On the 1887 OS map, however, we found *Church (site of)* further to the east of here (grid ref: 842182), immediately west of Hartgrove Farm. In the field today can be seen a sunken platform, 30ft x 40ft and orientated E-W. So was there a single church, shown in the wrong place on one of the maps, or was there two?

The Methodists were later to build not one, but two, chapels in this tiny village, both of which were even closer to the axis of the Central line. The first was built in 1826, but in 1881 a larger one, dedicated to St Peter, was built just yards to the east, which is now *The Old Chapel*. The earlier chapel was thereafter used as a sunday school hall. These two chapels served the sparsely populated areas of East and West Orchard and Margaret Marsh, whose populace were said to have been, *"... fervent and supportive"*. The chapel was closed in the mid-70's and both buildings are now

The former Methodist chapel at Hartgrove stands close to the Central Axis, with fine views south to Hambledon Hill,

private houses. Standing in front of the chapel, the round window is noticeable for its six-petalled design – six was with us again. And, of real relevance, was the fact that the chapel axis was aligned with Hambledon Hill, visible to the south. We had come across this before; at Avebury, for example, the chapel opposite the pub is almost N-S aligned with the Michael and Mary energy flows. At Knowlton, on Cranborne Chase, the ruined church is aligned with the Beltaine sunrise, and there are countless other examples.

From outside the chapel we could see Hambledon Hill in the distance, and we were aware of how high we were above the Blackmore Vale. We were satisfied that the location of three (or four?) former places of worship, one of which is in alignment with the line, and all of which stood on a prominent ridge, was not coincidence.

East Orchard church is sited just 300m from the axis, and contains the font from the lost church at Hartgrove; the two churches must have been intervisible. The line then continues south, crossing Fontmell Brook just west of Farrington Bridge, before striking right through Applin's Farm.

Farrington is another small hamlet north of Hambledon Hill, and which is notable today for the Dorset Centre for Rural Skills. Older OS maps show a chapel at the road junction (grid ref: 842151). This is the redundant chapel of St John the Baptist, the saint whom we know was venerated by the Knights Templar. It was rebuilt in 1839 and at that time still retained a 12th C font, described by John Hutchins in the 19th C. On the 1891 map there is also a *Chalybeate Spring*, just north of the crossroads. We arrived at the spot not knowing if the chapel had been demolished or, as has often happened, been converted into a residence; it turned out to be neither. We found a padlocked door barring us from the small, and very obviously closed, chapel. At least it had survived and, looking at the well-tended churchyard lawn and potted plants, was still being lovingly cared for by local residents. On our second visit we obtained the keys from a cottage opposite; but going inside was depressing indeed – all the fixtures and fittings had been stripped away and the interior was full to bursting with household goods, boxes and furniture, which were obviously in storage. Our sadness was relieved somewhat as we saw one delight, a stained glass window behind where the altar would have been. A scene of the Crucifixion was depicted, and at the foot of the cross was the sole figure of a mourning, praying Mary Magdalene, alabastar jar at her feet, a scene we had seen elsewhere on Astrum lines.

The former chapel of St John the Baptist at Farrington.

The lane opposite runs past thatched cottages and comes to a stile, leading to a path that continues south to Hambledon Hill itself, the southern terminal point of the Wessex Astrum, looming high to the south. The line then passes right through the centre of Shroton Brake, a small wood shown on the 1891 OS map.

The Central Axis then climbs the steep slopes of Hambledon Hill where it terminates at the 604ft spot height (marked on the map on page 117). Here it also converges with the Magdalene Line that comes down from Glastonbury. We stood here on this hallowed spot on a beautifully calm and sunny October afternoon, looking down the Central Axis Line, It felt incredible that we had stood at the other end of the line, on Wotton Hill, some 52 miles to the north, just a few weeks earlier, looking in the opposite direction towards where we now stood. We could see the twinned wooded peaks of Duncliffe Hill before us, and the uplands of Wiltshire basking in the mist beyond. We really got the feeling that everything was connected on the sacred landscape of our ancestors, and that nothing existed in isolation. We only need a shift in our perceptions to see our world like this today. We are all part of the whole.

Chapter 22
The Beltaine Alignment - St Michael Revisited

X Chalice Well
X Glastonbury Tor

X North Wootton
X Knowle Hill

X Shepton Mallet (north side)
X Downside

X Stoke St Michael

X Vobster

X Buckland Dinham

X Laverton

X Rode

X Trowbridge (Studley and moat)

X Seend Cleeve
X Seend

X Sells Green/Martinslade

X Mother Anthony's Well
X Oliver's Castle/tumuli

X Three Barrows tumuli

X Beckington (stones and barrow)
X Avebury

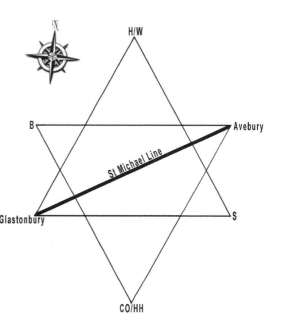

One of the most convincing arguments for the Wessex Astrum being authentic is that the St Michael Line, the world-famous Beltaine sunrise alignment, is one of the defining configurations of the hexagram. The diagonal axis connecting two points of the Astrum, namely Glastonbury and Avebury, follows this alignment. The stretch involved is 43 miles in length and the angle is around 63° off true north, or 66° off the Glastonbury-Brockley line. This alignment is where the sun rises today between May 3-6th today, which was formerly during Beltaine festivities. In the opposite direction the line marks sunset around 2nd-5th November, just days after the traditional date for Samhain. This Beltaine sunrise line also forms one side of a triangle defined by Glastonbury, Stonehenge and Avebury, one angle of which is almost exactly 90°. We set out to revisit the sites that fell within the Astrum, seeking new insights and further confirmation that the designers of the hexagram were aware of the existence of this ancient alignment. Before we tell of our site visits, a short recap of the details and history of this famous line might be timely.

The alignment was named from the number of churches and hills dedicated to St Michael, the dragon-slaying Archangel, that stand on it. Two of the key factors are that the line is aligned with the rising of the sun around May Day, originally Beltaine, one of the ancient fire festivals; it is also the longest line one can draw across England from the west to the east coast. The axis of the alignment runs for over 350 miles, from Carn Lês Boel in Cornwall up to Hopton in East Anglia, passing through many important sacred sites *en route*, such as St Michael's Mount, Avebury, Glastonbury, Royston Cave and Bury St Edmonds.

Reference was first made to the alignment in the 1950's by mystic Ithell Colquhoun in her book *The Living Stones*, linking it to the Knights Templar and Arthurian traditions. In *The View Over Atlantis,* published in 1969, John Michell noted how often St Michael sites stood on the alignment. His proposal that Christian sites dedicated to St Michael had replaced former pagan places on ancient alignments was controversial at the time, a process now known as site evolution or site continuity.

With this in mind, Paul Broadhurst and Hamish Miller entered centre stage. Their study of the alignment proceeded quite literally step-by-step, dowsing rods in hand, up and down the ley over several years. Miller and Broadhurst advocated that at many places ancient esoteric knowledge was used to position sacred places, and that symbolism used in church architecture reflects this lost knowledge. Many see *The Sun and the Serpent* as a masterpiece of dowsing and geomantic study, whilst others have dismissed it.

Over several years, they tracked the ley and its two energy flows, finding dragons, serpents, spirals, and other strange carvings in Church architecture, confirming to them that earth energy currents were somehow interacting with the axis of the ley. They likened this phenomenon to the caduceus of classical mythology and architecture, seeing the two serpents entwining around a central staff as symbolic of the two energy currents associated with the ley. They named these flows Michael and Mary, which were the male and female, yang and yin cosmic forces. In many places the two energy courses leave the main axis for miles, ambling across the land in a serpentine manner. When they converge, such as at Glastonbury, Avebury, St

Michael's Mount, Bury St Edmunds, Royston Cave and Creech St Michael, the yin and yang energies are powerfully balanced and in fact determined the original design and choice of location of these sacred sites.

Miller and Broadhurst came across many images of St Michael slaying a dragon, but on occasions it was St George or St Margaret who were slaying the poor beast. Churches and wells dedicated to Mary also cropped up, and it was suggested that these replaced former places of the Goddess. Where churches were not dedicated to these saints, Miller and Broadhurst often found that dedications of several had *originally* been dedicated to dragon slayers.

An image encountered several times on our Astrum travels is that of St John the Apostle (otherwise known as John the Divine) holding a chalice from which is emerging a beautiful blue dragon. This man was particularly loved by Jesus and was in fact the first disciple of John the Baptist. Officially, it is said that the serpent is rising from the chalice that represents either the "cup of sorrow" foretold by Jesus, or that John survived the drinking of poison from a cup, due to his faith. To us, it represents the life force of the Earth (the dragon) rising out of the Divine Feminine (the Chalice). What is relevant here is that one of St John's feast days is on May 8, during the Beltaine festivities, a time associated with the St Michael Line.

One thing that became apparent to us was that Miller and Broadhurst's emphasis had been to follow the two energy currents, which meant that *most of the sites on the actual axis of the alignment were not described by them*; their remit was to track the energy currents, not the axis. This meant that we really were going over new ground, in describing churches and other places that were located on, or very near, the actual alignment. We were visiting many sacred sites that had not been described in Hamish and Paul's classic book.

What we find of interest is that Miller and Broadhurst quote (on page 23 of *The Sun and the Serpent*) the findings of statistician Robert Forrest: *"... if the St Michael Line is regarded as a "corridor" or "route" rather than a straight line, then the coincidences [of churches associated with the line] multiply. If a tolerance of 500 metres is allowed either side of the line its entire length, then no less than 63 churches fall within the boundary."* It is interesting that we had reached a similar conclusion as far as regarding the Astrum lines as "corridors", and we had quite independently decided that our corridors should be a maximum 1 km wide, i.e. 500m each side of the axis!

John Michell calls the alignment, *"... one of the wonders of prehistoric engineering."* But, as already mentioned, David Furlong has cast a critical eye over the accuracy of the St Michael alignment, in his book *The Keys to the Temple*. His computer analysis of the axis found that although Burrowbridge Mump, Glastonbury Tor, Avebury and the church at Ogbourne St George lined up to within metres, other sites, such as St Michael's Mount, The Hurlers and Bury St Edmunds, were out by up to 2718 metres. He concluded that, *"...the rest of the St Michael Line is merely wishful thinking."* We found it comforting that the only truly straight section of the St Michael Line falls within the Wessex Astrum. So the question has to be asked; which came first – the St Michael Line or the Wessex Astrum!

Recent work by David Furlong, announced by him on the stage at Megalithomania 2008, has shown that the St Michael Line was also in alignment with Orion's Belt around 2,800 BC, confirming the work of other writers that we should look for stellar alignments for leys, and not just solar and lunar ones.

Glastonbury Revisited

The Beltaine Line, as defined by the Wessex Astrum, begins at the Chalice Well, one of the most sacred and peaceful localities of Glastonbury. The water rises from the ground at a steady rate of 25,000 gallons per day and has never been known to dry up, even in the severest drought. The water has a high iron content, leaving a red deposit on the rocks, leading it to being called the Red Well. This would have been a healing locality in prehistory, the colour being viewed as the blood of the Goddess. The Holy Grail is said to be hidden beneath the well, brought here by Joseph of Arimathea, and which bestows healing powers to the water. One man in the 18th C issued a sworn statement of how, after suffering from asthma for thirty years, he was miraculously cured after taking the waters of the well on seven consecutive Sundays. 10,000 people descended on the well in one month alone and it became a popular spa.

Energetically, the well and gardens are very powerful, at times uplifting, at other

The Chalice Well. This ancient sacred place is said to be the resting place of the Grail. The vesica piscis is seen on both the well-head cover and at the large pool.

times calming and grounding. Both the Mary and Michael flows of the St Michael Line surge through the gardens, and cross each other twice, at the waterfall and the Lion's Head fountain. The Mary flow follows the water from the wellhead down the slope, through the waterfall, between two yews and through the vesica piscis pool.

From here the alignment goes through the White Well, which was recently reopened and is now beautifully bedecked with altars, shrines and indoor pools, created with much love and reverence by Glastonbury people. The rooms are damp, dark, candlelit and full of peaceful energy and atmosphere.

233

The earliest record of a Christian church on the Tor is from 1234, when Henry III gave his royal seal of approval for a fair to be held *"... at the monastery of St Michael on the Tor"*. It is hardly surprising that a church was built on this major Goddess centre, and St Michael is a common dedication at hilltop locations where pagan worship had been rife. He is the dragon slayer, a fitting figure to place on the Tor, with its serpentine spiralling path and powerful earth energies. On one side of the tower is a much-eroded figure of the archangel with dragon under foot.

It is well-known that the Tor stands on the St Michael Line. The long axis of the Tor actually aligns with the ley, running approximately WSW to ENE. The Michael and Mary flows do not, however, beat a direct path to the summit, but rather travel in spiralling trails, often following geological/processional ridges. To their surprise, Miller and Broadhurst found that at the summit both currents make a point of avoiding the tower, before descending the hill to resume their journey to Avebury and beyond. They found that around the summit the pattern of the Mary current formed a chalice, into which the Michael energies flowed. They saw this as a *"ritual mating"* of the two polarities, a harmonious cosmic interaction on the sacred hill. In his book, *Energy Secrets of Glastonbury Tor,* Nicholas Mann sees the Tor as a vehicle channelling a huge vortex of energy, *"... the point of connection with and energy input from the heavenly dimension"*, playing out the ancient concept of the Axis Mundi, the World Mountain which, mythologically, received

Glastonbury Tor, capped by the tower of St Michael. It is one of the defining sites of the St Michael Line, and powerful energies flow around its sacred slopes.

lightening (i.e. cosmic energy *and* Divine knowledge) from the Gods. Various myths link the hill with King Arthur, the Goddess, and the Fairy King. Certainly the hill has a pull of two dimensions; there is the physical desire to climb a sacred hill and follow in the footsteps of our ancestors. But this act also fulfils a spiritual need, to symbolically reach toward our own aspirations. The Goddess was invoked at hilltop ceremonies in ancient times, and no doubt there would have been processions from the town, as there are today at certain festivals. The labyrinthine pattern on the slopes of the Tor is a result of enhancing natural features and is thought by many to have been created long before Celtic times, its designers making good use of the natural striations offered by the geology. Labyrinths are archetypal patterns of the human mind, representing the turning path we take to inner enlightenment. In her book, *In the Nature of Avalon,* Kathy Jones beautifully describes in detail how to walk the labyrinth, relating its seven circuits to the human chakras.

Standing on top of the Tor is an exhilarating and uplifting experience. The Somerset levels are spread out below, with the Mendips rising to the north. To the northeast, the tower of North Wootton church can be seen in the distance, with the summit of Knowle Hill beyond. These are our next destinations on the Beltaine Line. Before then, the axis passes close to Gog and Magog, the sacred ancient oaks of Avalon, before passing through three farms on the Somerset Levels.

North Wootton is the next village on the line, and we approached it from the west, along the road from Launcherley, where a large white dragon, recently created on Launcherley Hill, gazes back to the Tor. We approached the village and noticed apple orchards thickly endowed with countless clumps of mistletoe, a sign of powerful earth energies. The village was visited by Miller and Broadhurst, where they dowsed the Michael current of the St Michael Line flowing though the church, which is dedicated

to St Peter. They describe it as, *"... an intimate little gem with a remarkable drunken font, which leads you to consider that the holy water hereabouts must be a lively brew"*. They do not describe any more details about the church, which is situated in the quiet village served by the babbling River Redlake, which flows off the Mendips. The exact age of the church is unrecorded, but thought to be 15th C. Up the tower, fine gargoyles returned our gaze and to the left of the porch is a guttering feature dated

Hexagram on the lectern at North Wootton.

1869 that incredibly displays a six-pointed star! Noteworthy inside is a copy of Botticelli's *Madonna with Child*, near the altar, and there is also that lopsided font. We were delighted to find a carved six-pointed star on the wooden lectern, a feature we had seen carved on pulpits elsewhere, and tiles around the altar with six-petalled flowers. The east window shows Jesus in the centre, St Peter to the left, and St Andrew, patron saint of nearby Wells Cathedral, on the right. The windows of the two saints are bordered by the *Mystic Rose* of the Virgin Mary.

From North Wootton the line crosses **Knowle Hill**, just yards north of the summit, before passing just south of a small rise known as Friar's Oven. The line soon encounters a ridge at the ancient crossroads of Stump Cross (grid ref: 597432). It is named as such on 1888 OS maps but no other features appear at the crossroads. Was there once an old stone cross here, or perhaps a megalith? There is a *Stump Cross* megalith at Mereclough in Lancashire. We could not see the Tor from here, because of the trees that now cover Knowle Hill, but from a small lay-by just to the south we could see virtually the entire Tor, right down to the lower slopes. We think this might be the furthest point east, *on the St Michael Line,* that the whole Tor can be seen.

Looking back to Glastonbury Tor, as seen from the lay-by just south of Stump Cross.

The line then skirts the north side of Shepton Mallet, through the small hamlet known as **Bowlish**. Old maps show it as a separate village, with its own school, mill and manor. The line crosses its main street, Ham Lane, where two roads meet and where both the Old Manor and Ham Manor are sited. From the entrance to the latter we could see a large stone projecting out of the wall to our right, and further east along the lane another large stone stood next to a wooden gate. We wondered if this rough stone, later used for milk churns or mounting horses, was an ancient megalith. Rising above the stonewalls we could see large, mature yew trees and the locality felt ancient and powerful. Other properties along Ham Lane are called Sunny Mount and Sunny Hill (suggesting possible solar rituals in the past) and from certain points we could look down to Shepton Mallet in the valley below. Bowlish House nearby was built in the 18th C and has an underground spring rising in the cellar that is said to always remain around 50° F and to link up with an underground river. This Georgian property is very close to the axis and is open to the public as a restaurant.

In the valley below, Shepton Mallet developed into a small Roman town, benefiting from being on the Fosse Way. Down at the parish church Miller and Broadhurst noted a powerful and wide flow of the Michael current of the St Michael Line, as it meandered away from the axis and through the town.

The axis then passes through the busy crossroads at **Downside**, named after the Abbey to the north at Stratton-on-the-Fosse. It then crosses the Fosse Way (at grid ref: 636452) where the raised banks of the Roman track can be seen either side of the modern road. Some large stones are lying by the side of the bridle path at this point, but we are not sure if

The St Michael line passes these stones, which lie alongside the Fosse Way.

236

these are ancient or modern (see image above). From here the line crosses another Roman road at the east end of **Beacon Hill**, around the 290m mark, just east of woods containing tumuli and earthworks. On the 1888 OS map, *stone* is shown on one of these mounds. In an article in *Newsletter #26* of the Society of Ley Hunters (May 2008), Jimmy Goddard confirms the survival of the stone (grid ref: 638458). He also comments that from Glastonbury Tor the sun rises out of Beacon Hill on May Day. He also cites a local archaeologist who believes the stone to be the remains of a medieval cross, whereas Jimmy dowsed it as being prehistoric. He also found, independently from us, the stones on the Fosse Way, mentioned above.

The line then passes through a boundary stone (marked on 1:25,000 maps, grid ref: 647459) and then just north of a stone marked on the 1888 OS map, to the SSE of Three Ashes (at grid ref: 653461 – where four field boundaries meet).

The Beltaine line then descends to **Stoke St Michael,** a village that was formerly the site of St Dunstan's Well. The centre of the axis passes through the main crossroads, The Square, and on the east side we found a large rough stone at road level, about 3ft long and painted white on its upper surface. Now used as a corner protector, we

Stoke St Michael. Left: the well pool next to the former Methodist chapel, which is on the alignment. Right: the large stone at the crossroads.

wondered if this stone was once an ancient marker, or the remains of a larger ancient site, situated as it is at such an important crossroads – and on the St Michael Line.

About 100yds south from the crossroads is the old Wesleyan Methodist Chapel, built in 1861. It is now the property of MJW Architects, who use the adjoining schoolhouse as an office. The owners are a couple called Michael and Michelle, which seemed quite fitting considering where they were situated! Michael was already very interested in the St Michael Line connection and he copied for me some information he had on the history of the village. Outside is a pool receiving water from a local spring and Michael told me that villagers and travellers still partake of the water. Back at the crossroads, the elaborate entrance to a small park has a carving showing local heraldry - four griffins and a five-pointed star.

It is interesting that Miller and Broadhurst's map of the area shows the Michael current flowing through the vicinity of the well, the chapel and the crossroads! They

St Michael and the dragon at Stoke St Michael.

recorded the flow going through the south porch and the north door of the parish church, situated north of the crossroads; it is dedicated to St Michael (who else?). Only the tower of the old church remains, the rest having been rebuilt in 1838-9. Fine winged gargoyles embellish the tower and inside the porch a brass plaque shows a very androgynous-looking patron saint slaying a semi-human beast. The energy is certainly powerfully felt as one enters the delightfully atmospheric church. Most of the windows show beautifully simplistic designs of white lilies, sometimes with a border of doves. One window near the altar, however, is different, for it shows St Michael slaying a poor green dragon (left). The scene was powerful as the afternoon winter sun streamed through the south-facing window. Other features of note are the Tree of Life on an old chair next to the altar, and the stone pulpit with a carved Templar cross.

From here the line crosses over the Mendips and descends down the steep road into the tiny, hidden hamlet of **Vobster.** The line passes through the old bridge that spans Mells Stream, an idyllic spot. The old church of St Edmunds is north of the bridge, past the Vobster Inn and down a track to the left at the bend. It is now a private residence and is just about the largest church we have ever found that has been turned into a dwelling place. The graveyard is accessible to the public; huge yews and a circular perimeter pointed to this being an ancient site, on a prominent mound overlooking the village. Both the 1891 and modern 1:25,000 maps show a perfectly circular wall around the church. Google Earth shows the circular perimeter clearly, and the fact that the church is aligned about 15° north of due east. Miller and Broadhurst map the Michael current as going through the church, but do not give any further details, and do not describe visiting it in *The Sun and the Serpent*.

The owner of the church was again called Michael, but he was unaware that his village stood on the alignment. He was kind enough to show us around an interior that held many hidden treasures. A fine green man is carved in stone just as one enters the church and below it an old pew bench with a six-pointed star on the end! *What a start!* Stained glass windows showing John the Baptist, favoured saint of the Knights Templar, and St Margaret (of Antioch) slaying a green dragon are noteworthy. Margaret was eaten by a dragon, but was regurgitated after her crucifix agitated the beast's innards. St Margaret and the dragon occur elsewhere on the St Michael Line, such as in a window at Trull church, also in Somerset; the very last church on the St Michael line, at Hopton in East Anglia, is also dedicated to her.

Upstairs in the church we were able to look closely at the stone carvings that decorated the roof beam supports, once only visible from several feet below. Nearly every carving was a head surrounded by foliage and acorns, some feminine, some angelic, and one with a sickle and wheat, symbolising the fruitfulness of the harvest. The church was atmospheric and we felt privileged to have been allowed to see inside. Michael can be contacted at the church on 01373 812290, for an appointment to view; the churchyard is open to the public.

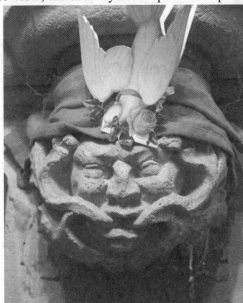 

Left: the Green Man inside the former church at Vobster.
Right: the ancient cross in the churchyard at Buckland Dinham.

A Methodist chapel once stood at Upper Vobster, and the naming of White Cottage and Holwell Farm nearby may further indicate sacred places in ancient times. Further to this, just south of the line, north of Lily Batch Lodge, a stone is shown in a field east of the track on the 1891 map (grid ref: 712492).

Buckland Dinham is the next stop. St Michael's church is a typical dedication on the St Michael Line. It is a fine Norman building, and even as we approached the porch we could see, either side of it, small windows which enclosed six-pointed stars! The window behind the altar in the 13th C Lady Chapel is interesting, for it shows Christ on the cross, but above, below and around him are two intertwined lines – are these the Mary and Michael flows of the St Michael Line? The main east window is again the Crucifixion, and this time Mary Magdalene is sobbing at the foot of the cross. From inside, we could now see those small windows on the south side to better effect, and how the elements of the hexagrams were red and green. The font is Norman and the north chapel has two 14th C effigies inlaid into the floor, reminiscent of those in Temple Church, but here they are very worn.

Back outside, there are fine dragons up the 15th C tower and to the NE of the church is the old village cross, with its medieval base. Peter dowsed an energy flow going from the cross, through a nearby yew and onward into the church (image above).

The charming, isolated church at Laverton, where fire festivals still take place.

The church is usually locked but keys can be obtained from a small box on the step of No.1, St Michaels Close, opposite the church. Whilst in the area it is worth visiting the Orchardleigh Stones, a megalithic site to the south of the village. Miller and Broadhurst describe the stones as being on the Michael energy current.

The line then goes through Luxgrove Wood and then to the south side of **Laverton (St Mary)**, a tiny hamlet. The manor is the property of the Duchy of Cornwall and his shield, with 15 spherical byzants (coins of the Byzantine Empire, used by the Crusaders), can be seen in the church. The dedication is to St Mary, and it is sited just 200yds north of the axis, near the convergence of Wheel Brook and Henhambridge Brook, which feed the Frome; dedications to women are typical of churches near rivers. The roof is in three levels, reflecting different building stages, and the whole delightful building is pleasing. The main window is of the Crucifixion, with Mary Magdalene praying at the foot of the cross; the words *It is Finished* are below. Although the walls have been plastered, the tiny chapel retains atmosphere, a quiet haven in a tranquil backwater of Somerset. There are images of the annual bonfire lit near the church each Easter at sunrise, a ritual that we were to find elsewhere at nearby Norton St Philip (see pages 252-253). They remind us of ancient fire festivals of ancient times. There was also once a Baptist chapel in the village.

Rode was introduced earlier in Chapter 21, as it is located where the Beltaine, Samhain and Central Axes all converge. The Beltaine Axis passes right through Christ Church, at the north end of the town; it also stands on the Samhain Line. It is unexpectedly grand, with two spires. It is now a private dwelling, but the owner, violin dealer Andrew Hooker, told us the churchyard is open to the public, so we were at least able to check out the exterior of the church. It was built in 1824 and largely paid for by Charles Daubeney, who was Archdeacon of Sarum. At that time Rode fell within Wiltshire and he felt that villagers shouldn't stray over to the church of St. Lawrence, Rode, in the rival diocese of Somerset. The building is to the design of Henry Edmund Goodridge, a Bath architect who was also responsible for Cleveland Bridge and a number of early Gothic churches in the area. In *The Buildings of England* (Penguin, 1958), Nikolaus Pevsner records the church as, *"remarkable… a fantastic exterior"*. The building was designed to seat 700 but little of the original Georgian fittings remain, save for red and white-ribboned stained-glass windows either side of the sanctuary, and some plaster faces, one of which is a green man. The church was made redundant in 1995, and for views of the interior follow the link on Andrew's website (www.aviolin.com).

On our visit, Peter spotted a large stone, at least 4ft long, protruding from a verge just

west of the church, on the corner of Langham Place. We beamed with delight at the possibility that this might be another ancient megalith, either in situ or brought here from somewhere nearby. The site marks where the Beltaine and Samhain lines cross! On perusing the 1890 OS map (scale: 1:10,560), we also found three stones in the field immediately northeast of the church (centred around grid ref: 807542). There was also once a *Barrow Farm* locally, just south of the north bridge, more evidence of prehistoric ritual and burial.

This stone lies next to Christchurch at Rode, where the Beltaine and Samhain lines cross.

Trowbridge

The line then skirts around the southern flanks of Trowbridge, once the administrative centre of Wiltshire due to wealth generated by the cloth industry. Miller and Broadhurst followed the Michael current into the church of St James, with its fine spire and uplifting interior. The flow aligns with the axis of the building.

The fact that our line misses the centre of the modern town is more than made up for by the places we were to encounter. The line first passes midway between the church

on White Row Hill and Southwick Court Moat. This spot is where White Row Bridge crosses the stream that flows from the moat. The moat and the element *White* for both the hill and bridge may point to a sacred place long ago (White or Whit = *Holy*). Southwick Court was the capital messuage of the district, but it is not known if manorial rights were ever exercised. The house stands at one side of an extensive medieval

The moat at Southwick Court is just south of the Beltaine Line.

241

moated site. The L-shaped building bears two stones dated 1567 and the southwest end of that wing was completely rebuilt in the late 17th C. Attached to the house is a two-storied gatehouse, thought to date from the 16th C. The drive to the Court starts just south of the bridge, and then forks right at the sign Southwick Court Chapel, where a car park will be found. A gap in the trees allows access to a wooden bridge, which spans waters of the moat at this very pleasant locality. (Please note that beyond the bridge is private property).

The church north of the bridge is St John the Evangelist, but it is usually locked. Attached to the older parts are less pleasing additions, which detract from the overall appearance. At the west end of the church the top of the window is in the form of a six-pointed flower.

The line leaves the bridge and crosses Silver Street Lane, before passing just south of the site of the old hospital, and going precisely through the *Manor House* of the 1890 OS map. The alignment then goes straight through the centre of Mount Pleasant Cottages (grid ref: 858568), before passing just south of Dursley House (named on older maps) at Lower Studley. Further on, a 38m spot height marks where the line crosses Blackball Bridge, before it crosses Green Lane at Green Lane Farm.

Hag Hill and Hagg Hill Farm are on the Beltaine Line.

The alignment then crosses the flanks of **Hag Hill** (significantly named – *Hill of the Witch or Crone*), which can be viewed from the entrance to Hagg Hill Farm, on the A350. It then crosses fields north of Great Hinton before ascending the ridge as it enters the parish of **Seend** at Seend Cleeve, where old maps show several wells and springs. A little further on, at Seend, one of these is Black Well. This can still be seen today behind Blackwell Cottage, accessed down a steep path from the car park of the Bell Inn. We pulled a large slate block back, revealing a small round brick receptacle containing water. John Aubrey, writer and antiquarian, stayed at Seend in the 1660s, making note of the mineral springs here. He in fact did his best to get Seend developed as a Spa, but nothing came of the plan, he suggests, owing to the jealousy of doctors in Bath. There is a tradition that two bottles of Seend water were sent each week to King George III in London, in an effort to stem his impending blindness.

The Beltaine Line then passes north of the main road at Seend and in fact the main A361 road runs parallel with the alignment for 1½ miles. The locality attracted a settlement at an early date and by the Domesday Book there was a well-established village with a church, which formed part of the royal hunting forest of Melksham, the trees of which once reached the foot of Seend Hill. In AD 1200, the King gave the land to Salisbury Cathedral, who still appoint the local vicar. In the 15th – 16th C, Seend prospered from the Wiltshire wool industry, due to its many springs, and at this time the church was rebuilt and enlarged. In the 18th C, when the wool trade was languishing due to foreign competition, Seend was given a fresh lease of life by the construction of the Turnpike road in 1750, linking Devizes and Trowbridge. At that time the road was one of the main arteries from London to Bath.

At Seend, Toni was again in an area of her ancestors; Wiltshire is the heartland of the Perrotts. In Seend, there were 67 baptisms of the Perrott lineage (in its variant forms) between 1619 and 1873, and 43 burials of her forebears between 1630 and 1888. There was once *Perret's Spout*, a spring which periodically flooded Perret's Lane, as in 1721.

The church of the Holy Cross, Seend, is a grand structure, approached through 19th C

Left: Black Well at Seend.
Right: St John with a golden dragon emerging from a chalice, at Seend Church.

wrought iron gates. It has some surviving 15th C features and fine gargoyles. The main window behind the altar shows Christ in Majesty, surrounded by angels. Other windows depict Faith, Hope and Charity, St Michael, and, next to the altar, Jesus appearing to Mary Magdalene, with her jar at her feet, after the Resurrection. Near the west end of the north aisle is a fine window showing St John, with a resplendent winged dragon rising from his Chalice (see image above). It touched Toni to think that her ancestors had used the Black Well and the church.

John Wesley preached in Seend on a number of occasions, and in 1775 he opened the Methodist Chapel (next to the pub!), which has been a continuous place of worship ever since. A commemorative plaque of the opening can be seen over the door. Below the brick structure, we found courses of older stone, and the worn cobbles leading up to the chapel may be of a similar age. Seend used to have a festival in early May, with stalls and a fair, which dated back at least to John Aubrey's time. There are two records of alleged witches being ducked in the river. The first, in 1773, speaks of a certain Mary Jenkins, who could turn herself into a white rabbit that could only be killed with a silver bullet. A second ducking took place as late as the 19th C.

The line then passes through **Sells Green** and **Martinslade**. Miller and Broadhurst dowsed an energy node where the Michael current crosses the axis, north of Martinslade. The line then skirts around the northern edge of Rowde, crosses the southern bridge over the Frome, and goes through the site of Rowde Mill.

It then crosses the Stonehenge to Wotton Holywell line (see Chapter 7) at the footbridge (grid ref: 976632) that spans the river that flows from Mother Anthony's Well (see below). The alignment then passes through Rowdeford School (a special needs establishment), which was formerly Rowde Ford House. It is an imposing Grade II listed Georgian house standing in 20 acres of parkland. Built in the late 18th C, the house has a long and interesting history and it wasn't until 1946 that the building became a school.

Directions to Mother Anthony's Well

To access the spring, walk down the valley between Oliver's Castle and the Roundway Covert (Wood) and keep on through the pasture up to the stock fence. At the fence go left and over the stile into the next field. Immediately after the stile, duck down through a hole in the hedge on your right to the field on the other side. Follow this hedge back in the direction you came as it curves around the wood. There are suitable openings into the wood so be patient – you don't have to battle the nettles. Once in, head for the middle to find the water. (Note: the woods are not a right of way; visitors enter at their own risk.)

From here one can see the towering heights of Oliver's Castle to the east, over which the line passes. At the foot of the scarp is **Mother Anthony's Well**, a sacred spring in a small wood, which is located just yards from the very centre of the Beltaine Line (grid ref: 999642). There is no report of buildings having been at the spring, but a Romano-British dwelling is recorded in the vicinity. English Heritage, in *Avebury Archaeological Research Agenda*, officially regard the spring site as Roman, describing it as being, *"... a major shrine associated with a spring..."*

From the well, the alignment goes up the valley and ascends the steep and sculpted slopes to **Oliver's Castle**, with its three attendant tumuli, through which the line runs.

The towering heights of Oliver's Castle, seen from near Rowde.

A family of tall slender trees stand guard at the top, as if gazing across the land below. The locality can be approached from a parking space (grid ref: 004647) and the walk is level, giving little clue to the spectacular views that wait at the top of the scarp. The camp was more anciently called Roundway or Rundaway Castle, and its present name seems to have arisen out of a popular local tradition that Oliver Cromwell once occupied the hill. The only foundation for this folklore is that the Battle of Roundway of 1643 was fought on the neighbouring Downs, although Cromwell himself was not present. Miller and Broadhurst followed the Michael and Mary flows of the St Michael Line into the hillfort, where they converged in the vicinity of the dewpond. This is the first site since leaving Glastonbury where the two energy currents converge actually on the Beltaine Line. Hamish and Paul poetically describe their visit: *"...One looks down on the world like the Gods of Olympus, amused at the triviality of human lives."*

At **Roundway Down** a headless ghost is said to walk. A certain Mr R Coward, who farmed at Roundway, stated that on three occasions prior to 1848 the apparition appeared to people he knew, and that the ghost was drawing them to an almost imperceptible barrow. A mound was excavated in 1855 and a skeleton (not headless!) was found. Since the barrow was opened the ghost has not appeared, although the area is haunted by a black dog, whose arrival is announced by the sound of rattling chains. The line passes through the site of the 1643 Battle of Roundway Down.

The alignment then passes almost exactly midway between the churches of Calstone Wellington and Bishops Cannings. These are both on the west circle of David Furlong's proposed landscape vesica piscis, outlined in his book *The Keys to the Temple*. From a car park (grid ref: 028660), just south of Morgan's Hill and Furze Knoll, one can see a well-defined track heading off east, and it is this ancient route that the line follows for over five miles to Avebury, crossing Wansdyke and turning into the modern road further on.

Just past the dyke the line comes to Baltic Farm, with three attendant tumuli, which can be seen from the A361. Approaching the Avebury landscape, the line goes very close to a track for one mile, past the farm, before joining the A361, which it mirrors for two miles, before following the A4361 for another mile into Avebury. Terence Meaden, in his ground-breaking book, *The Secrets of the Avebury Stones,* plots a megalith on this road (stone IX on his map on page 12), which seems to be on our Beltaine Line. Variations in the route of the alignment have been shown by different writers. In *The View Over Atlantis,* John Michell has the line exactly following the track

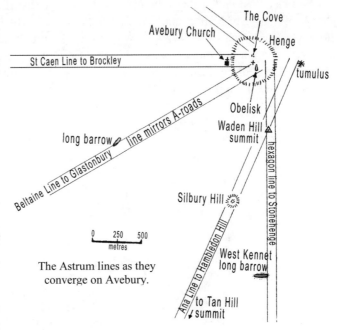

The Astrum lines as they converge on Avebury.

and the A361 as it approaches Avebury, whereas Miller and Broadhurst show the alignment as crossing the fields some 200m north of the A-road. The axis of our alignment leans more towards Michell's line.

Avebury has been dealt with in some detail in previous chapters, with respect to the four other Astrum lines that converge on it. The Beltaine alignment goes through the southern part of the henge, in the vicinity of the Obelisk and the two large entrance stones (No's 1 and 98). In *The Measure of Albion*, John Michell plots the exact axis as passing just a few feet south of these two giant megaliths. His map (Fig. 7.3) shows the alignment coming into Avebury just north of Beckhampton Road, which confirms our Beltaine Astrum line. Miller and Broadhurst's map seems to show the line going right through the stones, but we are aware of the limitations due to scale on both maps.

The St Michael Axis of course continues further east. Beyond the henge, the route runs for over a mile up to Fyfield Down, marked by an ancient track once named as the *Herepath*. This makes a total of over five miles of track and road aligned with the Beltaine Line – again, Alfred Watkins would have loved this! Leaving the henge, the track goes past Manor Farm. Between here and the church at Ogbourne St George the line goes through Temple Farm, which sits in Temple Bottom. The Knights Templar had their preceptory of Temple Rockley here (see page 27 for map). The land was given to the Templars in 1155-6, which they held until 1313, when it was passed on to the Knights Hospitallers.

As we stood at the site of the Obelisk at Avebury, now a large concrete pyramid, we recollected the wonderful and magical sites that connected us to Glastonbury Tor, 43 miles away. We had walked at times in the footsteps of John Michell, as well as in those of Hamish Miller and Paul Broadhurst; we had diverted from their path, however, for much of the way, as we had not so much followed the St Michael Line energy currents, but more the astronomical alignment itself. We felt that St Michael himself was looking down on us – and we hoped that he was satisfied with what we had found, both on the Land and within ourselves, during our Quest.

William Stukeley's 1723 drawing of the 21ft long Obelisk, now destroyed. The Beltaine Line of the Astrum terminates here.

Chapter 23
The Samhain Alignment

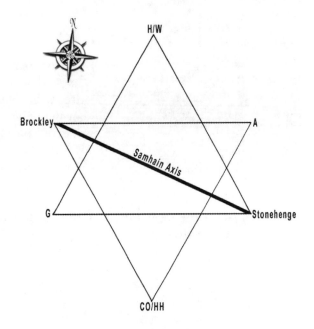

W e have named this line the Samhain Axis, because it aligns with the sunrise around the ancient festival of Samhain, now much degraded into the modern Halloween activities so loved by children. The azimuth of this line is 111° from the north, which is the sunrise point, from the latitude of Bristol and London, around 23-26 October each year, just days before Samhain. This direction has only changed by less than one degree in the last two thousand years. The line is 43 miles long and runs from Brockley to Stonehenge (see map page 184), and the mid-point is the village of Rode, where the line crosses both the Beltaine Line and the Central Axis, as described previously.

The unsymmetrical hexagrams at Brockley reflect the shape of the Wessex Astrum hexagram.

The apex point is just yards south of **Brockley** church, which is dedicated to St Nicholas. It is currently under the care of the Redundant Churches Fund, who provide for an informative booklet inside. Services are only held twice yearly now, on the Sunday nearest 6th December (St Nicholas' Day) and another around midsummer. We obtained keys from a nearby cottage (see notice in porch).

We approached the church through an iron arch on a sunny October morning and were greeted by a tree to our right that resembled a dragon rearing up from the earth! Toni also spotted large clumps of mistletoe hanging on a tree over the wall to our right (in the grounds of the neighbouring nursing home, the former manor house), a sure sign of powerful energy flows. We entered a churchyard that was shaded by yew trees, huddled together to create a powerful atmosphere, just as the clock up the tower chimed the hour.

Inside is a Norman font, but the majority of the fabric of the building is 13th C. The atmosphere and energies were immediate as we entered the long, narrow church and several fine monuments and paintings suggested that the church had once enjoyed good patronage. This was in the form of the Smyth-Pigots, lately of Brockley Court, who were related to the Royal Family. Large pews, high quality fittings and paintings of Royal emblems bore witness to this wealth. After restoration work in 1842, a local newspaper commented that, *"Brockley church may now be considered one of the gems of church architecture..."*. But what really struck us were the stained glass windows, which date from 1825. Above several scenes were hexagrams, in a woven or roped design. And they were not symmetrical, but were just like the shape of the Astrum! We were elated with the discovery of such hexagrams in a church at this apex of the Astrum. (We have since discovered almost identical hexagrams above windows at St Anne's in Manchester.)

It is worth mentioning that in *The Ley Hunters Companion,* Paul Devereux and Ian Thomson plot a ley line that goes from Brockley Church down to Glastonbury! The nearby chapel of St Bridget, not far to the north, is also worth visitng. It is a charming chapel with a fine medieval churchyard cross.

From Brockley church the Samhain Axis heads along **Brockley Combe** (known as Wolf Combe in a Saxon charter) towards Bristol Airport and beyond. The line runs down the length of the magical, tree-covered ravine, full of mysterious walks and hidden caves. The axis goes along the road immediately below Yorkhouse Cave, the terminal point of the Brockley-Glastonbury hexagon line. This sacred locality was covered more fully in Chapter 20 (pages 205-8).

From the Combe the line crosses the golf course before going straight through the terminal buildings of **Bristol Airport**! Work by Robin Heath suggests that airports seem to be located on alignments, and that they mark modern power points; we wonder if this connection is also to do with shamanic flight?

The next stop is **Felton Hill**, where the axis of the line cuts through the southern edge of Felton Common. Walking south from St Katherine's, which appears to stand on an ancient mound, we walked across open ground until we came to a prominent, overgrown mound near the south-west corner of the common (grid ref: 517648 – only shown on 1: 25,000 scale OS maps). This is an oval mound up to 1m high and strewn with several large stones, thought to be from a collapsed Neolithic burial chamber. The next site on the common is two tumuli (marked on all maps at grid ref: 519648), a rare example of confluent Bronze Age barrows, defined by converging ditches. We had seen examples previously, high up on Nine Barrow Down in Dorset. Both mounds are around 1m high and 21-22m in diameter. Their position affords commanding views of the valley below and Dundry Hill to the north-east. Locally there is a record dating from 1923 that speaks of a *Bully Well* (from the deity Bel?), whose waters were, *"... good for the eyes."*

The church of St Andrew at Chew Magna. Left: we dowsed a powerful energy current going from the block of stone in the foreground, through the cross and into the church.
Right: Toni experiencing the energy around this magnificent medieval cross.

249

Chew Magna is the next centre of habitation on the Samhain alignment. It is recorded from Saxon times and the church is Norman. The manor belonged to the Bishop of Bath and Wells from 11th-16th C and it was visited by Henry II in 1250. It has a Tudor manor house, home in the 1700's to Sir William Jones, the Attorney General of England. Raised pavements are a feature of the village and they are in fact Grade II listed. The Tun Bridge, a scheduled ancient monument, spans the River Chew and dates from the 15th C. The Samhain Line passes close by the bridge.

The church is dedicated to St Andrew and is approached from the main street by passing the Old School Room, which has a carving of St George slaying a dragon on the front. On entering the churchyard, a large upturned octagonal cross base is encountered and, beyond it, the most magnificent medieval cross we have ever come across. Six steps lead up to a slim stone cross shaft.

The church itself is imposing, with a tall tower decorated with gargoyles and some 12th C surviving stonework. Inside, two effigies of knights are notable, one of whom lies nonchalantly with his head on one hand! The Lady Chapel has a fine and delicately executed window showing various scenes of Mary, as well as a depiction of the sun and moon either side of a radiant vesica. The energy in this chapel was very powerfully felt. Another "hot spot" was around the wooden altar in front of the rood screen. Toni dowsed energy currents flowing from this spot, through the font and out through the walls. Outside, the flow continued to the medieval cross, which was a powerful energy focus, and onward through the large stone by the gate. From here it forked, one branch of which continued along one raised pavement and down to Tun Bridge, the other went along the other raised pavement past the shops. Across the bridge we noted how Dumpers Lane ran parallel with the alignment.

The alignment then traverses the northern slopes of Blackberry Hill, before crossing **Barrow Hill,** at Barrow Vale. Just 2 miles south of the axis is Temple Cloud, reminding us of the strong Templar legacy in the area. It then crosses Cam Brook at the old mill, and goes up to **Carlingcott,** land formerly owned by the Priory at Montecute. The hamlet is known to have existed prior to 1800 but the modern

Above: megalith at Carlingcott.
Right: Buddha on the roof of a private
Buddhist temple at Carlingcott.

development began in the 19th C when the Somerset coalfield was expanded as the Industrial Revolution increased the demand for coal. The axis of the line passes within yards of the Methodist Chapel, a fine stone building built by local miners in 1851. Prior to this, people had worshipped at the Wesleyan Methodist Chapel, which still stands, even though it is no longer a place of worship. The desire for a form of Church government that was less restrained led the founders away from the Wesleyan Chapel. Two stone pillars at the door, topped by foliation, reminded us of the twin initiatory pillars of Freemasonry.

Next to the chapel we saw a sign, *Laurel Farm and Temple,* by a lamp post which had multi-coloured patterned glass! We enquired within and found some really nice people who invited us to look around and dowse. At the rear of the property is a room called The Temple, which was built by the previous Buddhist owners some years before. A statue of the holy man himself sits on the roof. We thought it relevant that these people had felt inclined to set up a sanctuary here, right on the alignment.

We were also delighted to come across an unrecorded stone at Carlingcott, about 200yds west of the Chapel, at the corner of a road junction (grid ref: 697582), at the end of a long wall. It protrudes from the wall, and about 3ft x 2ft of uncut rounded stone is currently visible, with an unknown quantity embedded in the wall (see image above).

The line then climbs Keel's Hill into **Peasedown St John,** which is situated on a hilltop on the Fosse Way, around which Roman and Saxon settlements grew. From archaeological evidence it appears there has been continuous occupation of the area since at least the early Iron Age. There is good evidence of Roman and Saxon villages locally; Saxon settlements in the area appear in several entries in the Domesday Book of 1086. A red dragon appears on the Parish Council's coat-of-arms. More recently, Peasedown was a coalmining village, but the last pits closed in the 1950's. The parish church is dedicated to John the Baptist, and two other chapels can be found in the village. The Methodist Chapel is still active, as well as a Catholic Church. The old parish church was dismantled in 1893 and was re-erected as the Church of St John the Divine in Fishponds, Bristol. The present church was built in 1893-4.

The line then proceeds through Double Hill, crosses Wellow Brook at Greenacres, and passes just a quarter of a mile south of **Stony Littleton (Wellow) Long Barrow** (grid ref: 735572), within the tolerance we had allowed ourselves for sites to include. This beautiful Neolithic sacred site has recently been restored and a signposted car park is now nearby. This has been described as one of the most notable chambered tombs in all of England, and we could not disagree with that. Standing at 30m long and 3m high, it has a crescental opening, with a large fossil ammonite built into the door jam; further ammonites can be seen on internal stones. Was this once taken as the magical spiral, symbol of the Goddess? Aligned with the midwinter sunrise, the passage is long and low and six side chambers are passed before the end chamber is reached. The sun still comes into this chamber every year for a few days around the solstice, entering the chambers just before 9.00am (later than the actual sunrise due to the elevated skyline). Places such as this were certainly more than ancestral tombs, but rather were also places where our shamanic ancestors would come to contact the spirits of *their* ancestors.

A bonfire is still lit every Easter at the church of Norton St Philip, a relic of pagan spring fire festivals. (Anon.)

The line then cuts through the southern end of **Norton St Philip**, a hamlet mentioned in the Domesday Book, where it is recorded as *Nortune*. However, a settlement was established during the Saxon period, probably in the shelter of the valley head around a possible church site. Until the 13th C, Norton was a small secular manor of little importance. But in 1232 ownership was transferred to the recently founded Hinton Priory, in the possession of which it remained until the Dissolution. Norton was granted its own fair in 1255, and a market was first held here in 1291. In 1345 the Priory was granted permission to transfer the Hinton Charterhouse Fair (first chartered in 1245) to Norton, because its success was disrupting the Priory's religious life! Norton thereafter became one of the county's more important wool trading centres, and the fair, held around The George, was comparable with some of the great national fairs. The success of this fair is reflected in periodical disputes with the city of Bath.

Norton St Philip was the site of a battle during the Monmouth Rebellion in 1685, and the George Inn, one of a number of establishments that claims to be Britain's oldest tavern, is located in the centre of the village. With 14th-16th C features, such as old beams and a cobbled courtyard, it is well worth a visit. The Duke of Monmouth himself stayed at The George.

Down the side of the Inn a sign directs you along a passage to the church, which stands at the bottom of the hill, unusually. Its position, however, is much nearer the Astrum line than if it had been sited at the top. The church of St. Philip and St. James, dating from the 14th C, has some 15th-17th C features, but was restored in 1847 by Sir George Gilbert Scott. In some of the windows we found very ornate six-pointed patterns and fine carvings in the wooden reredos and altar frontals in the SE (Lady) Chapel. One of these was Mary Magdalene, holding her jar. She is visible again in the main east window, tenderly kissing Christ's feet as he hangs on the cross. In a window dedicated to St Ann (= the Goddess Ana) is another six-pointed figure in glass. There are also photos on display of the annual bonfire held in the churchyard every Easter morning, surely a continuance of pagan fires lit of long ago.

Also in the village is the little-known Lyde Spring (grid ref: 772561) on Wellow Lane Could this name possibly have derived from the old sun God Llud? Opposite the church, go down The Barton, which turns into Wellow Lane further on. Soon on the right you will hear running water coming from the woods, which is the spring. (If you come to The Old Mill then you have gone too far). It is a pleasant, peaceful place and on our visit the water was flowing very strongly from two sources.

The waters of Lyde Spring at Norton St Philip.

In *The Pattern of the Past*, Guy Underwood speaks of several examples of "magic pavements" in the village, crazy paving that marked the flow of energetic water lines. He surmised that this phenomenon might be the origin of the tradition that it is unlucky to step on the cracks in the pavement.

The Samhain Line then crosses a Roman road that once ran from Bath to Poole. It then scales Rode Hill, on the northern side of **Rode**, where it crosses both the Central Axis and the Beltaine line. The line is marked by Christ Church, as well as a megalith we found just outside the churchyard (see page 220 for details of both). Incredibly, the megalith sits in the vicinity of where the Beltaine and Samhain lines cross. On perusing the 1890 OS map (scale: 1:10,560) we found three stones recorded in the field immediately northeast of the church (centred around grid ref: 807542). The Samhain Line passes right through this field! Miller and Broadhurst tracked the Michael current through the parish church of St Lawrence, to the south.

Westbury - Town of the White Horse

Westbury had two moats locally, and the town is said to be the location of a royal palace used by the ancient kings of Wessex. The line enters the town via a small settlement known as The Ham, where it passes right through the crossroads (grid ref: 861522). Neolithic and Bronze Age remains have been found locally and it was the site of a Romano-British settlement – the origins of historical Westbury. Land and property in Westbury has been variously owned by both the Priory of Monkton Farleigh and Lacock Abbey. The town grew partly as a result of the line of springs that flow out of the steep slopes to the east, notably at Wellhead, and the town has an ancient market place.

Westbury has five churches and is centred on the historic Market Place, with the churchyard of All Saints' Church (14th C) behind it. Mentioned in the Domesday Book, it is thought to be the site of an earlier wooden Saxon church. The present building is imposing and unexpectedly large, and is noted for its 17th C faceless clock. All Saints' boasts the third heaviest ring of bells in the world, an Erasmus Bible and a 16th C clock with no face, constructed by a local blacksmith. On the exterior of the south side, east of the porch, is a fine three-faced head, with a single larger head above it. The energy inside the church is powerful in some places, particularly in the

Left: the grand parish church of All Saints, Westbury;
Right: these chapels at Westbury Cemetery are aligned with the Samhain Line!

14th C Lady Chapel. The main east window is of the Crucifixion, with Mary Magdalene in attendance, and behind the altar is a fine stone carving of St George and the dragon. The Chapel of the Holy Name, on the north side, is very small but very peaceful. The local choir often sing in here because of the renowned acoustics.

The church is usually locked outside service hours but the keys can be obtained from the adjacent parish office, open on certain weekdays (tel: 01373 859450), or from keyholders listed on the porch gate.

But Westbury held more suprises for us: from the centre of town the line goes up the slopes and passes just north of a former chapel, on the corner of the B3098. It is a fine stone chapel which is now home to White Horse Pottery. The line crosses the road just east of the chapel and cuts across the cemetery at an acute angle. A site visit to the cemetery revealed, amazingly, that the two chapels, as well as two enormous mortuary buildings, were almost aligned with the Samhain Line as it crossed the cemetery.

The Westbury White Horse.

From Westbury the line climbs the steep scarp onto Salisbury Plain, to the south of the Westbury White Horse. It is sometimes claimed that the horse was first cut into the chalk as long ago as the year 878 AD, to commemorate the victory of King Alfred the Great over the Danes, at the Battle of Eðandun (possibly at the nearby village of Edington). However, scholars believe the horse dates from the 18th C, for there are no records of it prior to the 1720's. The form of the current White Horse dates from 1778, when it was restored. The horse is best seen from the special viewing point on the B3098 (grid ref: 883515).

The Samhain Line then passes through MOD land for several miles, until it passes by **Imber,** a small, deserted village, isolated in the middle of MOD land on Salisbury

Plain. Its residents were evicted in 1943, as part of the Allied preparations for D-Day. Interestingly, the troops who were sent there said Imber was haunted. Fervent campaigns have taken place in the past to allow people to return, and today the Imber Conservation Group are active in preserving the area's landscape and heritage.

St Giles at Imber, now closed and gutted but which once contained interesting relics.

Considering the size of Salisbury Plain and the lack of villages in the area, we thought it amazing that the line passes just 150yds south of the church! The village has an ancient history and stands in an area rich in prehistoric remains, and several Roman tracks cross the area. It is recorded as a Saxon community in 967 AD and the village had a population of fifty in the Domesday Book. Most of the original cottages have been replaced by mock army training buildings, but the church of St Giles still stands (now redundant and sadly out of bounds behind a wire perimeter). The church dates from the 13th C and contains notable 15th C wall paintings on the north wall. The state of the building had deteriorated until it was eventually restored in the 19th C, but all fixtures and fittings were removed to other Wiltshire churches in 1943.

The village and its roads (but not the church) are usually open to the public during

We joined the annual peace vigil held in Imber on New Year's Eve 2007.

Easter, much of August and through Christmas and the New Year (for details ring the MOD training office on 01980 620819). Once a year a service is held at the church on the nearest weekend to St Giles Day in September (known as Imber Day), and we learnt that in recent years a Peace Vigil takes place in the village at noon on New Year's Eve.

So we found ourselves in Imber on 31st Jan 2007, where we joined peace activist and organiser Ruth and eighteen other souls in the chilly car park. We held up cards with peace affirmations and discussed various political and peace issues. Along a fence Ruth put

255

out dozens of laminated photos of Imber when the village was still occupied, as well as others showing some gatherings of evicted villagers and their subsequent protests. To our delight, some of these were of the interior of St Giles, access of which is now denied. These included amazing images of two monuments depicting figures in full armour – they were knights! More than this, one displayed a heraldic shield that had three six-pointed stars! The tombs are now housed at Edington Priory, to the north of the MOD ranges. In another image the altar was adorned with a red engrailed cross, a type associated with the Knights Templar, displayed, for example, at Roslyn Chapel. On another old photo, we had a close-up of the tiles in front of the altar and some of these showed a circle, enclosing a square, which itself contained a six-pointed figure – more sacred symbolism. Even here, miles from anywhere on the army ranges of Salisbury Down, we had found esoteric links with the Wessex Astrum.

From Imber the line goes through a stretch of inaccessible MOD land, and study of the 1889 OS map failed to turn up any features of interest. The next accessible point is the Chitterne to Tilshead road, where the line crosses at grid ref: 011464. Of interest is that at this exact point an ancient earthwork also crosses the road, before heading east for nearly a mile, enclosing a long barrow en route. The line then passes along the entire length of an elongated and gradually descending plateau, the axis of which points towards Shrewton and Maddington, mirroring a parallel old track.

The axis of the line approaches **Shrewton** straight through the road junction known as the Gibbet, and then through the site of the old windmill (grid ref: 064444) shown on the 1889 map. Standing just north of the line, Shrewton Church is dedicated to St Mary and was given over to Lacock Abbey in 1236 by Sir Robert Bluet. It has a short and solid tower but is kept locked outside services. The line crosses the bottom of a road called Furlong Lane, just yards north of the Methodist Chapel. This building is dated 1861 and above the door are fine window paintings of peace doves and lilies. The old Manor House was just south of this locality. On the corner of the lane is Furlong House and on the side of it is a plaque, pronouncing that it was the birthplace of Sir Cecil Chubb, "… who gave Stonehenge to the Nation on 26 October, 1918."

The line follows the A344 to **Stonehenge**, passing between two tumuli either side of the road east of the Fargo Plantation (shown on the 1889 map), before going along the road, passing just yards south of several tumuli in the field east of the woods. With pinpoint accuracy, the axis of the line goes right into the heart of the sarsen circle of Stonehenge (see map on page 184), an incredible feat considering that the line started 43 miles away at Brockley Church, and was predestined to follow Samhain around sunrise.

(Postscript: Toni map-dowsed the Astrum to see if there were any major energy flows, such as had been found around the St Michael Line. Early indications suggest that there may be a significant energy flow entwining the Samhain Line between Brockley and Stonehenge, continuing along the extensions of the line to the Preseli Mountains in one direction, and Winchester and Chichester in the other. Could this be an enticing explanation as to why the Blue Stones were brought all the way from Preseli, a known place of special energies? Of course, there are no doubt countless other energy flows crossing the area awaiting discovery, so please check Toni's website for further developments.)

Chapter 25
The Way Forward

"We cannot solve the problems we have created with the
same thinking that created them."
Albert Einstein

So what has been the point of our Quest, this pursuit of alignments that we have come to know as the Wessex Astrum? Was the Quest for our own gratification; were we in a rush to be the first to publish? Were we being driven by selfish motives? Or had we been on a voyage that was more than simply the discovery of some lines on the landscape?

It seemed at times that when we ventured out onto the Wessex landscape, we often found more than we had bargained for. We discovered sacred geometry in churches; we found former chapels and holy springs on old maps; we revealed many "lost" and unrecorded standing stones, which would surely now have a better chance of survival;

we dowsed, and even felt our bodies tingle with healing pulses of energy at sacred sites and, more than this, found that these flows continued through the most developed of areas – the flow of the Earth's life force would not be denied; we have stood midst some of the most beautiful, and isolated, scenery in the South, places we would never have visited but for following Astrum lines.

The Monument in London. The dragon rises to heal sick Albion;
we all share in the responsibility for healing her.

But it has been more than this. In going out into the Astrum landscape, we found a little more of what makes *us* tick – for going out is ultimately going within. So often we felt that we were being guided to places, and we would duly follow, not always knowing why. Studying the lines and sites of the Astrum was at times a logical, left side of the brain process, and inevitably so. But we also found wonder, and experienced magic, following our feelings and intuition, boldly going where we felt drawn to go, not merely where our brains dictated. And perhaps this was the whole point, to reconnect with the wisdom of the land, and the processes within us that operate beyond logic and reason.

We had already come to the conclusion, prior to writing this book, that we would not put out knowledge and information for the sake of it. It is knowledge, after all, that has got this planet into such a mess. Surely it is wisdom that is required now, and knowledge and wisdom are not always congenial bedfellows. For this reason, while we realise that further geometrical forms may be generated from the hexagram, we have not attempted this for the current book, leaving it for others if they wish to do so. We feel that the *Wessex Astrum,* above all else, should be a vehicle for people to venture out once more onto the sacred landscapes of this beautiful planet. Reading is no substitute for direct experience, as our ancestors knew thousands of years ago.

We show here two of Toni's "doodles", as she calls them, quick automatic or unconscious drawings, which she sometimes draws either whilst tuned into sacred sites and their elementals, or at other quiet moments elsewhere. Other drawings will be shown in her forthcoming book *London Dragon Paths*. This is just one of many ways we can connect with a sacred site. Other means

One of Toni's automatic drawings, channelled and drawn on site at Sutton Waldron spring. It shows this site on an energetic level, as well as other dimensions. (See also her drawing *Spring Sprite* on page 137.) © T Perrott.

are through yoga, tai chi, meditation, dowsing, drumming, chanting, singing, sitting silently, and venturing into the pitch black of ancient chambers, to make that special connection with beings of other dimensions, guardians of deep, ancient wisdom.

Take no one's word for anything, including ours. What is required nowadays, we would suggest, is for people to once again connect with their spiritual roots, to frequent the ancient places once more, to leave the hustle and bustle of everyday life, to walk in quiet solitude up hill and down dale, to truly "find ourselves". As pilgrims of old have done over the millennia, we need only *be* rather than *do*, listen rather than speak, experience rather than reason, open our hearts and let our intuition guide us.

As a species we have disconnected ourselves from the Planetary Spirit, from Gaia. The results can be seen all around us, inhaled with every urban breath: fumes and light pollution, destruction and decay, concrete and tarmac, skyscrapers and corporate logos, new housing quotas from Government forcing regional councils to build a huge number of new houses over open fields. We have also allowed the Sovereignty of the Land, our vital sacred connection, to slip away quietly in the legislative chambers of the EU; our ancestors are surely turning in their graves. The British Isles have always been renowned as sacred, which is why, through the strong sovereignty bond, we still have one of the few sovereigns left in the western world.

Spiritually, we are children who have been separated from our mother, roaming aimlessly, without direction or purpose. This loss of connection is being numbed by consumerism, stimulants and power games. But our mother never abandoned us, and we can begin today to extend our hands out to her, and with them our hearts.

By visiting sacred sites and walking the old tracks, we believe humankind will come to see the Land as our ancestors once saw it, to regard the Earth as they once did - as sacred. For when we hold an object as sacred, be it a crucifix, rosary beads, or holy book, we cannot possibly destroy it. Holding the Earth as sacred may be Man's only way of surviving the present chaos we find ourselves in. We all share a responsibility for the state of the planet, and we all share a responsibility for healing sick Albion. If our work helps just a few people to regard our Planet as sacred, then it will all have been worthwhile.

Toni's drawing below is entitled **Albion Deflating.** As soon as her conscious mind saw it, she realised that it looked like a balloon in the shape of Britain, becoming distorted and misshapen as the air was escaping; she saw it was Britain losing its vitality and identity. We have lost our sense of Self, and cultural individuality as a cohesive tribal group. We have become like a tree; we can only see the leaves and higher branches – we have lost sight of our roots, both historically and spiritually.

On a recent trip to the top of Glastonbury Tor, Toni had a vision of a male figure blowing a horn, like the herald Mercury, across the landscape below, with the message "Wake up, Albion!" As part of Albion, it is time for us all individually to awaken spiritually. Shamanic cultures have long included the idea that the world is sung into being, and this created a reciprocal relationship between us and our environment, making us aware that we are part of a greater web of life. The Bible also states, 'In the beginning was the Word". Toni's vision seems to be telling us that we need to reconnect with our song and bring it into harmony with the universe. Shamanism was the way of our ancestors, and they used visualisation to connect with the symbols and archetypes in the Universe. Once we understand that the mind does not differentiate between what is seen by the eye, and what is seen in our imagination, then we realise we can change our world through our minds. Although maligned by the Church, shamanism is not a religion, and can coexist happily with other belief systems.

If nothing else, the energy of sacred sites serves us well by balancing the two halves of the brain, logic and intuition, yang and yin, dark and light, rational thought and intuition, conscious and subconscious, and further polarities. Our ancestors knew this balancing quality of sacred places; just being there is healing. If we could, we would make everyone spend time at such healing sites, including all our world leaders!

You could say that our Quest has really been part of our overall mission in life, to spread the message. But at the end of the day, we are all on a mission. The way forward for Mankind will be the way forward for Planet Earth, for we and She are umbilically connected in both a spiritual and physical sense.

If you have appreciated any part of our book, we would ask you to **pass on the message**, with a smile, to prospective pilgrims and let it ripple around the globe. The more people the merrier, literally. Visualise the Wessex Astrum pulsating vibrantly in the landscape, sending out beautiful beams of healing light all around the globe, a beacon for the lost to receive and be guided by. We shall be posting people's experiences and visions on our web pages.

In Peter's novel, *Thirteen Moons – Conversations with the Goddess,* the Earth Mother gives the hero lessons and insights on how we as a species can once again regard the Earth as sacred, before it is too late. We feel the last words are best left to her:

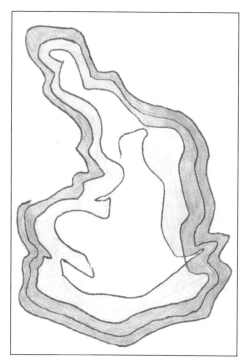

Toni's automatic drawing *Albion Deflating*, which represents Britain losing its energetic vitality and national identity. © T Perrott

'Whenever you wish to hear me just listen to birdsong, or the crashing of waves on the shore, or my soft whispers in the wind as it rustles through the trees, or my shout in a crash of thunder. More than this, you will find me in the silence of an ancient tomb, in the tranquility of a still pond, or in the stillness of your sleep.

I am always with you. How can I not be? Follow your heart always. Go play with the joy of life. Rejoice with the Land. You and I are one.

And finally, I urge everyone to come and stand on that edge, looking across the precipice. For if you do I will surely push you off – so be prepared to fly!

The healing has begun. Yes, it has begun.'

Resources –
Maps, Websites and Groups

Ordnance Survey Maps

The following sheets cover the Wessex Astrum:

1:50,000 scale (1¼ ins to 1 mile):
Sheet 172 – includes Bristol and the Wotton/Holywell apex points.
Sheet 173 – Wiltshire, including the Avebury apex point.
Sheet 182 – Somerset, including the Glastonbury and Brockley apex points.
Sheet 183 – including Glastonbury and Rode at the geographical centre.
Sheet 184 – Wiltshire, including Salisbury Plain and the Stonehenge apex.
Sheet 194 – Dorset, including the Hambledon Hill apex point.

1: 25,000 scale (2½ ins to 1 mile):
Sheet 117 – Dorset, including the Hambledon Hill apex point.
Sheet 118 – includes the Hambledon Hill apex point and Shaftesbury area.
Sheet 129 – includes hexagram lines at the Dorset/Somerset border.
Sheet 130 – includes Salisbury Plain and the Stonehenge apex point.
Sheet 141 – Somerset, including the Glastonbury apex point.
Sheet 142 – Somerset between Glastonbury apex and Rode.
Sheet 143 – Wiltshire, including Rode and part of Salisbury Plain.
Sheet 154 – Gloucestershire, including Brockley apex and part of Bristol.
Sheet 156 – includes the Somerset/Wiltshire border area.
Sheet 157 – Wiltshire, including the Avebury apex point.
Sheet 167 – Gloucestershire, including the Wotton/Holywell apex point.

An excellent resource for the early editions of OS maps is: www.old-maps.co.uk

Recommended Related Websites

The Authors:
Peter Knight: www.stoneseeker.net
Toni Perrott: www.dragonseeker.co.uk
Stone Seeker Tours and **Stone Seeker Publishing:** www.stoneseeker.net
Dragon Seeker Tours (tours of London): www.dragonseeker.co.uk

Groups and Societies:
Dorset Earth Mysteries Group: www.dorsetmysteries.org
Wessex Research Group: www.wessexresearchgroup.net
Society of Ley Hunters: www.leyhunter.org
The Antiquarian Society: www.theantiquariansociety.com
Avalon Rising: www.avalonrising.co.uk
British Society of Dowsers: www.britishdowsers.org
Wessex Dowsers: www.wessexdowsers.co.uk

Individuals:
Steve and Karen Alexander: www.temporarytemples.co.uk
Gary Biltcliffe: www.belinusline.com
Paul Broadhurst: www.mythospress.co.uk
David Furlong: www.kch42.dial.pipex.com
Palden Jenkins: www.palden.co.uk
Anthony Kennish: www.tonykennish.co.uk
Nicholas R Mann: www.britishmysteries.co.uk
Terence Meaden: www.stonehenge-avebury.net
Hamish Miller: www.hamishmiller.co.uk
Tony Peart: www.templarmechanics.com
Chris Street: www.starcircles.info

Other:
Convention of Alternative Archaeology & Earth Mysteries: www.stoneseeker.net
Megalithomania: www.megalithomania.co.uk
Out of the Ordinary Festival: www.outoftheordinaryfestival.com
The Megalithic Portal: www.megalithic.co.uk
The Modern Antiquarian: www.themodernantiquarian.com
The Henge Shop (Avebury): www.hengeshop.com
Glastonbury Online: www.glastonbury.co.uk
Chalice Well: www.chalicewell.org.uk
Glastonbury Abbey: www.glastonburyabbey.com
Mystical Glastonbury: www.isleofavalon.co.uk
Old Maps online: www.old-maps.co.uk

Dorset Earth Mysteries Group

Peter Knight is Chairman and co-founder of this active and friendly group who meet for regular monthly meetings, hosting lectures by prominent people in the earth mysteries field. Its members also go on field trips to sacred sites, such as pilgrimages into the inner sanctum of Stonehenge to experience the sunset, and also hold social events. Members are entitled to a reduced entrance rate at talks, as well as discounts on Peter's field trips. Non-members are welcome at talks, although membership is open and a warm welcome awaits you. For membership enquiries, or to obtain a list of forthcoming events, visit the DEMG website at:

www.dorsetmysteries.org

Wessex Research Group

The Wessex Research Group is a coalition of local groups, societies, centres and organisations, founded by the late Nigel Blair. It networks and exchanges information about talks, available speakers, events and field trips. It issues a monthly newsletter about forthcoming events across Wessex and other areas.
For further information, visit their website:

www.wessexresearchgroup.net

Further Reading

The following works are recommended for further study of Astrum localities and of issues raised in this book. Most have already been referred to in the text, and some, unfortunately, are now out of print.

Karen and Steve Alexander, *Crop Circles Yearbooks*, www.temporarytemples.co.uk

Philip Ball, *The Self-Made Tapestry – Pattern Formation in Nature,* Oxford University Press, 1999.

Gary Biltcliffe, *Secrets of the Masonic Isle – Uncovering the Magic and Mystery of Ancient Portland.* Published shortly. Website: www.belinusline.com

Robert Coon, *Spheres of Destiny: The Shaftesbury Prophecy.* 1989. (Out of print, but is now online: http://members.lycos.co.uk/glastonbury/contents_shaftes.html

Michael Dames, *The Silbury Treasure,* Thames and Hudson, 1976.

Michael Dames, *The Avebury Cycle,* Thames and Hudson, 1996.

Paul Devereux, *Symbolic Landscapes,* Gothic Image, 1992.

David Furlong, *The Keys to the Temple,* Piatkus, 1997.

John Gale, *Prehistoric Dorset,* Tempus, 2003.

Robin Heath and John Michell, *The Measure of Albion,* Bluestone Press, 2004.

Palden Jenkins, *Map of the Ancient Landscape around Glastonbury,* Gothic Image, 2005.

Kathy Jones, *The Goddess in Glastonbury,* Ariadne, 1990.

Anthony John Kennish, *The Glastonbury Chronicles,* self-published, 2002-8.

Peter Knight, *Ancient Stones of Dorset,* Power Publications, 1996.

Peter Knight, *Sacred Dorset – On the Path of the Dragon,* Capall Bann, 1998.

Peter Knight, *Dorset Pilgrimages*, Power Publications, 2000.

Peter Knight, *Earth Mysteries – An Illustrated Encyclopaedia of Britain* (CD-ROM), Stone Seeker Publishing, 2003.

Peter Knight, *Thirteen Moons – Conversations with the Goddess,* Stone Seeker Publishing, 2007.

Henry Lincoln, *The Holy Place: The Mystery of Rennes-le-Château,* Jonathan Cape, 1991.

Nicholas R Mann, *Energy Secrets of Glastonbury Tor,* Green Magic, 2004.

Nicholas R Mann and Philippa Glasson, *The Star Temple of Avalon,* The Temple Publications, 2007.

Nicholas R Mann, *Sedona – Sacred Earth,* Light Technology Publishing, 2005

Nicolas R Mann, *The Sacred Geometry of Washington DC,* Green Magic, 2006

Terence Meaden, *Stonehenge – The Secret of the Solstice,* Souvenir, 1997.

Terence Meaden, *The Secrets of the Avebury Stones,* Souvenir, 1999.

John Michell, *The View Over Atlantis,* Sago Press, 1969.

John Michell, *City of Revelation,* Garnstone Press, 1972.

John Michell, *The New View over Atlantis,* Thames and Hudson, 1983.

Hamish Miller and Paul Broadhurst, *The Sun and the Serpent,* Pendragon Press, 1989.

John North, *Stonehenge – Neolithic Man and the Cosmos,* Harper Collins, 1996.

Nigel Pennick, *Sacred Geometry,* Turnstone Press, 1980.

Toni Perrott, *London Dragon Paths – A Sacred and Mystical Landscape Revealed* (in preparation).

Lynne Picknett, *Mary Magdalene – Christianity's Lost Goddess,* Robinson, 2003.

Michael Poynder, *Pi in the Sky,* Rider, 1992.

Ann Proctor, (ed.), *This Enchanting Place – Facets of Chalice Well,* Chalice Well Trust, 2006.

Jackie Queally, *The Spiritual Purpose to Rosslyn: Key to a Hidden Matrix,* Celtic Trails, 2007.

Philip Rahtz and Lorna Watts, *Glastonbury: Myth and Archaeology,* Tempus, 2003.

Christopher Street, *Earthstars – The Visionary Landscape (Part One: London, City of Revelation),* Hermitage Publishing, 2000.

Guy Underwood, *The Pattern of the Past,* Abacus, 1969.

Alfred Watkins, *The Old Straight Track,* 1925. Abacus reprint, 1970-93.

About the Authors

Peter Knight

Peter is well-known for his lively and enthusiastic workshops and field trips on topics relating to sacred sites, leys and dowsing. He has been leading tours to sacred sites since 1995 and has spoken at several international conventions, such as in the USA, Malta, and across the UK. He is co-founder of the Dorset Earth Mysteries Group, is an Adult Education Tutor on archaeology and earth mysteries subjects, and has held seminars at Bournemouth University. Peter has published five books previously, as well as having written for magazines. He has appeared on radio and TV, such as on Channel 4's *Don Roamin'* with Monty Don. Peter is the founder and organiser of the Conventions of Alternative Archaeology and Earth Mysteries, held annually in Dorset, which gives a platform to new and leading researchers. In 2006 he founded Stone Seeker Tours, promoting holistic tours to sacred sites across the UK and Europe. He also envisioned and hosts the *Ancient Ambient Chill-Out*, combining funky world music with large-screen images of sacred sites and tribal cultures.

His interests include walking, drumming, world music, dowsing, prehistoric art, shamanism, and photographing Nature. He is a father, vegetarian and follows a Goddess-orientated spirituality, whilst honouring spiritualities and religions.

Contact Peter by e-mail at: stoneseeker@waitrose.com
Web site: www.stoneseeker.net

Toni Perrott

Toni Perrott is an earth mysteries researcher, dowser and writer, as well as artist and traveller. She is based by Hambledon Hill, in North Dorset, an area of outstanding ancient sacred sites, which she spends a lot of time exploring, and experiencing and guiding people around, along with her fellow researcher, Peter Knight. Toni has been a speaker at Megalithomania and at the Out of the Ordinary Festival (see her website for past and forthcoming events). She spends time exploring sacred sites, not only in Stonehenge and Avebury, but all around Britain, Europe, the USA and beyond, passing on the message of *Seeing the Landscape in the Old Ways*, as our Ancestors once did. She lived in Japan for several years, studying Japanese art, and explored South East Asian sacred sites. Her next book, *London Dragon Paths*, detailed below, is about earth mysteries of Central London, and brings together her interests in shamanism, walking, local history, dowsing, symbolism, shamanic and spiritual art. She is currently setting up guided walks around ancient sites in London.

Contact Toni by email at: toni_perrott@hotmail.com
Website: www.dragonseeker.co.uk

Stone Seeker Tours
with Peter Knight and Toni Perrott

Are you planning to bring a group to visit sacred sites in the UK, who are looking for spiritually inclined outings? Do you have seekers wishing to truly experience places like Stonehenge, Avebury, Glastonbury, Dartmoor, Jersey, Ireland or Dorset?

Stone Seeker Tours specialises in tailor-made excursions. You bring the pilgrims and we will provide the expert guides, and the unforgettable experiences. The following subjects will be expertly covered, and individual topics can be included or excluded, depending on the focus and requirements of the group:

Sacred archaeology ~ Ancient astronomical alignments ~ Ley lines ~ Sacred geometry ~ Myth and folklore ~ Earth energies and dowsing ~ Crop circles Church symbolism ~ Drumming and healing circles

Peter and Toni are the guides of Stone Seeker Tours. They have been taking groups around sacred sites for many years, including a wide variety of 'alternative' groups, such as dowsers, healing circles, and self-growth groups. They have a good sense of humour and are both very enthusiastic, making for entertaining and informative tours. Their trips are a spiritual experience, as pilgrims interact with the Goddess landscape.

List of localities:
Stonehenge (can also include the Cursus, Woodhenge and Old Sarum) – Avebury (including West Kennet Long Barrow and Silbury Hill) – Ancient Dartmoor – Glastonbury (Tor, Abbey, Chalice Well, etc) – Dorset stone circles and leys – Neolithic Jersey – Winchester – Megalithic Brittany – Knowlton and Cranborne Chase - Sacred Cornwall – Dorchester and Cerne Abbas – Malta - Da Vinci Code & Knights Templar sites - Prehistoric Ireland – Shamanic drumming in tombs.
Peter and Toni also have in-depth knowledge of other areas too, so please enquire! Retirement and disabled parties can be catered for with special wheelchair-friendly itineraries. Tours can be accompanied with or preceded by illustrated talks on a variety of subjects. For a full list of subjects, visit the Stone Seeker web site at:

www.stoneseeker.net

Dragon Seeker Tours
with Toni Perrott

Toni is currently setting up earth mystery tours around Central London, as well as a few sites further from the centre, based on her *London Dragon Paths* research and experience. Check her website:

www.dragonseeker.co.uk

Other Books by the Authors

(A) Peter Knight

Ancient Stones of Dorset
Published in 1996 by Power Publications. £12.99
Still the most comprehensive work on Dorset's megalithic sites
208 pp (gloss finish), 147 photographs and 132 drawings
Maps of ley lines and sites, with grid references
Earth energies, astronomy, newly discovered stones and ancient crosses
Recently reprinted - thousands of copies now sold!

Sacred Dorset ~ On the Path of the Dragon
Published in 1998 by Capall Bann. £12.95
292 pp, 119 photographs and 82 line drawings
A thorough work on Dorset's ancient spiritual heritage
Includes hillforts, wells and springs, the Cerne Giant, sun and moon, the green man,
fairies, dragons, trees, ley lines, and more.

Dorset Pilgrimages ~ A Millennium Handbook
(with Mike Power)
Published in 2000 by Power Publications. £6.95
144 pp (gloss finish), over 100 photos and line drawings
Newly envisaged day-long pilgrimages across Dorset
Churches, stone circles, megaliths, wells, etc are visited en route
Signed copies are available from the author

Earth Mysteries ~
An Illustrated Encyclopaedia of Britain (CD-ROM)
Published in 2003 by Stone Seeker Publishing. £9.99
Over 350MB of information –
the biggest overview of British earth mysteries ever published
Compatible with Windows Word (Windows 98, XP, etc)
Over 250 colour and b&w illustrations, maps and line drawings
A-Z format, plus resources and fully cross-referenced
Like a giant website – with over 1000 hyperlinks

Thirteen Moons ~ Conversations with the Goddess
Published in 2007 by Stone Seeker Publishing. £9.99
Peter's first novel, which has been receiving rave reviews.
The book's hero is contacted by the Earth Spirit on thirteen full moons at sacred sites across Europe (such as Roslyn, Stonehenge, Avebury, Glastonbury, Ireland, the New Forest and Brittany; Peter and Toni went to dozens of sites across Europe researching the novel). The Goddess gives him lessons concerning leys, sacred sites, earth

energies, ecological issues, the Grail, Mary Magdalene, crop circles, sacred geometry and how to connect with the Earth Spirit. She divulges what the human experience is really about and how we can live fulfilling lives in harmony with the Planet and the Land – before it's too late! The culmination is the gift of **13 Insights**, by which we can live spiritually conscious lives.

The book is laced with the author's caustic humour, and is also semi-autobiographical, as the author draws on his many experiences at sacred sites – his own inner journey unfolded whilst researching this book across Europe. The book also includes an extensive listing of all the localities visited in the novel, so people can also walk the path of *Thirteen Moons.*

www.stoneseeker.net

(B) Toni Perrott

London Dragon Paths – A Sacred and Mystical Landscape Revealed
(In preparation)

Toni reveals her discoveries of an ancient pre-Roman sacred centre in Central London, through old maps, historical records, folklore and dowsing earth energies. She finds mounds, a possible henge, ancient trackways and processional routes, wells, maypole sites, alignments, plus old crosses, which often replaced megaliths. There are major energy flows, or *Dragon Paths*, that seem to have defined the position of this sacred centre and on which a major dynamic city has grown up on. A Sovereignty Path, a sacred processional way follows three combined Dragon Paths.

It is Toni's experience of Avebury, Stonehenge, Glastonbury, and other ancient sacred landscapes, that led her to see this new vision of London. This book started out with a trip to Temple Church in London, and curiosity about this amazing atmospheric Templar site inspired further exploration of the earth mysteries of the area. She has walked and dowsed several sections of the paths to feel at first hand how they were meant to be followed, as a modern pilgrim, and has told the story of her experiences.

The importance of London came also from its siting on the River Thames, by the sacred twin hills and sacred island, as well as being a crossing point on the major goddess river, with fabulous votive offerings to her found in the river, such as the Battersea Shield. It is significant that the Thames follows the intertribal boundary between five Celtic tribes, and London would have been well-placed as a major intertribal sacred centre. London was also at the centre of an extensive road system, which is acknowledged by some archaeologists, and this may have been based in part on prehistoric trackways.

www.dragonseeker.co.uk

Index

Note: Dorset, Wiltshire, Somerset and Gloucestershire do not have their own entries in the index, because the sheer amount of such entries would be impractical and meaningless.

271

272